SPICE
HEALTH HEROES

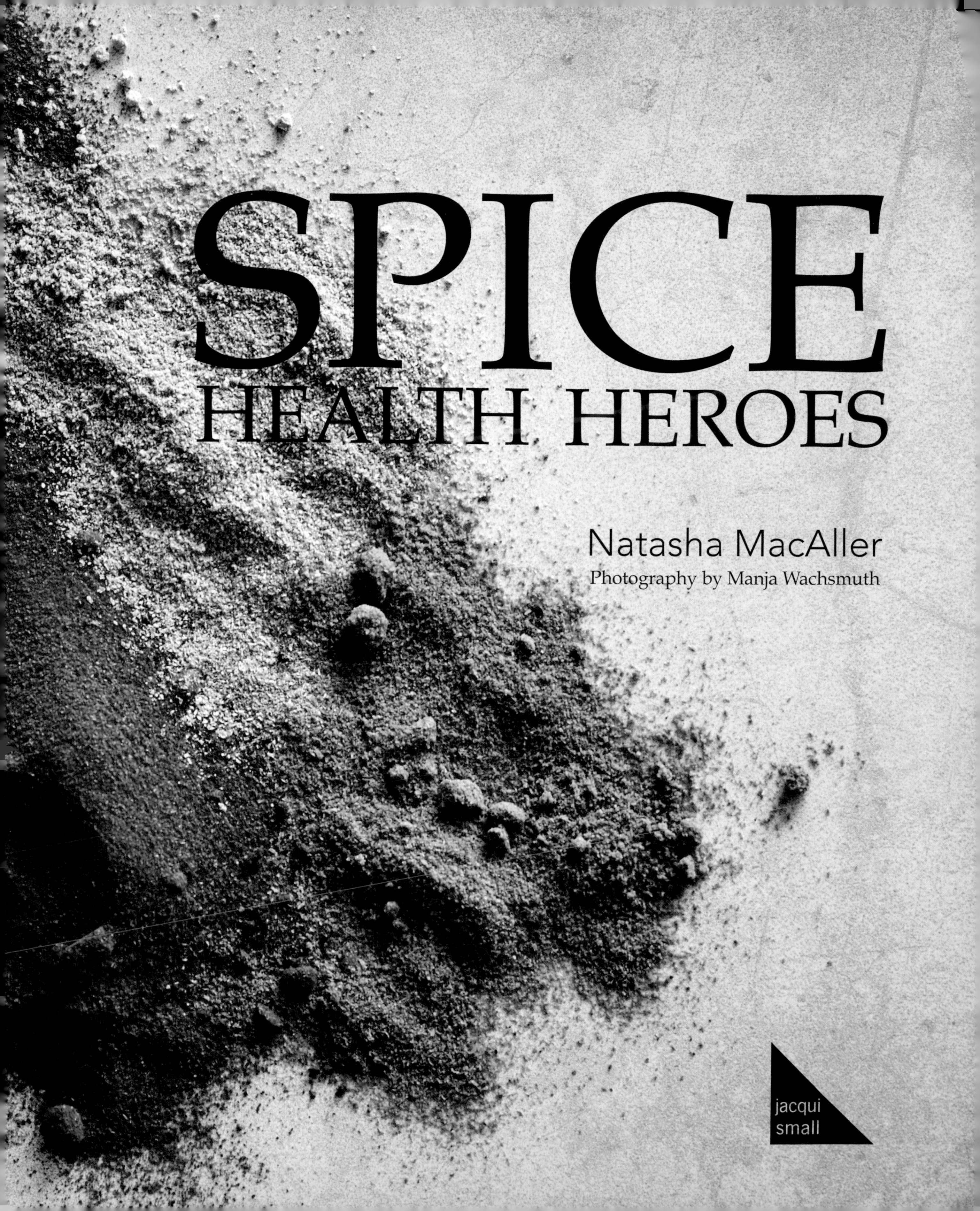

SPICE
HEALTH HEROES

Natasha MacAller

Photography by Manja Wachsmuth

jacqui
small

First published in 2016 by
Jacqui Small LLP
74–77 White Lion Street
London N1 9PF

Publisher: Jacqui Small
Senior Commissioning Editor: Fritha Saunders
Managing Editor: Emma Heyworth-Dunn
Editor: Anne McDowall
Designer: Maggie Town
Production: Maeve Healy

ISBN: 978 1 910254 77 6

A catalogue record for this book
is available from the British Library.

2018 2017 2016
10 9 8 7 6 5 4 3 2 1

Printed in China

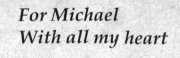

For Michael
With all my heart

Quarto is the authority on a wide range of topics.
Quarto educates, entertains and enriches the lives
of our readers — enthusiasts and lovers of hands-on living.
www.QuartoKnows.com

Contents

Foreword

My own experience of spices was formed during my childhood in Northern Greece. Nearby was Crocus, a small village in the mountains named after the plant that produces saffron, the most precious and expensive of all spices. In Crocus and the wider area of Kozani where saffron is grown, people often start their day by drinking a cup of tea made of an infusion of just two fine saffron filaments. They understand the potency of this spice and use it sparingly and respectfully in their food and drink.

Spices, earth's refined alchemy, discovered and cherished by our ancestors, enhance the flavour of our food, bringing life to our mealtimes. As this wonderful book shows, we can use spices not only for their culinary delights but also for their impressive healing qualities to support our health, inner balance and wellbeing.

Along with flavour, spices add texture and colour to our plate. Eating a tasty, aromatic, nutritious meal mindfully in a pleasant environment nourishes the mind, body and spirit. When our food satisfies our tongue, then our brain is content and doesn't look for pleasure and satisfaction elsewhere. If our diet is bland or unbalanced, lacking one of the six tastes: sweet, sour, salty, pungent, bitter and astringent, then we can feel something is missing. That's when our body turns to the 'easy' tastes – sugar and salt – and overeating, which, as we know, contributes to obesity and the increasing prevalence of chronic diseases.

Spices, I believe, are the heroes that can save us from disease and poor quality of being. As the title *Spice Health Heroes* suggests, spices have extra-special properties, including recently confirmed antidepressant effects. Trust spices to help us find happiness.

Spice Health Heroes takes us on a journey through history, folklore and science to our kitchen with unique recipes gathered and artfully created by the charismatic Natasha. Her ideas convince us to grab our apron and explore further in our own kitchens these beautiful spice recipes.

In my own 'Medical Kitchen Wisdom' workshops for professionals and 'Cooking on Prescription' groups for the public, people explore how to use 'Food as Medicine'. Hippocrates said that 'The best doctors cure by changing the diet and lifestyle of their patient'. My intention, in my medical practice as a specialist in Nutritional Medicine and Ayurvedic Nutrition, is to help people find what foods suit their 'type', and spices are often the forgotten or unknown ingredient that can help. *Spice Health Heroes* will be on my 'prescription list'.

I love spices and use them everyday in my cooking. My wish is that, by the time you finish reading this book, you too will come to love and respect our spice health heroes.

Eleni Tsiompanou, MD, PGDip, MSc Nutritional Medicine
Founder, Health Being Institute, London, England

Introduction

Spices are the flavour of life and may be the source of wellbeing for life, too.

The word spice, derived from the Latin word *species*, originally meant 'merchandise, goods, wares or a commodity from the Far East'. The definitions of what constitutes a spice and what constitutes a herb are rather fluid, and opinions differ, with herbs often turning into spices and vice versa. For example, garlic is considered a spice – the garlic clove is a flower bud – but it is also listed as a culinary herb. Plant leaves are the most confusing and argued about: a fresh basil leaf is referred to as a herb, but the moment it is dried it becomes a spice. Therefore, after much researching, analyzing and pondering, I believe that a spice is the seed, berry, bark, root, rhizome (creeping rootstock), branch, leaf, aril (a fleshy coating of some seed varieties e.g. pomegranate) or sap of a plant.

Spice history… in a nutshell

Spices have been part of civilization, culture, myths and medicine for tens of thousands of years. One of the first records of spices being used, dating back to at least 1600BC, was found on the Greek island of Santorini, where frescoes display a scene of young girls and monkeys picking saffron, presumably for medicinal use. The earliest evidence of spices being traded dates back to a pharaoh queen's funerary monument, which depicts spice-trade routes linking the Nile by camel and boat to the Horn of Africa some 3,500 years ago, including voyages to the ancient isle of cinnamon, Sri Lanka.

Thousands of years later, saffron was introduced to Eastern America by German religious groups fleeing persecution, who brought with them their penchant and passion for saffron. By the 1730s, the Pennsylvania Dutch, as they became known, had become famous for cultivating, selling and exporting saffron. Although the acres of crocus are now small kitchen gardens, saffron is still grown there by Mennonite, Amish and Lutheran families. Saffron recipes from centuries back are still made in these devoutly religious communities – and at 10,000 US dollars a pound of stamens, saffron-growing remains a very profitable, albeit labour-intensive, hobby.

Spices have been tasted, traded, stolen and the cause of bloodshed for many millennia all over the world. One of the most bloody and significant battles that rewrote spice history took place over the span of around 200 years, between the 15th and 17th centuries. The battling participants in the murderous Spice Wars included Spain, Portugal, England and Holland as each country fought for dominance and control of the Spice Islands. Two of the Banda islands, a tiny set-apart chain of ten volcanic islands in Indonesia, were the only place where the coveted nutmeg grew and, at that time, the spice was worth its weight in gold because not only was nutmeg thought to be an aphrodisiac but it was also believed to cure the plague.

In countries and climates near and far, other familiar and exotic spices flourished: Middle Eastern Persia and Ancient Greece, Rome and later the first European spice-trade capital of Venice were rich with an abundance of oregano, rosemary, bay leaf and pomegranate, all used for medicines. India, the land of holy basil (tulsi), cardamom, fenugreek, tamarind, cassia cinnamon and today's rock-star turmeric, to this day still grows 15 per cent of the world's spices and leads the way in health studies of turmeric. China has a wealth of flu-fending star anise, star rhizome ginger and super-C citrus, while Africa, a continent of ancient spice routes, where, ironically, no spices actually originate, is the creative hub of some of the world's most popular and colourful spice blends. In the New World, Grenada in the Caribbean now grows the majority of allspice, nutmeg and clove, planted hundreds of years ago from Spice Island seedlings by the British colonialists. Lastly, in the Americas, land of fiery-hot chilies, heart-healthy cocoa and body-cleansing hibiscus, these spices have been revered as healing medicines by the ancient indigenous populations of both North and South America.

Spices for flavour and health

Historically, spices have been used throughout the ages as aromatic flavourings for food and as perfumes to sweeten the scent of battle-weary knights when they were in attendance to the king. However, more importantly, spices have been used throughout the ages as medicine, to heal the body and extend life. Different spices have different talents and can be used to warm, cleanse, restore, soothe, boost energy levels and support the vital body-balancing immune system. Spices are concentrated full of phytonutrients (nutrients and chemicals in addition to vitamins and minerals), which, while not vital for keeping you alive, may help prevent disease in addition to keeping your body systems working at their best.

Spices used as medicine remain relevant as natural sources of active compounds for treating human conditions or disorders, including immune-imbalanced and inflammatory

> Spices have been used for so many centuries not only as flavour enhancers but as medicine as well. There must be some benefit; there is something more to spices than simply taste.
>
> Luigi Fontana, MD, PhD

diseases and cancers. There are hundreds, if not thousands, of current cancer-research projects investigating the promising potential of medicinal plants to discover new possible therapies utilizing complementary medicines that lack the toxic effects of chemotherapeutic drugs and may have the same, or better, curative effects as current chemical therapies.

Spice Health Heroes is not a diet book, nor is it a medical treatise. (I am not a doctor, but rather a ballerina-turned-chef with a passionate interest in health and, particularly, in spices.) However, it does include contributions from a number of revered international medical doctors, who are weighing in on the promising research, trials and conclusions relating to the medicinal uses of these 30 spice health heroes, which it is thought may relieve, assist and have genuine benefit to health and wellbeing.

There are also contributions here from 21 lauded international chefs, whose spice stories and recipes began from their very first taste of a spice then developed over years of cooking, creating and tasting into their own individual spice signature.

These two professions, culinary and medical, have come together and are working as a team to bring attention to the simple fact that good food equals good heath. Culinary medicine is not about following a diet, nor is it about removing entire food groups from your life, but rather it consists in eating fresh food that is free from a long list of artificial ingredients: just simple, wholesome, fresh food, full of flavour, health-giving properties – and spice.

'Spices have been used for so many centuries not only as flavour enhancers but as medicine as well. There must be some benefit; there is something more to spices than simply taste', suggests Luigi Fontana, MD, PhD, Professor of Medicine at Washington University and at University of Brescia, Italy. Dr Fontana is a very lean man. This is not so surprising considering one of his areas of study: calorie restriction (CR). 'From yeast to mice, if you reduce calorie intake (without causing starvation), animals are healthier and live much longer! We are now studying this in humans.' As with many matters relating to diet, Dr Fontana and his colleagues are learning that things are never simple. 'We are finding that it is not *just* CR that gives benefit. It is an

interaction of many factors, one of which is the friendly bacteria that live in our gut, the microbiome. For example, we recently published a paper showing that mice that are 1) fed turmeric, and 2) contain the microbiome of a human from Bangladesh show an increase in the amount of time the body has to absorb nutrients, compared to mice that are identical except that they have a microbiome from a human from a European country. It is not just turmeric that gives this benefit, it is the interaction of turmeric with the healthful flora that live within us!'

Storing and using spices

Do you open your spice cupboard to a collection of dusty tins, dog-eared paper boxes and no-longer-see-through small glass jars of reddish or brownish powders of… what is that? Spice? Is there any smell to them? Check that neither the colour nor the scent of the spices has faded: if it has, toss it out. Don't keep spices you want to use on a rack above the stovetop: they will perish within weeks. Keeping spices in tightly sealed glass jars will prevent the volatile oils from becoming humid and oxidizing. Stored in a cool dark place, whole spices, including leaves and flowers, will keep for 1–2 years, seeds and roots for 2–3 years and ground spices for 6–12 months.

The single most important tip for ground spices is to buy only what you need for a few months. For the best value for money, purchase spices whole, then toast and grind them as you need them. Freshness is more important than origin, but if possible, choose organic, as many spices come from the tropical climates over long distances and non-organic ones are most likely to have been sprayed or irradiated to prevent pests and extend shelf life.

To warm and release their volatile oils, toast and swirl whole spices over low heat in a small dry pan until they release their scent, then allow to cool before grinding in a mortar and pestle or electric spice grinder. If you need to replace fresh spices with dried ones in a recipe, as a good rule of thumb, allow 1 teaspoon of dried for 1 tablespoon of chopped fresh (though in the case of dried sage, use only ½ teaspoon). The fragrance of fresh spice will fill the kitchen and your soul with its intoxicating aroma.

Spice blends

This international sampling of spice mixes are easy to blend into your favourite foods. Spice mixtures are often the secret and essential ingredient that will transform a so-so plate of food into something deliciously memorable! Use them to add a boost of flavour to anything from a soup to roasted nuts, finely grind your spices and stir into a drink, or invent your own blends as a creative idea for gifts.

1. Tash's Tamale and Taco Spice

A Mexican mix that pairs well with veggie, fish and meat dishes for that authentic 'south of the border' flavour! Hibiscus adds a bit of sour citrus; if unavailable, you can substitute the zest of 2 limes.

2 tbsp chopped fresh sage (or 1 tbsp dried)
2 tbsp mild chili powder
1 tbsp salt flakes
1 tbsp chopped garlic (or 2 tsp garlic powder)
1 tbsp onion powder
1 tbsp dried oregano, crumbled
5 tsp cumin seeds, toasted and ground
2 tsp guajillo chili powder
1 tsp ground cinnamon
1 tsp freshly ground black peppercorns
2 tsp crushed chipotle of chili pepper flakes
2 tsp hibiscus tea or 6–8 calyx petals, ground

Combine all the spices together and mix thoroughly.
Store in an airtight container.

2. Homemade Pumpkin Pie Spice

A blend to add healthy sweetness to your morning latte, lunchtime roasted veggie salad or evening dessert.

3 tbsp ground cinnamon
1 tbsp ground ginger
1 tsp ground cloves
1 tsp ground fresh nutmeg
¼ tsp ground cardamom
¼ tsp ground white pepper

Combine all the spices together and mix thoroughly.
Store in an airtight container.

3. Somoma Spice Mix

Inspired by California's top wine-growing region, this blend can be added to farmers' market finds, or to pizza or pasta dishes.

2 tbsp dried basil, crumbled
2 tbsp dried marjoram, crumbled
2 tbsp dried oregano, crumbled
1 tbsp dried thyme leaves, rubbed or ground
1 tbsp dried bay leaves, crumbled
4½ tsp dried rosemary needles, ground
2 tsp red pepper flakes
2 tsp fennel seeds, toasted and ground
1½ tsp dried mint, crumbled
1½ tsp garlic powder
1½ tsp onion powder
1 tsp lemon zest

Combine all spices together and mix thoroughly.
Store in an airtight container.

1

2

3

4. Rich Curry Blend

A full-flavoured blend for traditional Indian curry dishes, this masala can even be added to poached fruit or nut desserts for a rich, mysterious aroma and taste.

2½ tbsp sweet paprika
2 tbsp cumin seeds, toasted and ground
2 tbsp ground turmeric
1½ tbsp coriander seeds, ground
1 tbsp smoked pimentón
1 tbsp ground fenugreek
1 tbsp mustard seeds, ground
2½ tsp fennel seeds, toasted and ground
2½ tsp ground red pepper flakes
2½ tsp fenugreek leaves
2½ tsp ground cardamon
1 x 5cm (2in.) piece cinnamon stick, charred and ground, or ½ tsp toasted ground cinnamon
¼ tsp ground cloves
¾ tsp dried orange peel

Combine all the spices together and mix thoroughly. Store in an airtight container.

5. Citrus Salt and Pepper Spice

Add a little citrus zing with your pepper-and-salt blend on salads, appetizers or even fresh fruit.

zest of 6 lemons, or 2 tbsp dried chopped peel
zest of 2 oranges, or 1 tbsp dried chopped peel
zest of 6 limes, or 2 tsp dried chopped peel

6 tbsp coarse sea salt
3 tbsp black peppercorns
1 tbsp dried pink peppercorns
1 tbsp dried green peppercorns
2 tsp Aleppo pepper flakes

Spread out all the citrus zest (unless using pre-dried peel) on a lined baking tray. Put into the oven on the lowest setting and leave until completely dried, about 1 hour. When dried, transfer to a bowl, add the salt, peppercorns and pepper flakes and stir until well mixed. Store in a decorative glass jar or salt mill and grind as needed.

6. Oriental Five Spice Plus One Blend

The go-to mixture for stir-fries, clear soups, marinades and chicken wings.

2 tbsp + 1 tsp ground star anise
1 tbsp ground Sichuan pepper or black pepper
1 tbsp ground fennel seed
1 tbsp ground cinnamon
1 tbsp ground cloves
1 tbsp ground ginger or galangal
1 tbsp sea salt (optional)
1 tbsp dried orange zest

Combine all the spices together and mix thoroughly. Store in an airtight container.

Immune spice

Immunity is balanced strength, the ultimate support for bodies and minds. Through an astonishing and elaborate programme of checks and balances, our immune system strives to keep us healthy and well. This handful of spices gives support to the immune system, our body's power-plant protector.

Immune Spice Health Heroes

Turmeric ★ Cumin ★ Clove & Allspice ★ Citrus Zest ★ Star Anise

Some complaints and diseases identified as immunodeficiency diseases (where the ability of the immune system to fight infection is reduced) are assisted by immune-boosting action – the common cold and flu, for instance – while others, such as inflammatory reactive autoimmune diseases (where the immune system displays an increased/abnormal response to tissues or organs in a person's own body) like rheumatoid arthritis and multiple sclerosis, require immune balancers. Immune spice health heroes have qualities that may help support and enhance our body's extremely complex immune system. Complaints from the common cold to serious and life-threatening diseases are defined in a very simplified way as generally due to a disconnect somewhere in the immune system. According to the International Union of Immunological Societies, there exists today a shocking 150 primary immunodeficiency diseases. One of this extraordinary system's many vital functions is to inhibit the activation of cells that can cause cancers to develop, and this handful of spices may offer not only flavour but also immune reinforcement.

Turmeric has a multitude of talents and is thought to help prevent and alleviate the symptoms of rheumatoid arthritis and Alzheimer's disease. Cumin is being studied as a hormonal balancer and black cumin as an anticancer warrior. Clove and star anise both offer anti-inflammatory support, while super-C citrus zest provides protection against common colds and flu.

Other immune spice heroes

Garlic A powerful preventative used for centuries by fighting forces from Ancient Greek battalions to Russian World War II infantry, garlic kept soldiers fighting fit and ready to do battle with its antimicrobial properties. Garlic is thought be have strong anticarcinogenic attributes that help to support the immune system.

Rosemary A must-have for barbecues, rosemary has been well studied, tested and analyzed for its extraordinary ability to nullify the cancer-causing hetrocyclic amines (HCAs) that form when beef, pork, chicken, lamb or any other meat is grilled (broiled), fried, charred, smoked or cooked over an open flame, and thus protects the immune system from having to stave off these easily absorbed chemicals.

Pomegranate Sprinkle a generous handful of fresh pomegranate seeds on grain dishes and fresh salads: not only are these red jewels delicious, but this traditional Persian super-spice, which has been used as a medicine since ancient times, also provides great anti-inflammatory and immune support and shows great promise as an anticancer hero.

Fenugreek Considered a legume and full of protein, the maple-scented fenugreek can create a barrier to assist the immune system in disabling toxins found in our food and drink that are often unwittingly ingested. Fenugreek shows promise in preventing calcium oxalate from accumulating in the kidney and gallbladder, preventing not only kidney and gallstones but also a reactive inflammatory response by the immune system. It is believed that it may keep blood-sugar levels better balanced and lessen the immune system's workload and it shows great therapeutic potential in stunting the growth of cancer cells, notably in the pancreas.

Wasabi Another promising anticancer, antibacterial hero, wasabi is ranked as the strongest antibacterial against *E. coli* and *Staphylococcus aureus*. Wasabi also helps to prevent food poisoning by killing off the bacteria that could be lurking on the fresh raw fish (sashimi) with which it is often served. This green-coloured rhizome has a great concentration of active isothiocyanate (ITC) compounds and may have a chemopreventive effect on cancer.

Mustard These tiny seeds are full of cancer-preventative isothiocyanate (ITC) compounds. In the nutrient-rich and cancer-suppressing brassica family, mustard displays promising results: hundreds of lab studies have demonstrated the chemopreventive potential of this sharply strong-tasting seed.

igliving.com/magazine/articles/IGL_2009-06_AR_Immune-Deficiency-and-Autoimmune-Disease-A-Complicated-Relationship.pdf

Turmeric *The Master Spice*

Some consider turmeric the most powerful spice in the pantry. Not only does this rhizome give curry dishes their distinctive, rich earthy flavour, but turmeric is also possibly the oldest and most scientifically studied spice in the world. Thousands of years ago, it was used as a medical, culinary and sacred spice: archaeological digs in Southern India have unearthed ancient pottery shards with traces of turmeric, garlic and ginger dating back over 4,000 years, while the ancient Indian discipline of natural healing, Ayurveda, describes turmeric as 'one who is victorious over diseases'.

Most of the world's turmeric comes from India; the finest quality with the highest concentration of the active compound curcumin comes from Alleppey, a city in the southern Indian state of Kerala.

Exciting current studies from around the world show promising results for turmeric as an antioxidant and antiseptic with anti-inflammatory and analgesic benefits, and it is thought to support the liver with its LDL- and triglyceride-cholesterol-lowering punch. The active compound that gives turmeric its bright-yellow colour, curcumin (not to be confused with cumin), is also thought to help fend off Alzheimer's disease and is one of the ingredients found in acetaminophen (more commonly known in the US under the brand name Tylenol). Current trials are underway, testing elite Olympic-level athletes, to study curcumin's ability to combat pain, inflammation and joint damage (which can lead to osteoarthritis). As turmeric is not considered a drug, it can be used in competitive sport when drug testing is obligatory.

A kitchen staple in Asia, turmeric is a key spice in an uncountable array of curries and is found, too, in Mexico's chile con carne; Japanese teas, vinegars and noodles; the Moroccan spice blend ras-el-hanout; soups, stews, pickled fruits and vegetables; that bright-yellow American mustard; classic British piccalilli and coronation chicken.

When chopping or grating fresh turmeric root (as in the Tropical Turmeric Smoothie on page 54), it's a very good idea to use gloves: in Asian countries, turmeric is still traditionally used to dye clothing a stunning sunshine orangey-yellow and it will dye your hands as well! Choose roots from a reputable source that are large, smooth-skinned and free of mould. Crisp, well-dried turmeric root is easily grated using a fine-toothed grater such as a microplane and its slightly bitter, peppery earthy flavour will be more prominent.

‘There is a widespread belief that all inflammation is negative, and must be reduced at all costs. However, there are different types of inflammatory processes, and they are mediated by different chemicals. The gentle 'COX1' inflammation helps to heal tissues from everyday damage – it encourages the maintenance of the stomach and gut lining, for example. 'COX2' inflammation occurs in response to more immediate damage, like strains and arthritic problems. Normal anti-inflammatory drugs such as aspirin and ibuprofen inhibit both reactions, so the recuperative effects of COX1 are reduced alongside the desired loss of pain and swelling.

In practice this causes gastric problems in many people, and can lead to ulcers and indigestion. The loss of the positive COX1 action in joints has been shown to actually increase the rate that cartilage damage occurs – really bad news for hips and knees!

The search for selective COX2 inhibitors has been intense, and disappointing. Several promising drugs have been withdrawn due to serious side effects – and all the time turmeric has been virtually ignored! However turmeric may be just what we are looking for – it shows great promise as an ideal COX2 inhibitor, free from any serious side effects. Research is positive in many areas including arthritis, heart disease, colon cancer and inflammatory bowel disease. It may also reduce the side effects of chemotherapy and long-term anti-inflammatory drug medication.

If you use only one spice, make sure it's turmeric! ’

Margaret Papoutsis, DO, Raw Dips (SN) (NT), MBANT, CNHC

Cumin *The Global Spice*

This humble, dried, seed-like fruit has been around for so long that historians are unsure where it originated. Related to parsley, dill seed and its look-alike cousin caraway, cumin is a hardy annual grower that is both drought and flood tolerant. Planted from seed in the winter months in countries from Mexico, India, China and Japan to Spain, Italy and Africa, the eight-sided, ridged, khaki-coloured seeds are harvested in summer. The Bible (Isaiah 28:27) speaks of harvested cumin being spread on a cloth and beaten with a rod to extract the drab, dusty seed, which, when toasted and freshly ground, exudes the most alluring aroma.

Ancient records indicate that cumin was an important spice in early Roman and Middle Eastern cuisine. Traditionally, it has been used medicinally for a number of complaints and diseases, including to counteract the bacteria that causes food poisoning, as a poultice for swollen throats and digestive organs and as an aid to reduce stress and lower blood sugar; especially important for those with diabetes. On-going studies also indicate that oil of cumin (cuminaldehyde), which is rich in phytoestrogens, mimics HRT, and it is being tested on a large scale for its antiosteoporotic effects.

This nutty and familiar-smelling spice is welcome in cuisines and dishes throughout the world, from Indian to Mexican, Thai to Middle Eastern, African to Germanic and Caribbean to Cajun and Portuguese, and is particularly prevalent in spice mixes, famously in ras-el hanout, hot Caribbean colombo powder, Madras curry powder, garam masala, baharat, Mexican chili powder and, my favourite, dukkah (see page 206).

It is one of the easiest spices to grind, so purchase whole seeds, toast them lightly in a pan and freshly grind the seeds when cooled.

Black Cumin *The Imperial Spice*

Also known by the names black seed, kalonji, onion seed and nigella, black cumin (*Nigella sativa*) is not biologically related to common cumin but to the flowering Ranunculaceae family. Native to Southern Europe, North Africa and Southern Asia, it is grown in the Middle East, the Mediterranean region and the Indian continent. Matte black in colour when dried, these small, roughly surfaced, wedge-shaped seeds are pricier than common cumin and were once an important spice in Southern and Central Europe. The earliest mention of black cumin relates that it adorned the young Egyptian King Tut's sarcophagus to accompany him to the afterlife, along with fragrant cinnamon and rosemary, generously used as embalming spices.

Black cumin has been revered for centuries in India and the Middle East for its wealth of traditional healing properties and its great support of the immune system. It is considered a natural interferon remedy for autoimmune diseases such as Crohn's disease and immune-mediated diseases like multiple sclerosis. More than 100 health-related compounds are found in the oil extracted from these tiny flavourful seeds, the most powerful and potent of which is thymoquinone. As yet found only in this black seed, thymoquinone is thought to strengthen the immune system by increasing activity in the body's natural killer cells that fend off viruses and disease. Promising studies continue in South Carolina.

The pungent scent, reminiscent of oregano, and slightly bitter flavour of black cumin seed lend themselves to spicy curries, slow-cooked vegetables and sauces. Always used as whole seeds, they can be sprinkled on cakes, breads and lavash, used in dips and lightly toasted then sprinkled over salads and soups.

❛ In recent years, there has been enormous interest in the bioactive constituents and pharmacological activities of cumin. A number of chemicals, such as flavonoids, lignins and other phenolic compounds, have been identified in cumin seeds, as well as fatty acids, vitamins, minerals and dietary fiber. Useful antimicrobial and antifungal activity of cumin has been shown against some gram-positive and gram-negative bacteria and other animal and human pathogens. The anticancer ability of cumin against colon and liver cancer is highlighted in a number of animal studies. Further animal tests have repeatedly shown cumin products to be diuretic and to reduce high blood sugar, plasma and tissue cholesterol and triglycerides. Last but not least, cumin extracts were found to relieve coughs and have anti-epileptic activity. ❜

Eleni Tsiompanou, MD, PGDip, MSc Nutritional Medicine

Clove *The Enchanting Spice*

Derived from the Latin word *clavus,* meaning nail, the tack-shaped clove is the handpicked and carefully dried flower bud of a tree belonging to the myrtle family.

Discovered in the Moluccas, the exotic Spice Islands now known as Maluku, Indonesia, where nutmeg, mace and pepper once flourished, cloves are cultivated commercially today in Sri Lanka, Brazil, Tanzania, Mauritius and Madagascar, where these elegant trees with their shiny evergreen leaves and pink clove buds scent the tropical island air with a pungent sweet fragrance. The trees grow slowly – they take at least eight years before blooming – and the buds are harvested by hand just as they are beginning to turn bright pink.

This ancient spice arrived in the European kitchen in abundance during the Middle Ages, enchanting kings and commoners alike, who soon discovered the many medicinal and culinary uses of this tiny dried flower bud. Huge demand for this valuable spice soon made the seafaring explorers unimaginably wealthy – and eventually sparked the bloody Spice Wars.

For centuries, cloves have had numerous medicinal uses as well as acting as a food preservative. Ancient Chinese medicine from the third century used clove to treat a number of ills, including indigestion, nausea and toothache. The active compound in clove, eugenol, has powerful antioxidant, antibacterial and antifungal properties. Today's increasing bacterial resistance to antibiotics is concerning and on-going studies with essential oils, such as clove, to kill bacteria without creating resistance could hold a solution to this problem.

The tiny but powerfully fragrant clove is now well known in nearly every cuisine and wields great results in both sweet and savoury dishes. It is also a component of numerous spice blends, pastes and beverages throughout the world, including China's five-spice, France's quatre épices, India's garam masala, Morocco's ras-el-hanout, Britain's mulled wine spice and America's pumpkin pie spice.

The finest quality cloves are the Penang variety from Malaysia. Look for this spice with the buds intact. Store sealed in a cool, dark pantry and use them whole in stews, sauces, compotes and for studding the Christmas ham, but remember to remove before serving.

' Clove has been revered not only for its culinary delight but also for its medicinal qualities. Historically, it has been used as a breath freshener and is still used in some chewing gums today. From a nutrient perspective, clove houses key minerals (potassium, selenium manganese, magnesium and iron) and vitamins (A, C, K, pyridoxine, thiamin, riboflavin). Traditionally, clove has been used for a spectrum of benefits as an anti-inflammatory and antiflatulent when taken orally, and as a rubefacient (warming and calming) when applied topically to muscles and joints. Moreover, it is noted to have properties that serve as a robust antioxidant, antiseptic and local anesthetic. This is often credited to its essential oil, eugenol, which has been in therapeutic use in dentistry as a local anesthetic and antiseptic for teeth and gum health. Eugenol also has been found to reduce blood-sugar levels in animal studies when compared to placebo and thus may have benefits in diabetics, but further studies are needed to determine its future role in therapeutics. '

Param Dedhia, MD

Allspice *The Awesome Spice*

First 'discovered' by Christopher Columbus in Jamaica growing from an evergreen tree, allspice was mistakenly thought to be the prized and pricey black peppercorn and was named *pimenta* (Jamaican pepper).

From Europe to the Middle East, Africa to the Americas, Scandinavia to the Caribbean, allspice glides effortlessly from savoury to sweet and is a must in pickled vegetables, sauces, fish dishes and desserts.

Although they were discovered thousands of miles apart, allspice and clove are often confused because they share the active compound eugenol, a warming and powerful antioxidant and antiseptic. This single berry does triple duty in place of traditional cupboard-spice blends such as mixed spice, English spice and pumpkin pie spice. It is a bit more peppery than clove, but with a complex sweetness, and softer in fragrance, with a hint of toasted orange peel.

Most of the flavour and compounds are found in the shell. Dried berries will last 2–4 years; ground allspice considerably less time – six months at the most – so purchase a little at a time for the freshest flavour.

Citrus Zest *The Zing Spice*

Not only is a bit of citrus zest often the secret ingredient in a salad dressing, carrot and coriander soup or a sauce for fish, but it also contains compounds that can help fight a number of complaints and diseases, from aching feet to, according to new studies, cancer. The flavonoids (organic componds) in citrus fruits, particularly in the peel, are being used in tandem with chemotherapy in several cancer studies, including to treat prostate cancer.

The range of citrus varieties and peel preparations are numerous. Orange, tangerine and mandarin peel are traditionally used in liqueurs, confectionary, pastries and cakes, and smell of winter holidays when added to warming mulled wine. Lemon is the most popular citrus fruit, for both its juice and peel, and there are thousands of varieties around the globe. Thought to have originated in Northern India or China, the lemon was introduced into Sicily in 200AD, and to the Middle East a few hundred years later. My favourite lemon-zest variety is the curious-looking but exquisitely fragranced Buddha's Hand Lemon, or Fingered Citron, a citrus variety composed nearly entirely of peel, used for flavouring savoury dishes, desserts, cocktail infusions and for making preserves. In Chinese tradition, it symbolizes happiness and long life, while in Japan, it is believed to bestow good fortune.

But the scent of a tropical lime is an all-time citrus favourite. Originating in Southeast Asia, it is one of the few citrus fruits that is grown from seed rather than being grafted and is happiest in tropical climes, being more prone to frost damage than other kinds of citrus. Lime peel is generally thinner and more delicate than lemon, orange and grapefruit. Loomi, also known as dried or black limes, are a traditional Persian and Indian spice. The limes are preserved by boiling whole green limes in brine then smoking and/or drying them in the sun. Added to Middle Eastern dishes, these rock-hard balls impart a citrusy, smoky flavour and are the perfect addition to legume dishes.

Buy organic fruit, as the peel of non-organic citrus is sprayed before transport with any number of chemicals. If not available, wash thoroughly with a natural plant-based fruit wash (ironically, most are derived from citrus oil!). Using a potato peeler or zester, remove the peel from the pith and use it right away or tightly wrap it in cling film (plastic wrap) and refrigerate to prevent it from drying out and becoming brittle. Or make this easy preserved lemon peel recipe: thinly peel the zest from 4 unwaxed lemons, drop into a small pan of boiling water and blanch for 1 minute. Strain, discard the water and repeat with fresh water. Rinse in cold water, then pat dry. Transfer to a small storage container with a tight-fitting lid, add 2 tablespoons of salt flakes, 3 tablespoons of sugar and 6 thyme sprigs. Mix well then cover and chill for a week, shaking the container daily. Scrape the preserving mix off the peel you want to use, then, using the tip of a knife, slice the peel into thin matchsticks. Garnish dishes, adding additional thyme leaves to finish. Substitute Valencia orange or pink grapefruit peel for a twist on the classic lemon taste.

www.citrusvariety.ucr.edu/citrus/buddha.html / www.ncbi.nlm.nih.gov/pubmed/23673480

‘ Citrus zest is fun to say, use and taste: it's the essence of the fruit, distilled into a squiggle.

Zest is a part of the peel, and the peel is powerful medicine. In an Arizona study, those who reported drinking both hot black tea and citrus peel had an 88 per cent reduced risk of squamous cell carcinoma of the skin; people who drank iced tea with citrus peel had a 42 per cent reduced risk of skin cancer. Both groups were compared with those who did not drink tea or eat citrus peel. And people who just ate the fruit or drank the juice did not have the same anticancer effect.

Why do tea and citrus zest seem to knock back the risk of skin cancer? Tea's polyphenols [protective antioxidant compounds] may protect against the carcinogenic effect of UV radiation. The theaflavins of black tea is one class of those plant chemicals, which may work by stopping cancer cells from starting.

Gram for gram, citrus zest has much more vitamin C than the juice or pulp, and more of the plant chemicals that are likely protective against cancer formation: d-limonene, hesperidin, naringin and auraptene. D-limonene, which constitutes the vast majority of citrus oil, works on cancer cells directly. Several other components of citrus peel are being studied as anticancer agents. ’

John La Puma, MD

http://www.ncbi.nlm.nih.gov/pmc/articles/PMC45584/; http://www.ncbi.nlm.nih.gov/pubmed/18072821; http://www.ncbi.nlm.nih.gov/pubmed/11142088

Star Anise *The Sultry Fighter Spice*

Considered the most important spice used in Chinese cuisine, this photogenic spice, with its eight starry-tipped points, is also a wealth of health. Long used as a traditional Chinese medicine to treat inflammation, nervousness, insomnia and pain, star anise (*Anisi stellati fructus*) has been demonstrated to possess antibacterial, antifungal and antioxidant activities. There's also an active flu-fighter component in star anise called shikimic acid. Slowly extracted from the seeds over the course of several months, this acid becomes part of the recipe for a vital modern-day vaccine.

Plucked just before they are ripe from a small evergreen tree native to Southern China and Vietnam, the green flower-shaped fruits are then sun dried.

The major flavour component in traditional Chinese five-spice powder, a centuries-old Chinese-spice blend, star anise has flavour layers of cinnamon, citrus, clove and peppercorn and the pungent flavour is found only in the pod's pericarp or shell, not in the seeds. Stars can be added whole to long-cooking dishes (see April Bloomfield's Adobo on page 78 or the Blackcurrant Consommé on page 46) or ground in Garam Masala Bastilla (see page 28). Some popular recipes that use star anise include the Vietnamese soup pho, Chinese pork ribs and Peking duck, curries, Jamaica jerk chicken and masala chai tea. Add a bit of star anise powder and a little orange or mandarin orange zest to hot cocoa to enjoy a heavenly after-meal beverage.

Strangely enough, star anise, cultivated in Southern China thousands of years ago, and anise or anise seed, primarily from Spain, contain the same essential oil, anethole, but are botanically unrelated. In traditional recipes from Italy to Scandiniva, anise and the slightly grassier-flavoured fennel seed are the favourites. Today, however, star anise has the spotlight, as it has become less expensive and has a complex richer flavour. Similar-flavoured spices and herbs include fennel seed, licorice and tarragon, all of which also contain anethole. Ground star anise can be substituted for an equal measure of ground anise seed in most recipes.

Because this spice has an extremely long shelf life of several years, merchants may keep it on the shelf for too long. Check that it smells lightly of licorice; it should not smell musty or have no scent at all.

If grinding star anise at home, use a mortar and pestle or a rolling pin to rough grind it then grind finely in an electric grinder or high-powered single-serve high-speed blender.

---

6 Star anise has been popularized for its flavour and for its medicinal qualities. Containing minerals (calcium, potassium, iron, copper, manganese, magnesium and zinc) and vitamins (A, C, thiamin, riboflavin, pyridoxine and niacin), it has been used in traditional medicine as an antiseptic, antispasmodic, digestive, expectorant, balancing tonic and stimulant. The seeds have been chewed after meals for generations in the subcontinent to refresh the breath and promote digestion. Its key oils include thymol, terpineol and anethole, which have been used to treat chest infections and coughs.

Modern research has noted star anise's activity as an antioxidant: it has been found to reduce the amount of cancer development after exposure to carcinogens. In a most intriguing study, antibacterial properties from anise showed benefit when tested against dozens of strains of drug-resistant bacteria. Most celebrated is its effective use against several types of viruses by preventing viral replication. Shikimic acid is the ingredient extracted from Chinese star anise to develop the drug oseltamivir, which is prescribed to treat (but not to prevent) the influenza virus.

On-going research is looking at anethole, an essential oil found in star anise, for its anti-inflammatory properties. An experiment conducted with animals showed anethole compounds as effective as the powerful anti-inflammatory drug indomethacin. Anethole is also an antioxidant and has been demonstrated to kill fungus. (Safety note: Star anise should not be fed to infants.) 9

Param Dedhia, MD

CUMIN AND GOATS' CHEESE STICKS

Nutty, toasty cumin paired with earthy, calcium-rich goats' cheese make these crumbly sticks not only delicious but also good for your bones: the active compound in cumin is rich in phytoestrogens that helps stave off bone loss.

MAKES ABOUT 12 (1.5–2CM/½–¾IN. WIDE) STICKS

100g (3½oz./generous ¾ cup) plain (all-purpose) flour
55g (2oz./½ stick) unsalted butter, softened
140g (5oz.) goats' cheese, cold
½ tsp toasted ground cumin
pinch sea salt

½ tsp dried thyme leaves
1 tbsp fresh thyme leaves, plus extra to garnish
1 egg white, beaten, to glaze
1 tsp cumin seeds
sea salt and freshly ground black pepper, for sprinkling on top

Preheat the oven to 190°C (375°F/gas mark 5). Pulse the flour, butter, goats' cheese, ground cumin, fresh and dried thyme and a pinch of salt in a food processor until the mixture appears crumbly.

Turn out onto a lightly floured board or marble and press into a dough. Roll out a square or rectangle about 5mm (¼in.) thick on cling film (plastic wrap). Slice into thin strips approximately 1.5cm (½in.) wide and cover with cling film (plastic wrap). Chill in the fridge until firm.

Place the sticks on ungreased parchment paper or a silicone-lined baking tray and brush lightly with egg-white wash. Scatter with the cumin seeds, salt and pepper and bake for about 15 minutes, until golden brown.

COURGETTE AND RED PEPPER PARCELS

A simple light starter or tray pass/hors d'oeuvre to celebrate the humble and prolific courgette (zucchini) and luscious buratta mozzarella, seasoned with thyme, peppercorn and citrus zest: a winning combination of flavour and colour. Add a drizzle of your favorite olive oil or fresh thyme oil (see page 194).

SERVES 4

1 red (bell) pepper (about 140g/5oz.)
4 courgettes (zucchini), (about 165g/5¾oz. each)
2 tsp thyme oil, for brushing (see page 194)
250g (9oz.) fresh buratta or buffalo mozzarella
2 tbsp capers

15g (½oz.) preserved lemon or peel of ¼ lemon, shredded into thin strips
extra virgin olive oil, to drizzle
12 small thyme sprigs
a few grinds freshly ground black pepper

Roast the (bell) pepper over a gas flame or on a barbecue, or place under a hot grill (broiler) on the top shelf of the oven, until blackened. Put in small bowl, cover tightly with cling film (plastic wrap) and leave for about 20 minutes, then peel away the skin. Slice in half, discard core and seeds and cut into 12 wide strips. Set aside. Thinly slice the courgettes (zucchini) lengthways into 5mm (¼in.) thick strips, 24 in total. Brush with a little thyme oil then grill in a pan or on the barbecue for 1–2 minutes on each side until soft and supple. Set aside on a plate. Slice the mozzarella into 12 equal portions. Place two courgette (zucchini) slices lengthways on a plate, just overlapping one another. Lay a slice of mozzarella a third of the way up then place a pepper strip on top. Roll the remaining short end of the courgette (zucchini) over both, then fold the longer end over the top and tuck under. Place three parcels on each plate and sprinkle with capers and preserved lemon peel. Drizzle with olive oil, scatter over the thyme sprigs and add a few grinds of black pepper on top.

THAT '70s MANDARIN CHICKEN SALAD

This dish was all the rage in California at the time I was dancing with the Koniklijk Ballet van Vlaanderen in Belgium and I made it for a dinner party and invited a few of my Flemish ballet colleagues. Much to my embarrassment, a husband and wife from what was then Yugoslavia tasted this New World dish and refused to take another bite. I was firmly told that one does not mix fruit and meat! Clearly they had not sampled dishes from their medieval ancestors, who mixed fruit, meat and spices in many a recipe. All the more for us then! Star anise has been used in Chinese medicine for centuries to combat a host of complaints and is also the secret spice used to combat the avian flu – how extraordinary!

SERVES 4 AS A MAIN OR 6 AS A STARTER

2 chicken breasts, with skin, bone in	**For the Five-spice Sesame Dressing:**
10g (¼oz.) peeled fresh ginger, cut into 4 pieces	90ml (6 tbsp) kecap manis (thick sweet soy sauce)
1 star anise	60ml (¼ cup) lime juice
2 kaffir lime leaves (optional)	3 tbsp freshly grated ginger
½ tsp black peppercorns	2 tbsp sesame seeds
3 spring onions (scallions), green and white parts separated	2 tbsp grapeseed oil
approx. 500ml (2 cups) vegetable or chicken stock or water	2 tbsp black or clear rice wine vinegar
100g (3½oz.) cellophane noodles	1 tbsp wasabi powder
oil for flash frying	1 tbsp five-spice powder
400g (14oz.) Chinese cabbage, shredded	1 tbsp sesame oil
150g (5½oz.) kale, shredded	1 tbsp minced garlic
175g (6oz.) sugar snap peas or 115g (4oz.) edamame beans	1 tbsp soy sauce
2 or 3 Mandarin oranges (350g/12oz.), peeled and segmented	¾ tsp chili paste
85g (3oz./¾ cup) cashew nuts, toasted and roughly chopped	

Add the chicken breasts to a large deep sauté pan. Add the ginger, star anise, kaffir lime leaf, peppercorns and the green tops of the spring onions (scallions). Slice the white part of the onions on the diagonal, measure out 55g (2oz./½ cup) and set aside. Cover the chicken with the stock or water and bring to a gentle simmer. Poach until tender and cooked to the bone, about 20 minutes. Turn off the heat and set aside until cool enough to debone. Discard the bones, skin and liquid. Cover the chicken meat and cool, then break up into bite-sized pieces and chill until ready to use.

While the chicken is cooking, whisk together the dressing ingredients, cover and chill until ready to use.

Pour oil into a wok or deep pan to a depth of 3cm (1¼in.) and heat to 180°C (360°F). Flash fry the noodles in four batches and drain on kitchen paper.

Put the Chinese cabbage, kale, sugar snap peas, mandarin orange segments, chopped cashew nuts, reserved spring onion (scallion) and chicken into a large bowl, pour over the dressing and lightly toss. Gently add the noodles and serve immediately.

GARAM MASALA BASTILLA

This rich but vegetarian take on a medieval 'greyte pye' includes an unorthodox garam masala that is really more like a medieval spice blend. In this modern version, vegetables, dried fruit and pulses replace the traditional game or fowl, enabling these once exotic and sought-after fragrant spices to be savoured in a new way.

SERVES 4

2 or 3 small sweet potatoes, peeled and thinly sliced

400g (14oz.) can white cannellini beans or chickpeas, rinsed and drained well

70g (2½oz./½ cup) sultanas (golden raisins)

2 pieces preserved lemon peel, shredded (see page 20) or zest of ½ lemon

100g (3½oz./¾ stick + 1 tbsp) butter

about 5 tsp Garam Masala Spice Blend (see below)

6 filo (phyllo) pastry sheets, opened out flat, covered with a damp cloth

½ quantity Turmeric Melted Onions (see page 146)

200g (7oz.) baby spinach, rinsed and patted dry

3 large eggs

100g (3½oz.) punnet ricotta (or farmer's cheese or cottage cheese)

13 cherry tomatoes, with stalks

Preheat the oven to 190°C (375°F/gas mark 5). Lightly oil a 30 x 15cm (12 x 6in.) baking dish.

Blanch the sweet potato slices in boiling salted water until al dente, about 2 minutes. Drain well and set aside.

Mix the beans, sultanas (golden raisins) and lemon peel or zest together in a bowl and set aside.

Melt the butter with 2 teaspoons of the spice mix. Brush two filo (phyllo) pastry sheets with this spiced butter, fold them in half and lay them side by side in the bottom of the baking dish so that they just overlap in the centre and the edges hang over the sides of the dish.

Layer the potato slices over the bottom of the dish, then add an evenly spread layer of the Turmeric Melted Onions and sprinkle over ½ teaspoon of spice blend. Next add an even layer of the bean and sultana (golden raisin) mix then sprinkle with a further ½ teaspoon of the spice blend. Cover with the spinach.

Beat the eggs with 1 teaspoon of spice mix. Pour over the spinach and gently shake the pan to settle. Spoon dollops of ricotta on top. Fold the edges of the filo (phyllo) just inside the edges of the dish.

Brush spice butter on the remaining filo (phyllo) sheets, fold in half, then cut into a grid of eight rectangles. Scrunch the filo rectangles into kerchiefs and arrange over the top. Pierce each tomato then tuck randomly on top, scattering a big pinch of spice blend over all. Sprinkle salt flakes on top if you like.

Bake in the oven for 30 minutes, until filo (phyllo) is browned and vegetables bubbling. Serve hot or at room temperature with a nice flagon of wine or ale!

GARAM MASALA SPICE BLEND

2 tbsp cardamom seeds, toasted and ground

4 tsp coriander seeds, toasted and ground

4 tsp ground cinnamon (or 1½ cinnamon sticks; charred and ground)

1 tbsp fennel seeds, toasted and ground

1 tbsp ground nutmeg

2 tsp ground allspice

2 tsp cumin seeds, toasted and ground

2 tsp chili powder

1 tsp ground cloves

1 tsp licorice powder (optional)

½ tsp fenugreek powder

Blend the spices in a mortar and pestle and transfer to a jar.

DIVER SCALLOPS
WITH SWEET POTATO PURÉE AND PRESERVED CITRUS PEEL
Suzanne Goin

'In the Southern California winter, citrus comes on strong and stays for the long haul, so I am constantly challenged to come up with new ways to use the whole fruit. We use a lot of citrus peel, often candied, in desserts, so I thought it would be interesting to incorporate it into a savoury dish.' SG

SERVES 6 AS A MAIN COURSE

1.3kg (3lb.) Jewel or Garnet sweet potatoes

25g (1oz.) tamarind block

1 lemon, plus 1 tbsp finely grated lemon zest

1 lime

1 orange

½ grapefruit

½ cinnamon stick, or ½ tsp ground cinnamon

½ tsp curry powder

1 chili de árbol or Thai chili (small red dried chili), crumbled

¼ tsp ground cardamom

2.5 x 2.5cm (1 x 1in.) piece fresh ginger, peeled and thinly sliced

3 tbsp honey

85g (3oz./¾ stick) unsalted butter, cut into small cubes

2 tbsp whole milk, plus more as needed

18 Maine diver scallops, about 55g (2oz.) each

1 tbsp thyme leaves

3 tbsp extra-virgin olive oil

Kosher salt and freshly ground black pepper

12 dandelion or baby rocket (arugula) leaves to garnish

Preheat the oven to 200°C (400°F/gas mark 6). Prick the sweet potatoes all over with a fork, place on a baking tray and bake for about 1–1 ½ hours (depending on their size) until tender when poked with a paring knife.

Using your hands, break the tamarind apart into small pieces and place it in a small bowl. Pour 120ml (½ cup) of boiling water over the tamarind and let it sit for 5 minutes. Stir the tamarind vigorously with a small whisk or spoon to loosen all the pulp and emulsify it with the water.

Using a vegetable peeler, peel strips of zest about 2.5cm (1in.) wide from all the citrus fruits. (Use a light hand to avoid the bitter white pith.) Place the zest strips in a small pan, cover with cold water and bring to the boil. Boil for 1 minute, drain and rinse with cool water. Repeat the process twice more.

Juice all the citrus fruits (you should have about 240ml/1 cup) and put the juice and the blanched zest in a non-reactive (earthenware, glass or stainless-steel) pan that is small enough for all the zest to be submerged. Add the cinnamon, curry powder, chili, cardamom, ginger, honey and ½ teaspoon of salt. Strain 2 tablespoons of 'tamarind water' from the bowl of soaking tamarind and add it to the pan. Bring the mixture to the boil, turn down the heat to medium–low and simmer for 12–15 minutes until the sauce thickens and looks glossy. Set aside.

When the sweet potatoes cool enough to handle, cut them in half. Cut away any burnt pieces and scoop the hot sweet-potato flesh into the bowl of a food processor fitted with a metal blade. Add the butter, 1 teaspoon of salt and a few grinds of pepper and purée to a smooth consistency. With the blade spinning, add in 2 tablespoons of milk (plus a little more if needed for the potatoes to move fluidly around the bowl). Season to taste.

Season the scallops with the lemon zest, thyme, salt and pepper. Heat a large sauté pan over high heat for 2 minutes. Swirl in 3 tablespoons of olive oil and carefully lay the scallops in the pan. (You may need to cook them in batches or in two pans.) It will smoke, but resist the temptation to move the scallops. Cook for about 3 minutes until browned, then turn them over and turn off the heat. The scallops should be a nice medium–rare.

To serve, spoon the hot sweet-potato purée onto the centre of six dinner plates and place two dandelion or baby rocket (arugula) leaves, overlapping the stems, on each plate. Arrange the scallops on top of the purée. Spoon some of the warm preserved citrus peel and some of the juices over the scallops and around the plate.

★

CALIFORNIA GIRL PRAWN CURRY
WITH SAMBALS

Growing up on the 'So Cal' coast, it was normal for us to have enchiladas, sukiyaki or 'authentically British' fish and chips for dinner, but a curry? Sally-Mom would make a curry from scratch – including all the sambals – when we had company. The scent of a curry cooking was mysterious but alluring to us kids and we knew those little dishes – 'sambals' – of coconut, toasted chopped peanuts, diced bananas, cashew nuts, olives, pineapple, golden raisins, jars of Major Grey's, with 'Sunday-best' spoons placed carefully aside, would soon appear on the table. What a treat! We would pile plates high with rice, a little curry, mild chutney and lots of our favourite sambals.

SERVES 6

90ml (6 tbsp) peanut oil	**For the So Cal garam masala:**
1 large onion, chopped	1½ tsp cumin seeds
1 large garlic clove, minced	2 whole cloves
1 tsp finely freshly grated ginger	½ tsp black peppercorns
175ml (¾ cup) shellfish or vegetable stock	½ tsp black cardamom pods
375ml (1⅔ cups) coconut milk	½ tsp green cardamom pods
1.3kg (3lb.) prawns (shrimp), peeled, cleaned and deveined	2 tbsp coriander seeds
1 tsp lemon juice, or to taste	½ cinnamon stick
handful (about 25g/1oz.) roughly chopped coriander (cilantro)	¼ tsp ground chipotle powder – a So Cal addition!
	1 tsp ground turmeric

To serve:

Sambals should include salty, sweet, sour and savoury flavours. Choose 8–12 of the following and serve, finely chopped, in an array of small bowls: salted roasted peanuts, spring onions (scallions), hard-boiled eggs, raisins and/or sultanas (golden raisins), dried apricots, sugared crystallized ginger, shredded coconut, kumquats (or small Valencia oranges seeded, finely chopped, with skins), black and/or green olives, spicy lemon pickle or zested lemon rind, watermelon pickle, radishes, fresh pineapple, apple, banana, flaked (shredded) almonds, salted walnuts, pears, cashew nuts, crystallized violets, etc.

Chutneys: Major Grey's, lime-garlic, mango-ginger or other Indian relishes and chutneys.

First make the garam masala. Turmeric adds that grand yellow curry colour, while coriander (cilantro) adds the real curry flavour. Toasting the spices adds intensity to their flavour. Toast the spices, stirring often, until they turn a few shades darker and give off a sweet, smoky aroma. Do not raise the heat to quicken the process, or the spices will brown too quickly or burn. Toast the cumin and cloves in a dry heavy frying pan (skillet) over a medium heat, remove to a small bowl then toast the coriander seeds, cardamoms, peppercorns and cinnamon stick. Once the spices are cool, transfer them to a mortar and pestle (or spice mill or coffee grinder) and grind to a powder. Stir in the chipotle powder and ground turmeric.

Heat the oil in a large pan, then add the onion and cook over medium heat until translucent and lightly browned. Add the garlic and ginger and cook for a few more minutes.

Add the spice blend and stir gently for a minutes over medium–low heat until you can smell the spices cooking. Add 60ml (¼ cup) of water, the stock and 175ml (¾ cup) of the coconut milk. Cover and simmer for 20 minutes, stirring occasionally.

Remove the lid, turn the heat to low and add the remaining 200ml (scant 1 cup) of coconut milk. Bring to a simmer, add the prawns (shrimp) and cook for 4 or 5 minutes. Stir in the lemon juice, chopped coriander (cilantro) and salt and black pepper to taste.

Mound a ladleful of the curry on steamy seasoned rice, sprinkle on the sambals, spoon on your favourite chutney and enjoy!

TURMERIC, CUMIN, CLOVE, GARLIC

CREAMY CHICKEN TIKKA
(HALDI ZAFRAN AUR ELIACHIWALI MURG TIKKA)
Cyrus Todiwala

'The word "tikka" originates in Persia and has been adopted globally, but seldom do people know its meaning, often assuming it refers to a sauce. In fact, the word simply means "cube"! This tikka, which is surprisingly creamy and mild, is spiced with saffron, cardamom and turmeric, enhanced with puréed nuts, yogurt and cream and served with a simple, yet very delicious Pulao Rice and a sauce created with the leftover marinade.' CT

SERVES 4

800g–1kg (1lb. 12oz.–2lb. 4oz.) boneless chicken leg or breast, cut into 2.5cm (1in.) cubes

For the marinade:

2 tsp ground turmeric

juice of 1 lime

2 tsp sea salt

1 handful raw cashew nuts

1 handful skinned unroasted almonds

handsome pinch saffron threads (I favour Iranian saffron)

1 level tsp ground green cardamom

1 level tsp ground mace

2 fresh slender green chilies, chopped

4 garlic cloves, chopped

7.5cm (3in) piece fresh ginger, peeled and chopped

200g (7oz./¾ cup) Greek-style yogurt

50ml (scant ¼ cup) extra virgin rapeseed oil (or other vegetable oil but not olive oil)

100ml (scant ½ cup) single (light) cream

salt to taste

For the sauce:

1 heaped tbsp butter

7.5cm (3in) piece cinnamon stick, broken into 2 or 3

2 medium onions

reserved marinade (see method)

1 x 450ml (15floz.) can coconut milk

1 tbsp chopped coriander (cilantro), optional

To serve:

Pulao Rice (see opposite)

thinly sliced pink shallots, chopped fresh mint and coriander (cilantro), dash of lime juice and salt, to serve (optional)

Blend the turmeric, sea salt and lime juice in a large bowl. Add the chicken pieces and turn to coat well, using a rubber spatula to avoid staining your hands. Transfer to a lidded container and refrigerate for at least 2 hours while you prepare the rest of the marinade.

Put the cashews and almonds in a bowl and pour over boiling hot water until the nuts are submerged. Cover and set aside for a couple of hours to allow the nuts to soften. (If you don't soak them well they don't purée well.)

Preheat the oven to 130°C (275°F/gas mark 1). Put the saffron threads into a small ovenproof bowl and put into the oven, then turn off the heat and leave for 10–15 minutes until just crisp. Crumble the threads gently between your finger and thumb then add a tablespoon or so of warm water, cover the bowl and set aside for the saffron to infuse.

Drain the cashew nuts and almonds, put in a blender and pulse to crush them as finely as you can. Add the saffron, cardamom, mace, chili, garlic, ginger, yogurt, rapeseed (or vegetable) oil and cream and purée. Pulse for a few seconds then scrape down the sides and check. You want a smooth texture but, but if you keep the blender running continuously, the contents will get hot and the cream may separate, so do take care.

Add this marinade to the partially marinated chicken and stir to mix well. Taste the marinade and add more seasoning if needed. Place in an airtight container and refrigerate for a few hours before using.

Scrape off and reserve the excess marinade before roasting, grilling (broiling) or barbecuing the chicken.

To roast the chicken, preheat the oven to 220°C (425°F/gas mark 7). Lay the chicken pieces on a silicone sheet on a baking tray and place on the top shelf of the oven. Cook for 8–10 minutes, turning the pieces halfway through cooking.

Alternatively, cook them under the grill (broiler) in your oven. Place them on the wire rack and place under the grill (broiler) and turn every 2–3 minutes until the chicken is cooked through and is nicely coloured all over.

If you want to barbecue the chicken, don't place the pieces directly onto the grill as the tikka will stick to it. Instead, skewer the pieces and hold them just above the flames: they will cook and colour perfectly.

To make the sauce: heat the butter with the cinnamon stick in a medium pan over a low heat for about 2 minutes, then add the onions and sauté gently until the onions are soft and pale.

Add the leftover marinade and increase the heat slightly. If it starts to stick to the bottom of the pan, loosen the sauce with some water and continue cooking until the fat separates. Add the coconut milk, bring to the boil, reduce the heat and simmer for 2–3 minutes. Turn off the heat and remove and reserve the cinnamon sticks.

Purée the sauce using either a stick blender or a blender (cool the sauce slightly first if using the latter), starting off on a low speed to ensure it doesn't spill out. Return the sauce to the pan, add the reserved cinnamon sticks and bring to the boil. Check the seasoning and add a tablespoonful of fresh chopped coriander (cilantro) if wished.

Serve the chicken tikka with the sauce, Pulao Rice and – if you really want to impress – a salad made from thinly sliced pink shallots and fresh mint and coriander mixed in with a dash of lime juice and salt.

PULAO RICE

'We Indians say pulao or palav but you may know this rice dish as pilaf or pilav. If you already have a favourite recipe, feel free to use it, but make sure you include some sultanas (golden raisins) and/or dried cranberries and some chopped cashew nuts and almonds. My version is a simple one that seldom fails.' CT

SERVES 4–6

1 tbsp butter	2 or 3 cloves
1 tbsp rapeseed oil	2 or 3 black peppercorns
50g (1¾oz.) whole raw almonds, skin on, cut into 5 or 6 pieces	1 tsp cumin seeds
	2 or 3 green cardamom pods, flattened to open
100g (3½oz.) barberries (available in some supermarkets, specialty shops or online), or 150g (5½oz.) dried cranberries, chopped	1 medium onion, halved and thinly sliced
	1 litre (4¼ cups) clear stock or water
	500g (1lb. 2oz./2⅓ cups) basmati rice

Preheat the oven to 130°C (275°F/gas mark 1).

In a wide casserole that will fit into centre of your oven with its lid on, heat the butter and oil over a low heat. Add the chopped almonds and barberries or cranberries and fry until the almonds have coloured slightly. Remove using a slotted spoon.

Add the whole spices to the fat (adding more and reheating if necessary) and cook for a few seconds until the cloves have begun to swell and the cumin to colour. Add the sliced onion and sauté until soft and pale. Add the stock or water and season with salt to taste. Bring to the boil, then add the rice and stir well.

Cover the casserole but check it regularly to ensure the rice doesn't stick to the bottom. (The best way to prevent this is to stir it from the bottom up so that you keep the heated rice at the top.) Simmer until the water is nearly absorbed, then clean down the sides, cover the casserole and place it in the oven.

After 10 minutes, turn off the oven. Leave the casserole in the oven for a further 30 minutes then remove it and loosen the rice gently. Stir in the almonds and cranberries or barberries.

If necessary, you can heat the rice up before serving it: put it in a glass bowl in the microwave and reheat on full power for 3–4 minutes until the rice is very hot.

Illustrated on pages 34–5

CUMIN, TURMERIC, GARLIC

SLOW-ROASTED LAMB SHOULDER
WITH QUINCE, CUMIN AND CORIANDER

The aromas from the slow-roasting cumin, quince and onions create a wordless way to introduce your family to the secrets of combining spices to create a mouth-watering main! The fat and spices melt down into the onion-carrot bed, which can be served alongside the meat. This is also great with farro or couscous and seasonal wilted greens.

SERVES 4

3 large onions (350g/12oz.), unpeeled, sliced into rounds

3 large carrots (225g/8oz.), peeled and cut into 5cm (2in.) rounds

3kg (6lb.10oz.) lamb shoulder, bone in, lightly trimmed of fat

2 tbsp coriander seeds

2 tbsp cumin seeds

2 tbsp black peppercorns

1 tsp cardamom seeds

3 bay leaves, torn

1 tsp ground turmeric

6 garlic cloves

2 tbsp salt flakes

2 tbsp olive oil

8 thyme sprigs

3 quince (or tart, firm apples), peeled, cored and cut into sixths

3 tbsp brown sugar

3 tbsp rice wine vinegar

cooked farro or couscous, to serve (optional)

seasonal wilted greens, to serve (optional)

Preheat the oven to 160°C (325°F/gas mark 3). Scatter the onion and carrot rounds on the bottom of an oiled roasting pan. Trim and lightly score the fat on the lamb shoulder and place on top of the bed of vegetables.

Dry-toast the coriander, cumin, peppercorns and cardamom in a frying pan until the aromas are released, then crush with a mortar and pestle. Add the bay leaves, turmeric, garlic, salt and oil to the mortar and crush to a paste. Massage this paste all over the lamb. Scatter with thyme sprigs and tuck quince pieces around the meat.

Sprinkle the sugar and vinegar over the top, then pour 100ml (scant ½ cup) of water into the side of the roasting pan. Tightly cover the roasting pan with thick foil and slow-roast for 4 hours.

Raise the oven temperature to 180°C (350°F/gas mark 4). Remove the foil, skim off the fat and add more water if needed. Baste the lamb then return it, uncovered, to the oven. Cook for a further 35 minutes or until fork tender.

PORK CHILE VERDE

Anne Conness

'I can't speak for the scientific connection between spice and health, but what I do know is that eating spicy things makes me feel happy and satisfied. And when I feel happy, I feel less stressed, and that makes my doctor happy!' AC

SERVES 4

1 tbsp cumin seeds	1 head garlic, cloves separated and peeled
1 tsp black peppercorns	60ml (¼ cup) canola oil
½ tsp cloves	2 tbsp lime juice
½ tsp ground cinnamon	1½ bunches coriander (cilantro)
½ tsp cayenne pepper	2 tsp cumin
2 tsp paprika	½ tsp cloves
2 tbsp salt	¼ tsp cayenne pepper
1.6kg (3.5lb.) pork shoulder, cut into 2cm (¾in.) cubes, most of fat removed	2 tsp paprika
	¼ tsp cinnamon
1.2 litres (5 cups) chicken stock	1 tsp salt
For the corn:	350ml (1½ cups) reserved cooking jus (see method)
3 ears of corn	**To serve:**
2 tbsp butter	1 tbsp sauce from chilies in adobo or chipotle paste mixed with 115g (4oz./½ cup) sour cream
30g (1oz./¼ cup) grated Monterey Jack or mild Cheddar cheese	
For the sauce:	1 dash Tajin (a classic Mexican dry seasoning of dried lime juice, chili powder and salt)
1 tomatillo, halved and stem removed	4 lime wedges
1 onion, roughly chopped	150g (5½oz./1 cup) pico de gallo (Mexican fresh tomato salsa)
2 jalapeños, halved and stems removed	
2 Anaheim chilies, halved and stems removed	small handful micro-coriander (cilantro) leaves

Preheat the oven to 180°C (350°F/gas mark 4).

Toast the whole spices, cool, then grind to a powder. Stir in the cinnamon, cayenne pepper, paprika and salt.

Toss the pork in the spice mixture and put in a roasting pan. Pour over the chicken stock, cover tightly with foil, put in the oven and cook until tender, about 1½ hours.

Strain the jus, skimming off the fat, and reserve 350ml (1½ cups) for the sauce. Break up the meat if necessary.

Char the sweetcorn: shuck the corn and remove the silks. Place the corn cobs on a baking tray on the top shelf of the oven or under the grill (broiler) on a high heat until charred. Leave to cool then place the corn cob in a cereal bowl and, using a sharp knife, cut the kernels from the cob in a downward motion; the kernels will collect in the bowl. Set aside.

For the sauce, toss the tomatillo, onion, jalapeños and Anaheim chilies and garlic in a bowl with the oil. Spread out on two baking trays and roast until caramelized, about 30 minutes at a medium–high heat. Leave to cool.

Blend the caramelized veggies in batches with the lime juice, coriander (cilantro), spices and strained cooking jus. Check the flavour and season to taste.

Put the pork in a pan with this sauce and heat up.

Melt the butter in a hot ovenproof pan then add the charred corn. Season with salt and pepper. Sprinkle cheese on top and put in the oven just long enough to melt the cheese.

To serve, put the pork on a plate and top with the corn. Garnish with the chipotle cream, a sprinkle of Tajin, a lime wedge and some pico de gallo. Finish with the coriander (cilantro).

CLOVE, STAR ANISE, ALLSPICE

SPICED PICKLED PLUMS

Served with a traditional Sunday supper of roast meats, these spiced pickled plums, full of the sweet comforting spices of autumn and winter, are readily transformed into a chutney for cheese and charcuterie (see recipe below).

MAKES 1KG (2LB. 4OZ.)

750ml (3¼ cups) apple cider vinegar	2 star anise
5g (⅛oz.) blade mace	10g (1½ tsp) orange zest
5 allspice berries	¾ tsp sea salt
2 tsp yellow mustard seeds	200g (7oz./1 cup) brown sugar
5 whole cloves	700g (1lb. 9oz.) pitted plums, quartered
1 cinnamon stick, charred	

Clean and sterilize one 1-litre (1-quart) or two ½-litre (½-quart) canning jars.

Put all the ingredients except the plums in a 1-litre (1-quart) pan and bring to a simmer for 3 minutes.

Put the plums in the sterilized jars then pour the liquid and spices over. Seal tightly with lids and set on the work surface until at room temperature. (You will hear the lids compress and create a vacuum.)

Store in a cool dark place for 2 weeks before using. The pickle will keep for up to a year unopened. Store opened jars in the fridge. Once opened, it will keep, chilled, for 6 months.

CLOVE, STAR ANISE, ALLSPICE

PICKLED PLUM AND SHALLOT CHUTNEY

A nice accompaniment for a cheese board, as pictured here, this chutney also makes a simple but tasty addition to a selection of cured meats and is delicious spread in a ploughman's ham and cheese sandwich.

MAKES 350G (12OZ./1 HEAPED CUP)

150g (5½oz.) shallots, unpeeled	1 tbsp vinegar from jar of Spiced Pickled Plums
2 tbsp extra virgin olive oil	1 tbsp honey
5 thyme sprigs	1 tbsp Vanilla Honey Mustard (see page 164)
2 tbsp port	1 tsp freshly grated ginger
30g (1oz.) sultanas (golden raisins)	1 sprig fresh thyme
200g (7oz.) Spiced Pickled Plums (see above), chopped into bite-sized pieces	

Preheat the oven to 180°C (350°F/gas mark 4). Trim the shallot root ends, leaving the papery skin attached.

Place in a small foil-lined baking tin and drizzle with olive oil. Top with thyme sprigs and roast in the oven for about 30–35 minutes, or until soft when pierced with the tip of a knife and golden brown.

When cooled, peel, discard the skins and slice the shallots lengthways into sixths.

Warm the port, add the sultanas (golden raisins) and leave to soak for about 10 minutes. Mix in the shallots and remaining ingredients and combine well.

Serve with your favourite cheeses and biscuits. The chutney will keep for 1 month chilled.

FLOATING SPICE ISLANDS
WITH LIME, RASPBERRY AND COCONUT JAM

A tropical-island tribute to the French classic, île flottante, a light, humble farmhouse dessert. Here, the 'islands' are baked in moulds then floated in a passion fruit-orange-pineapple (POP) 'sea' finished with citrus and nutmeg.

SERVES 4–6

For the lime, raspberry and coconut jam:
240ml (1 cup) coconut cream
1 vanilla pod (bean), split in half and cut into 4 pieces
4 large egg yolks
1 tbsp cornflour (cornstarch)
100g (3½oz./½ cup) palm sugar, or raw or white sugar
100g (3½oz.) frozen raspberries
6 whole allspice berries, toasted and cracked
zest and juice of 1 lime

For the POP crème anglaise:
175g (¾ cup) passion-fruit pulp seeded (about 8 passion fruit)
120ml (½ cup) orange juice
zest of 1 orange
100g (3½oz.) fresh or frozen pineapple chunks

1 tsp freshly grated ginger
100g (3½oz./½ cup) caster (superfine) or coconut sugar
4 large egg yolks
475ml (2 cups) full-fat (whole) milk

For the meringue:
1 tsp coconut oil or butter, for greasing molds
4 large egg whites, at room temperature
⅛ tsp cream of tartar
150g (5½oz./¾ cup) caster (superfine) sugar
1 tsp vanilla extract

To garnish:
2 kaffir lime leaves, cut into thin strips
½ tsp freeze-dried raspberry dust (optional)
large pinch freshly grated nutmeg

To make the lime, raspberry and coconut jam, in a medium pan, whisk the coconut cream, four pieces of the vanilla pod (bean), the egg yolks, cornflour (cornstarch) and sugar with a pinch of salt. Add the raspberries, allspice and lime zest and juice and cook over medium heat, scraping down the sides occasionally and gently stirring until the mixture is thick and custard-like, coating the back of a spoon, and has reached 70°C (160°F). Strain through a fine mesh sieve into a bowl set in an ice bath to cool the jam then chill.

To make the POP crème anglaise, in a saucepan over low heat, warm the passion-fruit pulp, orange juice and zest and pineapple chunks with the ginger, remaining four pieces of vanilla and 1 tablespoon of the sugar. Simmer for 10 minutes. Cool briefly, then using a bar or stick blender, purée until smooth. Set aside to cool. In a small bowl, beat the egg yolks with the remaining sugar. In a medium pan, warm the milk over medium heat. When the milk steams, slowly stream in the yolks, whisking until incorporated, then stir with a wooden spoon until the sauce thickens and coats the back of the spoon. Strain into a bowl inside an ice bath and whisk to stop it from cooking further. When cold, fold in the juice purée. Cover and chill until ready to serve.

To make the meringue, preheat the oven to 160°C (325°F/gas mark 3). Very lightly brush 16 dariole moulds or a mini-muffin tin with coconut oil or butter. Set aside. In the bowl of a stand mixer or electric mixer with the whip/whisk attachment, beat the egg whites with the cream of tartar and a large pinch of salt on medium speed until frothy. Increase the speed and add the sugar 1 tablespoon at a time. Add the vanilla and whip until the whites form shiny stiff peaks. Using a piping bag with a star tip, pipe the meringue into each mould until two thirds full. Place in a casserole or cake tin and place in the oven. Pour boiling water into the corner of the pan to come halfway up the moulds. Bake in the oven for 7–10 minutes until set, or until a temperature probe reaches 63–66°C (145–150°F). Remove the moulds from the water bath and unmould onto a parchment-lined baking tray.

To serve, arrange three or four meringues on the bottom of each flat-bottomed bowl. Fill a jug with the POP crème anglaise then carefully pour equally into each bowl. Spoon the jam into quenelles around the meringues and garnish with kaffir lime leaf strips, a sprinkling of raspberry dust (if using) and a grating of nutmeg.

BLACKCURRANT CABERNET CONSOMMÉ
WITH VANILLA MILK CUBES, CLOVE–CARAMEL APPLE AND CHOCOLATE 'NOODLES'

This divine consommé contains not only eugenol-packed clove but also delicious deep-purple blackcurrants, which are known to contain high levels of anthocyanins for optimum brain health.

SERVES 4–6

For the consommé:

1 star anise

½ tsp peppercorns

500g (1lb. 2oz./5 cups) blackcurrants, fresh or frozen

peel of 1 orange

700ml (3 cups) apple juice or water

250g (9oz./¾ cup) golden or cane syrup

60ml (¼ cup) Cabernet wine

2 tbsp fresh Key or Tahitian lime juice

For the vanilla milk cubes:

2 gold gelatin leaves (see page 86, or 1½ tsp powdered gelatin)

120ml (½ cup) double cream

120ml (½ cup) full-fat milk

2 tbsp golden or cane syrup

½ vanilla pod (bean), split and scraped, or ½ tsp vanilla paste

¾ tsp amaretto

For the clove-caramel apple:

1 crisp red apple

240ml (1 cup) apple juice or water

200g (7oz./1 generous cup) golden or cane syrup

10g (¼oz.) fresh ginger, peeled and cut into 4 pieces

½ tsp ground cloves

For the chocolate 'noodles':

1½ tsp agar agar powder (or 3 tbsp agar agar flakes)

85g (3oz.) dark chocolate (72% cocoa solids), chopped

1 tbsp cognac

To serve:

about 2 tbsp toasted sliced almonds

To make the consommé, toast the star anise and peppercorns and rough grind using a mortar and pestle. Put into a 2-litre (2-quart) pan with the blackcurrants, orange peel, apple juice, syrup and a pinch of salt and bring to a low simmer. Cook for 5 minutes then take off the heat, whisk in the wine and lime juice and infuse for 20 minutes.

Using a stick or bar blender, purée the liquid then strain and discard the pulp and spices. Strain again using a fine mesh strainer or cheesecloth. Chill the consommé until ready to serve.

To make the vanilla milk cubes, line a small rectangular plastic container with cling film (plastic wrap).

Put the gelatin leaves in a bowl, cover with cold water and leave to soften. (If using powdered gelatin, see page 86.) In a small jug, whisk together the cream, milk, syrup, vanilla, amaretto and a pinch of salt until smooth.

Squeeze out the water from the gelatin leaves then add the gelatin to a small pan and warm to melt. Whisk immediately into the cream mixture until dissolved, then pour into the prepared container. Place on a flat surface in the fridge until set, about 30 minutes, then cut into cubes.

To make the clove-caramel apple, slice the apple horizontally wafer thin using a mandoline or sharp knife. Pour the apple juice or water into a small pan, add the syrup, ginger and cloves and bring to a simmer. Add the apple slices and simmer gently until they are almost translucent. Cool, then chill and cover until needed.

Remove the ginger pieces, then simmer and reduce the cooking liquid until it is of a caramel consistency.

To make the chocolate 'noodles', dissolve the agar agar in 175ml (¾ cup) of water and bring to a simmer. Turn down the heat and add the chocolate and cognac, stirring to blend smooth. Pour into a plastic squeezy bottle with a small tip opening. Secure the top. Let the liquid chocolate thicken to a soft custard-like consistency.

Prepare an ice-water bath in a rectangular container. Gently squeeze the chocolate from the bottle to create squiggles over the ice bath, a bit at a time. Gently scoop the 'noodles' out of the bath using your hands and drain on baking paper. Repeat until you have four small piles of noodles.

To serve, divide the vanilla milk cubes amongst flat-bottomed bowls. Carefully ladle the consommé around them. Garnish with the apples, chocolate noodles, a drizzle of clove caramel and some toasted sliced almonds.

SWISS BERRY QUILT CAKE
WITH CARAMELIZED PEACH COULIS AND LEMON VERBENA SABAYON

Always a popular light dessert during long Indian Summer days – a reminder of autumn, but not yet – this is a low-gluten and, excluding the sabayon, dairy-free dessert.

SERVES 8–10

140g (5oz./1¼ cups) plain (all purpose) flour, sifted

¼ tsp ground cloves

280g (10oz./1½ packed cups) soft light brown sugar

14 large egg whites, at room temperature

1½ tsp cream of tartar

2 tsp orange zest

For the Swiss Berry Coulis:

450g (1lb.) blackberries

500g (1lb. 2oz.) raspberries

200g (7oz./1 cup) caster (superfine) sugar

2 allspice berries, toasted and ground

2 cloves, toasted and ground

1 tsp fresh lemon juice

To serve:

Lemon Verbena Sabayon (see opposite)

Caramelized Peach Coulis (see opposite)

fresh berries

edible flowers and/or lemon verbena or mint leaves

Preheat the oven to 180°C (350°F/gas mark 4). In a bowl, combine the flour with the ground cloves and half of the brown sugar. Place a piece of waxed or parchment paper on a flat surface. Sift the flour mixture onto the parchment, then sift again back into the bowl. Repeat then set aside.

In a stand mixer with a whisk attachment on medium speed, or in large bowl using a whisk, beat the egg whites until foamy. Ensure all equipment is clean, dry and grease-free. Sprinkle in the cream of tartar then continue to beat the whites until tripled in volume. Sprinkle the remaining sugar over the whites 1 tablespoon at a time and continue beating until the sugar is incorporated and the whites are thick and glossy. Turn the speed to medium–low and fold in the flour and sugar mixture in three additions. Finally, add the orange zest.

Spoon the cake batter into an unbuttered 25cm (10in.) angel-cake tin with a removable bottom. Run a knife through the batter to break up any air bubbles. Bake for 45 minutes, until golden and the cake springs back when you lightly press the surface. Invert, in its tin, onto a cooling rack and cool completely, at least 1 hour.

While the cake is cooling, make the coulis. Rinse and drain the berries, reserving about a quarter of each. Add the remaining berries to a large pan. Over low heat, add the sugar and spices and bring to a low simmer, stirring the sauce to break down the berries. Use a food mill or sieve to strain out the seeds then stir in the lemon juice. Cover and chill the coulis and reserved berries until needed.

Turn the cake right side up, then run a knife around the sides and centre tube of the tin. Release from the sides, then run a knife around the bottom to release. Slice the cake vertically into 2cm (¾in.) slices. Set aside.

Have a spring-form pan, reserved berries and berry coulis ready. Lightly moisten the pan then line with cling film (plastic wrap), letting the side of the film (plastic) fall over the edges. Sprinkle a third of the reserved berries in the bottom of the pan then add a ladleful of sauce. Press a layer of cake slices onto the bottom, filling in the cracks to make a 'patchwork-quilt' layer. Repeat these layers two or three times, finishing with a little more sauce on top. Tuck the cling film (plastic wrap) over the top then add another layer of film over the top. Weight the cake with a flat plate and a 500g (1lb.) weight or can on top. Chill in the fridge for at least 3 hours or overnight.

Make the Lemon Verbena Sabayon and Caramelized Peach Coulis (see opposite).

To assemble, peel away the cling film (plastic wrap) from the top of the cake tin and cover with a cake plate. Flip over onto the plate then release the sides then the top of the spring-form pan. Peel away the film. Cut the cake in wedges and place on individual plates. Spread a generous spoonful of peach coulis onto each plate then spoon the sabayon over the edge of the cake. Garnish with fresh berries and edible flowers and/or verbena or mint leaves.

LEMON VERBENA SABAYON

This sabayon is made with lemon verbena, but you can use the same technique for infusing cream with all sorts of spices and herbs.

SERVES 8–10

240ml (1 cup) double (heavy) cream

10–12 fresh lemon verbena leaves, roughly chopped

¼ vanilla pod (bean), split, or ¼ tsp paste

3 large yolks, at room temperature

55g (2oz./¼ cup) caster (superfine) sugar

120ml (½ cup) sparkling wine

Put the cream, lemon verbena leaves and vanilla pod (bean) into a pan and heat to a gentle simmer, stirring. Let cool, then cover and infuse for at least 2 hours or overnight.

To finish the sabayon, place the egg yolks in a heatproof bowl set over barely simmering water and whisk well. Slowly add the sugar a little at a time, then gradually add the sparkling wine and vigorously and continuously whisk for about 10 minutes until light yellow and fluffy. Have an ice bath ready. Transfer to the bowl to the ice bath and continue to whisk the mixture until completely cooled. You may set aside the mixture at this point until service, but keep it chilled.

When ready to serve, strain the leaves from the chilled cream, then whip the cream into soft peaks.

Fold the cream into the egg mixture in three stages, gently mixing until combined. You can make this up to 3 hours in advance, covering and chilling until needed.

Serve a generous spoonful over each wedge of quilt cake.

CARAMELIZED PEACH COULIS

SERVES 8–10

450g (1lb.) fresh yellow peaches (or apricots), pitted and quartered

2 tbsp brown sugar

2 tsp freshly grated ginger

¼ tsp ground allspice

1 tbsp grapeseed oil

large pinch salt

¼ tsp ground white pepper

Preheat the oven to 180°C (350°F/gas mark 4). Put the peach quarters in a large bowl, sprinkle in the sugar, ginger and allspice and toss to coat.

Oil a baking tray and arrange the peaches on it, cut side up. Sprinkle with the salt and white pepper. Bake on the middle rack of the oven for 30 minutes, until bubbly and caramelized.

When cool, run through a food mill to purée. Adjust seasonings, cover and chill until needed.

Illustrated on pages 48–9

TURMERIC, CITRUS ZEST

MANDARIN POPPY-SEED POUND CAKE

Zesty with mandarin, lime, the sweet crunch of poppy seeds and the tang of turmeric, this simple cake is delicious, can be adapted for any occasion and pairs perfectly with a steamy cup of Cardamom Chai Tisane (see page 208). If you can't find mandarin purée (available from specialty food shops), you can make your own by gently simmering and reducing 475ml (2 cups) of tangerine or orange juice by about three quarters to yield approximately 150ml (²⁄₃ cup) of purée. Leave to cool before using.

MAKES ONE BUNDT CAKE OR 12–14 SMALL CAKES

For the cake:

3 tbsp poppy seeds, plus 2 tsp for lining moulds

240g (8½oz./2 cups) plain (all-purpose) flour

2 tbsp cornflour (cornstarch)

½ tsp sea salt

225g (8oz./2 sticks) butter, softened

¾ tsp ground turmeric

200g (7oz./1 cup) castor (superfine) sugar

zest of 3 tangerines (or 2 oranges) and 1 lime

5 large eggs

80ml (⅓ cup) mandarin purée or orange juice concentrate (see recipe introduction)

For the icing:

60ml (¼ cup) mandarin purée

2 tbsp boiling water

250g (9oz./2 cups) icing (confectioner's) sugar

30g (1oz./2 tbsp) butter

pinch salt

Preheat the oven to 160°C (325°F/gas mark 3). Grease a ring cake mould (Bundt pan) or individual dariole moulds and line with the 2 teaspoons of poppy seeds, then place on a baking tray.

Sift the flours with the salt and 3 tablespoons of poppy seeds and set aside.

In the bowl of a stand mixer with a paddle attachment, or in a bowl using a spoon, cream the butter with the turmeric and sugar until light but not over beaten; about 2 minutes. Add the zest, then fold in the eggs one at a time on medium speed until blended, scraping down sides between additions. Add the purée and the flour mixture until just combined. Scrape down the sides and bottom of the bowl to blend well. Do not over mix. Spoon into the prepared cake tin or moulds, smoothing the top, and bake in the oven for 18–20 minutes for the small cakes, or about 50 minutes for the large one, until a knife or toothpick comes out clean.

To make the icing, in a small bowl, add the mandarin purée and water to the sugar. Beat with a whisk until smooth. Beat in the butter with a pinch of salt until combined.

To finish, cool the cake(s) for 10 minutes in the tin, then turn out on to a wire cooling rack. When completely cool, cover to keep from drying out. Glaze with the icing and allow to dry.

TURMERIC, CITRUS ZEST

TROPICAL TURMERIC SMOOTHIE

The combination of fruit and spice and rich-but-healthy coconut or cashew milk is my favourite before a workout or just as a get-to-work beverage! If you prefer, you can use papaya instead of mango and add three leaves of coriander (cilantro). For a thicker smoothie, freeze the coconut milk in cubes before blending.

SERVES 1

85g (3oz.) pineapple

115g (4oz.) fresh frozen mango

2.5 x 5cm (1 x 2in.) strip orange peel

5cm (2in.) piece (20g/¾oz.) turmeric root, or ¼ tsp ground turmeric

⅛ tsp cracked black pepper

¼ tsp cardamom seeds, toasted and ground

1 tbsp fresh lime juice

240ml (1 cup) coconut milk

4–6 ice cubes

1 tsp chia seeds

Put all the ingredients except the chia seeds into a high-speed single-serve blender-juicer and blend until smooth. Sprinkle chia seeds on top and serve.

TURMERIC, CLOVE, STAR ANISE, CITRUS ZEST

SPICED TURMERIC TISANE

This warming drink is spicy, aromatic and does not contain any caffeine or dairy. It is recommended that you add a little fat to any recipe containing turmeric as this helps activate turmeric's health properties. The alliance of peppercorn and turmeric makes for a powerful spice team!

SERVES 2

5cm (2in.) piece fresh turmeric, peeled and cut into 'coins', chopped

2.5cm (1in.) piece fresh ginger, peeled and chopped

1 cinnamon stick, toasted

6 black peppercorns

1 star anise

5 whole cloves

3 green cardamom pods, crushed to release seeds

2 x 2.5cm (1in.) wide strips orange peel

1 tbsp honey, or to taste

240ml (1 cup) coconut milk

Put the turmeric, ginger, cinnamon stick, peppercorns, star anise, cloves, cardamom and orange peel into a pan with 240ml (1 cup) of water and bring to the boil. Reduce the heat and simmer for 3–5 minutes or until fragrant. Turn the heat to low and steep for a further 3–5 minutes.

Remove from the heat and stir in the honey. Strain and discard solids.

Warm and froth the coconut milk, or other milk of your choice, and gently pour it into the tisane. Serve immediately.

Cleansing spice

The body's versatile and clever natural detoxification or cleansing systems have evolved over millennia to adjust to the increasingly hostile sphere we exist upon: Earth. These cleansing spices show promising ability to provide support to our natural detoxification systems, helping to cleanse the body and clear the mind.

Cleansing Spice Health Heroes

Cinnamon ★ Rosemary ★ Oregano ★ Bay Leaf ★ Hibiscus

Air, water and soil are necessary for survival, but many parts of the planet's surfaces and oceans are no longer considered clean; finding a pristine lake or ocean reef not affected by the disruptive human footprint has sadly become the exception. Despite our body's remarkable and sophisticated workings, ill health, disease or symptoms may present themselves at any time for any number of reasons, including ones we don't clearly understand.

Spices in this chapter abound with plentiful antioxidants, the most powerful support to fend off free radicals and aid in flushing out toxins. Rosemary can help focus our short- and long-term memory and aid us with complex brain tasks. Sweet-tasting cinnamon may provide additional support for the liver, pancreas and digestive system by aiding in balancing blood sugar. Very topically, oregano checks in to support the system's PH acid-alkali balance, which is constantly being challenged by the effects of stress, an unhealthy diet and exposures to pollutants. The humble and ancient-storied bay leaf, brimming with nutrients, including vitamin C, is an oxidation reducer and LDL-cholesterol fighter. Last but not least, the pink-party-girl hibiscus is thought to be a formidable foe in the war on cleansing and clearing the digestive system of excess fat and carbohydrates by blocking fat absorption and flushing it out of your system.

Other cleansing spice heroes

Turmeric With an encyclopaedic amount of promising healing capabilities, this extensively studied spice also shows benefit for suppressing fat-cell growth and provides tremendous liver-strengthening support. Research studies suggest that active turmeric compounds can lower LDL-cholesterol levels with their lipid-blocking properties, thereby aiding weight loss by reducing fat tissues overall.

Pomegranate This jewelled fruit aids in flushing out free radicals with its high levels of antioxidant polyphenols, the disease-fighting antioxidants found in plants. All parts of a pomegranate – the fresh or dried seeds, the leathery skin, the pulp, flowers and roots – are full of goodness and packed with a variety of powerful polyphenols ready to be utilized to aid in clearing the system.

Coriander The concentrated free-radical-fighting antioxidant compounds in coriander seeds may help to protect, cleanse and regenerate liver tissue damaged by lifestyle behaviours and a number of diseases, including NAFLD (non-alcoholic fatty liver disease). The cell-protecting antioxidant oils contain large amounts of linalool and geranyl acetate, which play a huge part in clearing the body of unwelcome bacteria and may also be helpful in clearing bladder and urinary tract infections.

Thyme The active oil of thyme, thymol, has a commanding antibacterial presence with its protective and clearing properties in the war on MRSA (methicillin-resistant *Staphylococcus aureus* – most well-known as the hospital skin-eating antibiotic-resistant staph infection) and other resistant bacterial strains. Thyme may also provide hangover relief with its detoxifying talents.

Tamarind It is thought that high-fibre tamarind binds to toxins that include cancer-promoting chemicals that may unknowingly be found in our food, thereby reducing their exposure to the digestive system and lessening the risk of colon cancer. Tamarind fibre also binds to bile salts, which are a component of the liquid secreted from the gallbladder during digestion to process the cholesterol-laden lipids and reduce their re-entry into the body via the colon. This process lowers LDL, 'lousy' cholesterol, which can form plaques in blood vessels.

Sage The polyphenol compounds in sage are packed full of antioxidants that may fend off the loss of natural enzyme acetylcholine, the primary neurotransmitter of the brain, giving it significant potential to help with memory, prevent Alzheimer's disease and increase cognition retention and focus in younger adults.

Cinnamon *The Good Sweet Spice*

Do you ever sprinkle cinnamon on your morning cappuccino? Or add a dash in your afternoon chai? Maybe you should. Not only does cinnamon add a bit of zing, it also gives our taste buds the suggestion of sweetness. On-going studies continue to make the connection between cinnamon and lowering blood sugar, which is of vital concern to those needing to reduce their sugar intake, especially as so many processed foods contain added sugar. How apt that this frequently used, sweet-tasting spice may actually *lower* blood sugar!

Loaded with powerful anti-inflammatory polyphenols, cinnamon is thought to help lower blood pressure and current research studies suggest that it may also help those afflicted with Alzheimer's and Parkinson's diseases. It is also thought to have skin-tightening and wound-healing properties and may boost libido in both men and women.

All parts (flowers, bark and leaves) contain cinnamaldehyde, and Ceylon cinnamon also contains eugenol; its leaves have a scented hint of clove.

During the Middle Ages, fantastical myths were born surrounding the indigenous 'true' cinnamon from Ceylon: devious explorers claimed that birds living on the Nile used cinnamon sticks to build their nests and only the Arab traders had the skills to shoo the birds away. The quest continued to find, acquire and trade this enchanting spice, which changed history as 15th-century explorers, including Christopher Columbus (who did find the other rougher cassia variety of cinnamon in Cuba), desperately searched to find the cinnamon that would make them, too, rich.

Cinnamon is found in an international array of dishes: in North America and Northern Europe, it is primarily added to baked-fruit desserts, cakes, bread, cookies and pastry. In Spain and Mexico, it is added to chocolate dishes, whereas Middle Eastern cinnamon is a common addition to dishes such as meat-based tagines and traditional chicken and brick-pastry *bastilla*. In India, China and Vietnam, it is laced through a multitude of spice mixes and dishes.

Cinnamon of both culinary varieties (see below) is best purchased as sticks (or quills). Cassia, with its strong sweet and familiar aroma, is brownish red and has quite a thick bark. It is generally pre-cut to fit in a spice jar. Ceylon (true) cinnamon is lighter brown and is made up of multiple paper-like layers. Its scent is mild and sweet. Cinnamon sticks will keep for about 3 years. Ground cinnamon loses fragrance easily in a few months so grind or buy only what you need. Toast cinnamon sticks in a pan over medium–low heat, turning occasionally until you can smell it; it will take about 5–7 minutes. Once toasted and cooled, it will be easy to grind in a spice or coffee grinder.

Bear in mind that ground cinnamon absorbs liquid very easily, so, when baking, if you want to add more cinnamon, add a little cinnamon oil rather than more ground cinnamon, which may either clump into a paste or make your finished recipe very dry.

❛ The cinnamon you buy at the grocery store is cassia (*Cinnamomum cassia*), aka Chinese cinnamon. It's warming and fragrant, and it also happens to lower blood sugar in people with diabetes and pre-diabetes.

Cinnamon is sort of magic: it helpfully changes your insulin receptors, alters the way the liver metabolizes blood sugar and even affects how your intestinal enzymes digest sugar. But it also contains a lot of coumarin, which can poison the liver... and might be responsible for each of the blood-sugar-beneficial effects! One good solution is Ceylon cinnamon (*Cinnamomum zeylanicum*), or "true" cinnamon. Ceylon cinnamon has a lot less coumarin than cassia, plus a sweet taste, delicate aroma and papery bark. Try a Ceylon cinnamon infusion: coumarin is oil soluble and will be left behind... though some of the blood sugar benefits may be as well.

By the way, cinnamon has even more antioxidants than mint, anise, licorice, vanilla, ginger or nutmeg, all of which are stocked with them. ❜

John La Puma, MD

http://www.ncbi.nlm.nih.gov/pubmed/26475130; http://www.ncbi.nlm.nih.gov/pubmed/24148965

Rosemary *The Remember-me Spice*

'**There's rosemary, that's for remembrance;** pray you, love, remember.' This timeless phrase spoken by Ophelia in Shakespeare's *Hamlet* rings true even today, when this remarkably powerful spice remains much written about and discussed by both the complementary and clinical medical communities.

Rosemary is a member of the mint family and indigenous to the Mediterranean region, but it grows over much of the world in moderately temperate climes. Strong and prolific with delicate flower blossoms of blue, pink or purple, rosemary takes hold easily, whether planted in containers or as vast hedges, and is drought tolerant and frost resistant. It is one of the most important spices medicinally, dating back to antiquity. Records of rosemary abound in ancient Greek and Roman legends and, in past centuries, this bountifully aromatic spice was touted for its importance medically far in excess of its use as a flavouring ingredient. Medicine men of the past who adhered to 'the four humours', a holistic Hippocratic medical discipline, believed, as many do today, that rosemary fortifies brain function, especially memory. (I am sniffing rosemary leaves as I write this!) The active compound in rosemary, cineole, which releases a piney-floral-eucalyptus aroma, may be the key to memory performance while another component, carnosic acid, is believed to be beneficial in fighting free-radical damage in the brain and the slow aging of the brain. Pretty heady stuff growing from a garden pot!

Rosemary's spiky leaves sprouting from strong solid stems make great skewers for barbecue or stovetop grilling (broiling) of lamb, chicken and even pineapple pieces. Rosemary is used in both sweet and savoury dishes, including alongside the familiar flavours of roast lamb, chicken, goats' cheese, preserved and fresh lemon peel, olive, garlic and tomato. In sweet dishes, it is wonderful in rosemary-infused olive oil polenta cake, rosemary and orange chocolate sorbet and in the rosemary-crusted Apple and Walnut Galette on page 88. As a teatime treat during pre-exam cramming, mix 1½ teaspoons of dried rosemary or 1 tablespoon of fresh chopped leaves with 2 teaspoons of cocoa powder in a cup. Stir in one cup of boiling water, cover and let steep for 5–7 minutes. Add a squeeze of orange juice and a little zest and/or sweeten if you like, then sip and study! The rosemary will help with clarity and the cocoa with energy.

❝ Rosemary leaf (the needles are the leaves!) is approved officially by Germany's Commission E, which is the US FDA somewhat-equivalent. Rosemary is approved for upset stomachs and has been widely studied – in Iran for improving occupational burnout, in the US for boosting cognitive function, in Scotland for reversing hair loss.

What we know is this: when you use a meat marinade containing rosemary, it both reduces the bacterial count in raw meat and drops the risk of intestinal and breast cancers from charred or overcooked meat.

Dried rosemary powder has reduced heterocyclic amine formation (a cancer-causing chemical created by high-heat cooking of meat and by charring) by up to 77 per cent in ground beef burgers grilled [broiled] at temperatures up to 200°C (400°F).

How? Whether it is powder-activating-detoxifying enzymes in the liver, or the scent triggering free-radical-scavenging activity, which is your body's healthy reaction to clean out damaging, inflammatory chemicals, or its powerful antioxidant and anti-inflammatory ability is not known. It is known that rosemary is delicious, easy to use and grow and widely available. ❞

John La Puma, MD

http://www.ncbi.nlm.nih.gov/pubmed/20492265; http://www.ncbi.nlm.nih.gov/pubmed/26579115

Oregano *The Pungent Spice*

Oregano, the 'pizza spice', is indigenous to the Mediterranean but is so hardy it will grow easily in temperate climates. This strongly scented beauty of the mint family has small oval-shaped green leaves, thrives in full sun and slightly acidic soil and has been used in food and medicine since ancient times.

Oregano's pungent, aromatic and slightly bitter flavour is available fresh, and oregano grows easily in most kitchen gardens, but it is best known and most commonly used in its concentrated dry form – look at that big plastic container of dried oregano leaves at the local pizzeria! The American craze for Italian-style food – pizza, spaghetti and garlic bread – began when World War II soldiers returning from Europe could not get enough of this pizza spice!

Oregano is often mistaken for marjoram, which is understandably confusing given that oregano is also known as wild marjoram, but the presence of a thyme aroma in the smaller leaves of true Greek or Italian oregano gives it a stronger flavour than the more delicate marjoram. It should also not be confused with Mexican oregano, which is related to the lemon verbena family, has a stronger flavour, with hints of citrus, and is frequently used in Mexican cuisine.

Oregano's primary essential oils, contained in its fuzzy leaves and stems, are thymol and carvacol. Oregano and its oil were used as health remedies not only by Hippocrates but also in numerous European, Asian and South American cultures and continue to yield many promising health features: there have been studies into using oregano oil as a possible LDL- and triglyceride-cholesterol-lowering aid, to slow or reverse the build-up of artery-constricting plaque and as a helpful cleanser/body rebalancer for thrush and other yeast infections. Make an orange-oregano infusion by pouring a cup of water over 1 tablespoon of chopped fresh (or 2 teaspoons of dried) oregano, a piece of orange peel and a clove for sweetness (optional). Cover and let steep for 5–8 minutes, then curl up and enjoy.

The pungent leaves are added, dried, to pizza-spice blends and used fresh or dried in Greek salad dressing, Chimichurri Argentina (see page 162) and Turkish lamb marinade. You can also enjoy it in the Stuffed Chicken Breasts with Artichoke Quinoa on page 76.

If drying your own oregano, air or sun dry it, as the low heat of an oven will reduce the strength of its active oils. Dried oregano leaves will keep tightly sealed in the pantry for about a year.

❛ Oregano is so much more than that dried herb you dust all over your pizza. In my practice, oil of oregano is one of my go-to medicines for respiratory and gastrointestinal infections.

It's the volatile oils in this spice, thymol and carvacrol, that have been shown to inhibit the growth of bacteria, including *Helicobacter pylori*, a bacteria that can cause gastric ulcers and reflux disease. The oils also serve as antivirals; I often recommend a few drops of oil of oregano in boiling water, and inhaling the steam for colds and upper respiratory infections. A recent study showed that a spray containing aromatic essential oils from five different plants, including oregano, was found to significantly relieve symptoms in those with upper respiratory infections.

It is also a good source of calcium and vitamin K, and has more antioxidant activity than blueberries! ❜

Geeta Maker-Clark, MD

Lambert RJ, Skandamis PN, Coote PJ, Nychas GJ, 'A study of the minimum inhibitory concentration and mode of action of oregano essential oil, thymol and carvacrol'. J Appl Microbiol 2001 Sep; 91(3):453-62. 2001. PMID:12450.
Evid Based Complement Alternat Med. 2011;2011:690346.

Bay Leaf *The Noble Spice*

Native to the Mediterranean, bay laurel (*Laurus nobilis*) belongs to the family Lauraceae, which also includes cassia cinnamon, Ceylon cinnamon, sassafras and the avocado. Bay varieties abound, including the California bay, which does not contain the cineole essential oils of the bay laurel, while bay leaves in India are likely to be cassia cinnamon leaves. An evergreen tree with hardy shiny tapered leaves, richly green on top and paler underneath, bay laurel grows in moderately temperate climates but manages quite well on many a London balcony. Bay leaf is probably the most used spice in the pantry.

During the Olympics in Ancient Greece, no gold, silver or bronze medals were awarded to the winners; instead, the Olympian was lauded with a prize of olive or laurel branches woven into a crown called *kotinos*. Bay leaves were sacred to the Greek god Apollo – the symbol of triumph – and the fresh crown of laurels was also awarded to poets, scholars and heroes, and still today is symbolic of great physical or mental accomplishment. The title baccalaureate ('bacca' meaning berry plus 'laurel', signifying the berry-laden branches) came into being during the Renaissance, when a newly graduated student was awarded a berry-laden laurel branch with their doctorate degree but had only moments to enjoy 'sitting on their laurels' before the challenging work of a doctor began!

The active compound found in laurel bay oil, cineole, is known as a strong antioxidant. Stronger than other naturally derived chemicals, such as vitamin C, the antioxidant compounds in bay leaves are released as the scent of bay infuses your food. Encouraging studies indicate that consuming bay leaf may help combat diabetes 2 by lowering blood sugar and LDL-cholesterol.

Bay leaf has a sweet aroma and a bitter taste but becomes creamy and luxurious when added to any number of recipes. One of the few leaf spices that retains its flavour and nutrients when dried, it lends itself to slow-cooking soups, stews and sauces. An essential component of bouquet garni, the classic blend of herbs (also including thyme and parsley) used to flavour meat and vegetable broths and stocks, bay leaf is also an essential ingredient in court bouillon for poaching fish, and is always a friend at a seaside lobster, clam or mussels boil picnic. Bay is also obligatory in pickling spices, an often-requested addition to marinade- and potato-based recipes and features in classic cream- or egg-based sauces such as Hollandaise and white sauce. The fragrance of bay leaves complements many an English custard or milk pudding and I often add bay to ice creams and panna cotta: the creaminess of bay enhances the rich mouthfeel of dairy.

www.ncbi.nlm.nih.gov/pmc/articles/PMC2613499/

' There are many different types of plants whose leaves are referred to as "bay leaves", so it's important to distinguish that a true bay leaf is scientifically known as *Laurus nobilis*, from the bay laurel tree. This leaf is very nutrient rich, unlike its imitators.

Bay leaves have been a part of culinary and medicinal culture for thousands of years, dating back at least to Roman times, and likely far beyond.

Bay leaves are powerful medicine for the gastrointestinal system; they are very effective for settling upset stomachs, soothing irritable bowel syndrome or even lessening the symptoms of inflammatory bowel diseases. Unique enzymes found in bay leaves help to improve digestion and nutrient intake, so they are wonderful to add to high-protein meals that might be harder to digest.

The essential oil of bay leaves has a strong aromatherapeutic effect and can even be mixed into a salve and applied to the chest to help alleviate congestion from colds. **'**

Geeta Maker-Clark, MD

Hibiscus *The Refreshing Red Spice*

Many types and colours of hibiscus grow prolifically in tropical, sub-tropical and moderately warm regions of the world, but only *Hibiscus sabdariffa*, the sour tea spice also known as roselle, Jamaica sorrel and karkade, has the concentrated health characteristics and benefits that have been known about and exploited in traditional medicine for centuries. Native to Africa, where it is still cultivated, *Hibiscus sabdariffa* is thought to have been domesticated in the Sudan region over 6,000 years ago. This beautiful hibiscus variety has large white, yellow, pink or red petals and a bright pink-red centre or calyx. The soft calyx (sepals), the red covering that protects the seedpod, is picked by hand in the morning hours, before it begins to harden, and is then dried in the sun.

Hibiscus is most often enjoyed as 'sour spice tea' and has been celebrated for its beneficial nutrients and traditional cures from Egypt to Mexico, Thailand to Brazil and Jamaica to China for millennia.

Hibiscus sabdariffa is being studied as a remedy for a number of conditions, including irritable bowel syndrome, fatty liver disease and metabolic syndrome. It has also gained an enormous amount of attention recently as a weight-loss spice because the active hibiscus acid (hydroxycitric acid) inhibits the production of amylase, an enzyme produced by the salivary glands and the pancreas to help the body digest carbohydrates. Where there is an excessive amount of unused carbs not needed as energy, the leftovers get stored as fat and it is thought that the hibiscus acid may allow this excess to pass through the system rather than being stored as fat. The stems and pectin-laden leaves of hibiscus are also thought to have possible anticancer benefit. Hibiscus contains very high levels of vitamin C and is considered to be a natural antiseptic, a diuretic, a gentle laxative and a natural body coolant.

This bright-red flowerbud is added to several fruit-tea blends and used as a natural food colouring and to give a rush of tart flavour to food and drink. The popular refreshing Mexican drink agua de flor de Jamaica is a blend of hibiscus boiled with water and sugar then cooled and served over ice. For a healthier option, replace the sugar with fresh fruit and fruit juices and add a few lime wedges for colour. This creative, colourful spice (doctors advise that we should 'eat a rainbow everyday') will inspire you to add a measure to food and drink, whether in a marinade for pork, sprinkled on crusted shellfish, as a seasoning for ceviche, in a sauce for poached fish or in a salad dressing or mixed into tonics, teas and martinis!

www.ncbi.nlm.nih.gov/pmc/articles/PMC2742648/; www.ncbi.nlm.nih.gov/pmc/articles/PMC4581252/; www.ncbi.nlm.nih.gov/pmc/articles/PMC3303862/

'Hibiscus is a really light and pleasant-tasting spice known for its deep-red colour, which infuses into beautiful teas. It owes this lovely colour to the plant pigment quercetin, which is an antioxidant, scavenging particles in the body known as free radicals, which damage cell membranes, alter the DNA and can cause cell death. By neutralizing free radicals, it may reduce or even help prevent some of the damage free radicals cause.

Hibiscus is also very rich in plant acids, including citric acid, malic acid, tartaric acid and hibiscus acid, which is unique to hibiscus.

The scientific evidence has grown over the years supporting the ancient use of hibiscus in many countries for blood-pressure control. On a recent trip to Senegal, I enjoyed many cups of hibiscus tea, which, I was told, was to support my "blood". A Cochrane review of hibiscus's effects on blood pressure published in 2010 included randomized controlled trials of three to 12 weeks in duration that compared hibiscus to either placebo or no intervention at all. All five of these studies found hibiscus had a blood-pressure-maintenance effect. Some of these trials look at hibiscus in tea form and others in extract. The best aspect? The safety profile of hibiscus is excellent, with no proven adverse reactions. '

Geeta Maker-Clark, MD

Ngamjarus c, Pattanittum P, Somboonporn C. Cochrane Database Syst Rev. 2010; Jan 20(1):CD007894.

HIPPOCRATES' HEALING BROTH

A comforting cleansing broth from Dr Eleni Tsiompanou, who reveals bay's health secret: 'Most of the ingredients in this recipe go back to antiquity, and Hippocrates would have used whatever meat was available according to season. For unwell people at the peak of their illness, he would have used just barley without meat in the soup and, as the patient got better, he would have given it in less dilute form. When you prepare the soup, chop the leeks, onions and garlic at least ten minutes before cooking them in order to stimulate their active ingredients. (If you use them in cooking immediately after they are chopped, they will have their characteristic taste and smell but not their anti-inflammatory properties.) This is a cheap and easy but highly nutritious dish that requires little preparation time. However, it works better if you cook it slowly over 4–8 hours.'

MAKES 700ML–1 LITRE (3–4¼ CUPS)

chicken wings or the carcass/bones of a roast chicken	1 celery stick
1.5kg (3lb. 5oz.) oxtail	1 or 2 leeks, roughly chopped
1 garlic clove, chopped	1 onion, finely chopped
2–4 bay leaves	115g (4oz./1 cup) chopped cabbage (optional)
2–4 thyme sprigs	175g (6oz./scant 1 cup) barley
2–4 parsley sprigs, finely chopped	pinch sweet paprika (optional)
1 tsp black peppercorns	dash of lemon or lime juice (optional)
1 tsp allspice berries	chopped fresh parsley (optional)
2 carrots, peeled and chopped	

Put the chicken wings or carcass and the oxtail in a large heavy-based cooking pot and pour over enough water to cover them. Bring to the boil slowly then skim the foam (which is mainly fat) from the surface.

Add the garlic, bay leaves, thyme, parsley, black peppercorns and allspice berries and simmer, covered, over a low heat for 2–4 hours. (The longer and more slowly you cook it the better.)

Remove the pan from the heat and strain the broth through a sieve or colander into a large glass bowl. Pick the meat from the oxtail and the chicken wings or carcass and either return some of it to the broth or keep it for another dish. Discard the bones, spices and herbs.

Add the vegetables and barley to the pan and season with coarse sea salt and pepper and sweet paprika if wished. Return to the heat and simmer slowly for a further 1–2 hours.

For a lovely Mediterranean sour twist, add a dash of fresh lemon or lime juice and sprinkle in some chopped parsley just before serving.

OREGANO

JERUSALEM ARTICHOKE DIP

This root vegetable, also known as sunchoke in the US, has nothing to do with Jerusalem but is derived instead from the Italian word for sunflower, girasole, *which sounds quite similar. This creamy appetizer dish can be made well ahead. It's beautiful simply on its own, but for a bit more rich nuttiness, add freshly grated Parmesan.*

SERVES 4–6

475ml (2 cups) vegetable stock

450g (1lb.) Jerusalem artichokes, peeled and sliced

2 garlic cloves

30ml (2 tbsp) lemon juice

1–2 whole chipotle peppers in adobo or 1 tbsp chipotle paste, or to taste

1 tbsp chopped fresh or 1 tsp dried oregano

120g (4¼oz./1 cup) grated Parmesan (optional)

Heat the stock to a simmer in small saucepan. Add the Jerusalem artichokes and garlic and cook until tender, about 20 minutes. Drain, reserving the cooking liquid.

Put the Jerusalem artichokes, garlic, lemon juice, chipotle peppers and oregano in a food processor and process until smooth, adding reserved stock as needed – it should have a hummus-like consistency.

Spoon into a bowl and fold in the Parmesan to combine (if using). Serve warm or at room temperature with breadsticks or crudités.

ROSEMARY, OREGANO, BAY LEAF, THYME

HERB AND SPICE OLIVES

For school lunchboxes, my creative Mum, Sally, would make black olive and cream cheese sandwiches, which my sister hated and I loved. This mélange is a long way from second grade!

MAKES 3 CUPS

4 whole anchovy fillets, drained

2 garlic cloves, thinly sliced

1 tsp orange zest

2 tsp lemon zest

60ml (¼ cup) extra virgin olive oil

2 tsp fresh lemon juice

2 bay leaves

2 oregano sprigs

2 rosemary sprigs

2 thyme sprigs

350g (12oz./2 cups) mixed green and black olives

12–16 piquante or sweet-cherry peppers

2 strips lemon peel

4 strips orange peel

½ tsp chili flakes, or to taste

240ml (1 cup) extra virgin olive oil

Using a mortar and pestle, grind the anchovies, garlic and orange and lemon zest. Fold in the olive oil, lemon juice, bay leaves, oregano, rosemary and thyme. Stir in the olives, piquante peppers and citrus peel. Season to taste with chili flakes.

Spoon into a decorative container with a tight-fitting lid, top up with olive oil, cover and refrigerate. The olives will keep chilled for up to a month.

HIBISCUS AND CITRUS-CRUSTED PRAWNS
WITH TART TUSCAN MELON

Tangy hibiscus flower buds or hibiscus tea, which can be purchased at health or specialty food shops or online, are full of vitamin C and anthocyanins. In this dish, the tart concentrated flavour of the deep-pink hibiscus calyx buds or dried hibiscus tea balances the rich prawns (shrimp) and delicately scented melon.

SERVES 6

½ Tuscan-style cantaloupe melon, peeled, sliced and cut into triangular pieces

zest and juice of 4 lemons

zest and juice of 4 limes

1½ jalapeños, minced

2 tsp dried hibiscus flower buds or tea, finely chopped or crumbled

55g (2oz./generous ½ cup) dry breadcrumbs

¾ tsp sea salt

65g (2⅓oz./⅓ cup) palm or soft brown sugar

4 tsp minced fresh ginger

3 tbsp dark rum

24 large prawns (shrimp), peeled, cleaned and deveined and butterflied

6 tsp grapeseed oil

2 spring onions (scallions), sliced on the bias, to garnish

1 handful micro-greens, to garnish (optional)

Put the cut melon in a medium bowl and set aside.

In another bowl, stir together the lemon and lime zests, jalapeño, hibiscus tea, breadcrumbs and salt. Set aside.

In a small saucepan, warm the lemon and lime juice with the sugar, ginger and 120ml (½ cup) water and heat until reduced to 120ml (½ cup). Add the rum and cook for 1 minute then remove from the heat, pour over the melon and toss together. Set aside.

Pat the prawns (shrimp) dry then coat with 2 teaspoons of the grapeseed oil. Heat the remaining 4 teaspoons of oil in a sauté pan over medium–high heat. Coat the prawns (shrimp) thoroughly in the prepared crust mixture, then sear in the oil in batches, adding more oil if necessary. Cook for 2 minutes then turn.

Spoon the melon and sauce onto individual plates or a serving platter, arrange the prawns (shrimp) on top and scatter with the spring onions (scallions) and micro-greens, if using.

ARCTIC CHAR
WITH HIBISCUS AND CELERY
Michael Kempf

'A light and vitalizing dish with a variety of consistencies and textures. When cooked, the char should have the consistency of a medium-boiled egg yolk. Sansho pepper is a very fresh, slightly spicy, citrus-like seasoning.' MK

SERVES 4

250g (9oz.) char, or brook trout, fillet
150g (5½oz./1⅓ sticks) butter
1 tbsp ground hibiscus
3 thyme sprigs
1 x 40–48g (1½–1¾oz.) jar char, brook trout or lumpfish caviar
1 tbsp walnuts
1 tbsp egg white
a little piment d'Espelette

For the celeriac confit:
150g (5½oz.) celeriac, peeled and roughly chopped
40g (1½oz./2¾ tbsp) salted butter
2 shallots, finely diced
1 tsp freshly grated ginger
salt and sansho pepper (Japanese pepper)
juice and zest of 1 lemon

For the celery emulsion:
150g (5½oz.) celery, leaves removed and reserved
4 parsley and 4 mint sprigs
2 pinches xanthan gum
1 tbsp hazelnut oil
1 tbsp rapeseed oil
1 tsp freshly grated ginger
½ Granny Smith apple, peeled, cored and finely chopped
salt and white pepper, to taste

For the celeriac rolls:
100g (3½oz.) celeriac
1 tbsp rapeseed oil
1 tbsp hazelnut oil
3 pinches sansho pepper
1 thyme sprig

First make the celeriac confit. Lightly salt the celeriac, place it in a plastic bag with the butter and vacuum seal. Put in a pan of lightly boiling water and cook for about 10 minutes. Remove from the bag and allow to drain, reserving the liquid. Cook the shallot down with the reserved cooking liquid until fully reduced. Mash the celeriac with a fork and add to the shallots. Season with the ginger, salt, sansho pepper and lemon zest and juice.

To make the celery emulsion, juice the celery with the parsley and mint and strain through a fine sieve. Blend 50ml (scant ¼ cup) of this liquid with the xanthan using an immersion blender, then blend this with the two oils and the remaining juice. Season with the ginger and a little salt and pepper. Stir the apple into the sauce and leave to stand. Season again to taste just before serving.

To make the celeriac rolls, peel the celeriac and slice thinly with a slicer, then cut into strips about 2 x 8cm (¾ x 3in.), three per person. Reserve the remaining pieces. Blanch the strips in strongly salted water, shock in an ice-water bath and drain well. Juice the remaining celeriac and strain the juice through a fine sieve. Mix with the two oils and season with salt and pepper to create a marinade. Add the celeriac strips and thyme to the marinade in a plastic bag and vacuum seal. Just before serving, remove the strips from the bag and form into rolls.

Lightly salt the char fillets, wrap in foil and refrigerate. Brown the butter slowly, stirring occasionally. Allow to cool, then slowly stir in the hibiscus until dissolved. Portion the char and place in a deep baking dish. Spread the hibiscus butter over it and place the thyme between the fillets. Bake in the oven at its lowest setting for about 10–12 minutes, until translucent. Sprinkle with coarse sea salt. Turn the oven up to 160°C (325°F/gas mark 3). Beat the egg with the piment d'Espelette and coat the nuts in this mixture. Using a slotted spatula or your hands, lift the coated nuts to a baking tray lined with baking paper and roast at for about 8 minutes, until golden.

To serve, portion the celeriac confit onto each plate. Arrange three celery rolls, three celery leaves and some walnuts on top. Pour the emulsion into the centre, place the char next to it and arrange a quenelle of caviar on top.

STUFFED CHICKEN BREASTS
WITH ARTICHOKE QUINOA

My good chef friend Kathy Kordalis shares her oregano-centric spice blend recipe, passed down through generations in her Greek-Australian family, as the seasoning for this moreish chicken and artichoke dish.

SERVES 4

4 x 170g (6oz.) boneless chicken breasts, skin on

1 tbsp butter or olive oil

For the Kordalis spice marinade (makes 200ml):

30g (1oz./¼ cup) fresh oregano leaves

2 tbsp chopped flat-leaf parsley

2 tbsp chopped mint

3 garlic cloves, sliced

1 tsp sea salt

1 tsp cracked black pepper

¼ tsp chili flakes

¼ tsp ground cinnamon

175ml (¾ cup) extra virgin olive oil

juice and zest of 1 lemon and 1 orange

drizzle (½ tsp) honey (optional)

For the artichoke quinoa:

4 whole artichokes (approx. 450g/1lb. each)

350g (12oz./2 cups) quinoa, rinsed well and drained

415ml (1¾ cups) chicken or vegetable stock

4 tbsp Kordalis spice marinade (see above)

¼ tsp salt

50g (1¾oz.) preserved lemon peel (see page 20)

For the chicken filling:

12 crushed green olives

8 sundried tomatoes, thinly sliced

1½ chopped artichokes (see above)

2 strips preserved lemon peel (see page 20), chopped

4 tbsp Kordalis spice marinade (see above)

4 sliced halloumi, grilled (broiled)

Whizz the marinade ingredients in a food processor or blender until smooth. Reserve 4 tablespoons of the marinade for the quinoa (see below), then submerge the chicken breasts in the remainder. Cover and chill for at least 2 hours.

Make the artichoke quinoa. Trim the artichoke stems and the leaves of thorns, then cut in half. Using a teaspoon, remove the feathery choke and discard. Put the artichokes in a large pan, add 2 tablespoons of the Kordalis marinade, then cover with salted water and bring to a simmer. Cover the artichokes with a plate to keep submerged and simmer for 20–30 minutes until the stem is fork tender. Strain and cool, reserving 60ml (¼ cup) of cooking water. Remove and discard the leaves from the artichoke, revealing the cup-shaped heart. Reserve 1½ artichoke hearts for the filling and roughly chop the remainder. Drizzle with a little olive oil and set aside.

Put the quinoa into a 2-litre (2-quart) pan (with a lid) and warm over medium heat, swirling the pan and stirring until dry-toasted. Add the stock, reserved cooking liquid and salt and bring to the boil. Lower to a gentle simmer, cover and cook for about 17 minutes. Remove the pan from the heat, leaving the lid on and let steam for 5 minutes. Test for doneness: if still crunchy or liquid remains, return to low heat and cook covered for a few minutes longer. Add the artichoke hearts, preserved lemon peel and the remaining 2 tablespoons of Kordalis marinade and heat through. Fluff with a fork, season to taste and keep warm.

Drain the chicken breasts, reserving the marinade. Combine all the chicken filling ingredients except the halloumi together in a small bowl. Cut a horizontal slit in each chicken breast, making a pocket, and stuff the filling inside. Slide a piece of grilled (broiled) halloumi into each and secure with kitchen twine.

Preheat the oven to 180°C (350°F/gas mark 5). Heat the butter or olive oil in a large ovenproof frying pan (skillet) or roasting pan over medium–high heat. Add the chicken parcels to the pan and sear until browned on all sides.

In a small pan, warm the remaining marinade to a simmer then pour into a little serving bowl.

Remove the kitchen twine, slice the chicken parcels in half and serve on a generous spoonful of Artichoke Quinoa. Drizzle the pan juices over the chicken and serve with remaining marinade.

CHICKEN ADOBO

April Bloomfield

'I've always been a big fan of bay leaves – the flavour goes well in pretty much everything – and I like using fresh ones for this dish. The cinnamon hiding in here adds just a touch of intrigue, but it's not too overpowering. The balance between the vinegar, soy and all these spice flavours simmering together has an unexpected, refreshing effect.' AB

SERVES 6

60ml (¼ cup) peanut (groundnut), grapeseed or canola oil

2.3kg (5lb.) bone-in, skin-on chicken legs and thighs

2 heads garlic, cloves separated but not peeled

1 large Spanish onion, peeled and cut into 8 wedges

55g (2oz./½ cup) fresh ginger, unpeeled, thinly sliced

10 black peppercorns, lightly toasted

2 star anise, lightly toasted

1 cinnamon stick, lightly toasted

4 fresh bay leaves, bruised, or 2 dried bay leaves

350ml (1½ cups) white cane vinegar or unseasoned rice vinegar

120ml (½ cup) soy sauce

rice, to serve

Heat the oil in a large pan that has a lid over high heat until it starts to smoke. Add half the chicken (so you don't crowd the pan), skin side down, into the hot oil and cook, turning the pieces over occasionally, until golden brown all over, 10–15 minutes. Transfer to a plate and repeat with the remaining pieces of chicken, then add those to the plate.

Add the garlic, onion, ginger, peppercorns, star anise, cinnamon stick and bay leaves to the pan. Cook, stirring every now and again, until the onion turns translucent, about 10 minutes. You'll start to see lovely, sticky brown bits on the bottom of the pan. Add the chicken, then the vinegar and soy. Raise the heat to bring the liquid to a boil, scraping the pan to release the sweet brown bits.

Cover the pan, lower the heat to maintain a gentle simmer and cook, stirring occasionally, until the chicken is very tender (it will come apart with a spoon), about 45 minutes. Serve in large bowls over rice.

ALLAN'S MARINATED LAMB SKEWERS
WITH CAULIFLOWER 'STEAK' SHAWARMA

Often used as a barbecue spice, rosemary contains a compound that offsets the toxicity of charred and cooked meat. Using rosemary branches as skewers creates clever healthy handles!

SERVES 4

600g (1lb. 5oz.) lamb (saddle or rump), trimmed and diced	1 garlic clove, minced
1 large onion, cut into 8 segments	2 x 10cm (4in.) rosemary sprigs
8 rosemary 'skewers' for grilling (broiling) lamb	4 thyme sprigs
For the marinade:	4 tsp port
60ml (¼ cup) lemon juice	1 tbsp olive oil
4 tsp Dijon mustard	**For the cauliflower 'steak' shawarma:**
4 tsp soft brown sugar	1 large cauliflower (approx. 1kg/2lb. 4oz.)
2 tbsp Worcestershire sauce	4–8 tsp Shawarma Spice Paste (see below), or to taste

Combine the marinade ingredients together in a large shallow dish. Marinate the lamb for 4 hours or overnight.

Preheat the oven to 200°C (400°F/gas mark 6).

Peel the leaves from the cauliflower and discard. Trim the stem, leaving the core intact. Put core side down on a work surface and, using a large knife, trim each end to create a flat edge, then cut in half through the centre and stem. Cut each half in half horizontally to give you four 'steaks'. Carefully arrange these slices in a steamer and cook until knife tender, about 6–8 minutes.

Carefully transfer the cauliflower to a foil-lined, oiled baking tray and brush the top and sides of each 'steak' with 1–2 teaspoons of Shawarma Spice Paste, or to taste. Sprinkle with salt flakes, place in the oven and roast for 10 minutes until golden brown.

Separate each wedge of onion into three or four layers. Thread two pieces of lamb onto rosemary skewers alternately with sections of onion. Season with salt and pepper. Lay the skewers on the hot grill or barbecue and cook for 10–15 minutes, turning two or three times, until the lamb is medium–rare, 8–10 minutes. Alternately, place the skewers on a baking tray and cook in the oven 10 minutes ahead of cooking the cauliflower, turning the skewers over as you add the cauliflower to finish in the oven.

Serve two lamb skewers and one cauliflower 'steak' per person.

SHAWARMA SPICE PASTE

This makes more than you need for the cauliflower steaks but you can store the remainder in a jar with a tightly fitting lid – it will keep chilled for 1 month – and add it to baked or sautéed potatoes or other vegetables, or brush it onto seafood or chicken.

1 tbsp fresh oregano leaves	½ tbsp ground mild or smoked paprika
3 garlic cloves, crushed	½ tsp ground turmeric
60ml (¼ cup) grapeseed or extra virgin olive oil	½ tsp ground cinnamon
1 tbsp cumin seeds, toasted and ground	¼ tsp ground fenugreek
1 tbsp coriander seeds, toasted and ground	¼ tsp ground cloves
1 tsp peppercorns, toasted and ground	

Put all the ingredients into a mortar and grind into a paste with a pestle.

MARINATED VENISON

WITH DASHI COCONUT CUSTARD AND CINNAMON TEA BROTH

Neil Brazier

'A spice presented to kings, queens and gods as presents through the ages, cinnamon does everything: its sweet scent is used for oil and for medicine and it's a spice that goes in wine, liqueur, chocolate, desserts, curries, buns and pastry as well as in savoury dishes, including this venison recipe. It really is a spice that knows no boundaries and can be used anywhere! My earliest memories of venison are ones of Christmas, roaring log fires and long winter nights.' NB

SERVES 4

300g (10½oz.) venison

quince paste, cut into cubes, to serve (optional)

For the venison marinade:

500ml (2 cups + 2 tbsp) red wine

90g (3¼oz./scant ½ cup) granulated sugar

40g (1½oz./2⅔ tbsp) salt

zest of 1 orange

zest of 1 lemon

4 bay leaves

2 rosemary sprigs

2 thyme sprigs

2 oregano sprigs

2 cinnamon sticks

3 garlic cloves, peeled and sliced

5 black peppercorns, lightly crushed

1 tsp juniper berries, lightly crushed

For the cinnamon tea broth:

60g (2¼oz.) cinnamon sticks

100g (3½oz./½ cup) granulated sugar

pinch salt

pinch cayenne pepper

For the coconut and dashi custard:

500ml (2 cups + 2 tbsp) coconut cream

300ml (1¼ cups) dashi

1 packet (12.5g) agar agar

For the coleslaw:

50g (1¾oz.) carrot

50g (1¾oz.) apple

50g (1¾oz.) celeriac

50g (1¾oz.) quince

4 tsp lemon juice

60ml (¼ cup) olive oil

For the marinade, put all the ingredients into a pan and bring to the boil. Remove from the heat and leave to cool. Place the venison in the marinade for 1–4 days in a sealed container, turning it over after 12 hours. Remove the venison from the marinade and slice, then place on to plates.

For the cinnamon tea broth, preheat the oven to 170°C (350°F/gas mark 4) and roast the cinnamon sticks for 4 minutes. Pour 600ml (2½ cups) of water into a medium pan, stir in the sugar, salt and cayenne pepper and bring to the boil. Add the cinnamon sticks then take it off the heat. Transfer the hot liquid into a plastic container and cover with a lid or cling film (plastic wrap). You can use it straight away or leave it in the fridge for 2–3 days. Strain the liquid through a sieve. Before use, dilute the cinnamon tea with two parts to one of water, then warm and serve.

To make the coconut and dashi custard, put the coconut cream and dashi in a pan and bring to the boil, then add the agar agar and mix well using a whisk. Cook for a further 3–4 minutes, then take off the heat, allow to cool and leave in the fridge to set overnight. Once set, blitz in a blender, adding water as required to create a custard-like consistency. Transfer to a piping bag. The custard will provide a creamy mayonnaise texture.

Julienne the carrot, apple, celeriac and quince for the coleslaw and dress lightly with the lemon juice, olive oil and a pinch of flaky salt.

To assemble, place venison pieces around each plate, spoon a coleslaw stack on one side, add some quince paste cubes, then pipe some custard dollops around the plate. When everything is on the plate, pour over the warm cinnamon tea, at the table if possible as the aroma of the cinnamon is fantastic.

BAY LEAF, CORIANDER

SYLVIA'S SAUERKRAUT

According to my friend Sylvia, who brought this naturally fermented recipe to New Zealand with her from her native Germany, classic Bavarian sauerkraut always includes caraway. This is my take on her classic staple.

MAKES ABOUT 1 LITRE (1 QUART)

1kg (2lb. 4oz.) cabbage, halved, cored and thinly sliced

1 large red onion, halved, cored and thinly sliced

2 tart green apples, peeled, cored and thinly sliced

2 tbsp salt

1 tbsp yellow mustard seeds

2 tsp caraway seeds, toasted

1 tsp coriander seeds, toasted

5 allspice berries

2 bay leaves

½ tsp sugar

¼ tsp crushed red pepper flakes

In a large mixing bowl, combine the cabbage, apple and onion. Sprinkle with salt and, using your hands, toss and squeeze the mixture. Add the mustard, caraway and coriander seeds, allspice berries, bay leaves, sugar and crushed red pepper flakes, mixing well. Set aside for 15 minutes.

Transfer to a non-reactive (earthenware, glass or stainless-steel) bowl and press the mixture down. Add a weighted plate just inside the container edges to keep the cabbage submerged in liquid. Cover with a clean cloth and store in a dark place at about 19–22°C (65–72°F).

Check the mixture daily, skimming off the scum that rises to the surface. Make sure the cabbage remains submerged. Taste after 5 days. For a stronger flavour, leave for a few more days. When ready, transfer the sauerkraut to a clean glass container, seal with a tight-fitting lid and store in the fridge for up to 3 months.

CINNAMON, BAY LEAF, CORIANDER

FERMENTED RAINBOW CARROTS

Thinly slice and add to salads, soups or main courses, or just enjoy them on their own – delicious!

MAKES ENOUGH TO FILL A 1-LITRE (1-QUART) JAR

3 tbsp kosher or flake sea salt dissolved in 700ml (3 cups) filtered water

1 bunch baby rainbow carrots (enough to fit snugly in a 1-litre/1-quart canning/mason jar)

3 fresh bay leaves

1 cinnamon stick, charred

¾ tsp coriander seeds, toasted

½ tsp cumin seeds, toasted

¼ tsp chili flakes

Dissolve the salt in cold water and set aside. Decoratively arrange the carrots in the jar and wedge in the bay leaves and cinnamon stick. Make sure the carrot tops are at least 1cm (½in.) below the rim. Place the jar on a tray or plate. Sprinkle in the remaining spices and fill the jar with brine, making sure the carrots are totally submerged. Cover with a small weighted plate that sits just inside the container edges – a water-filled jam jar on the plate works great.

Store in a dark place at about 19–22°C (65–72°F), covered with a cloth. Check daily, topping up with more brine if needed. After 5–10 days, taste the carrots (they will continue to ferment). When the flavour is to your liking, cover with a tight-fitting lid and refrigerate to stop the fermentation process.

COCONUT, MANGO AND LIME MOUSSE
WITH HIBISCUS GELÉE

Inspired by the beauty of a lotus flower opening and the taste of ruby-red hibiscus-flower tea, this rich but healthy, eye-catching dessert celebrates the superb benefits of hibiscus, whose clean taste is balanced with creamy mango, coconut, ginger and lime.

SERVES 4

For the hibiscus immersion and gelée:
8g (¼oz.) dried red hibiscus flowers or 3 hibiscus tea bags
6 tbsp sugar or agave syrup
60ml (¼ cup) lime juice
2½ gold gelatin leaves (see note, or 2 tsp powdered gelatin)

For the mango-lime mousse:
1½ gold gelatin leaves (see note, or 1¼ tsp powdered gelatin)
140g (5oz.) fresh or frozen mango pieces
100ml (scant ½ cup) thick coconut cream
2 tbsp lime juice
1 tbsp caster (superfine) sugar

1 tsp freshly grated ginger
½ tsp ground cardamom
½ tsp pure vanilla extract

For the coconut-lime mousse:
1½ gold gelatin leaves (see note, or 1¼ tsp powdered gelatin)
200ml (scant 1 cup) thick coconut cream
7 tbsp lime juice
5 tbsp caster (superfine) sugar

To serve:
toasted coconut shards

Wedge four flat-bottomed glasses snugly at an angle in a container on the shelf of the fridge. Set aside.

First make the hibiscus immersion. Boil 240ml (1 cup) water and hydrate the hibiscus flowers (or tea) until soft and the water is bright red. Add the sugar and lime juice and stir to dissolve. Cover and chill until needed.

To make the mango-lime mousse, soften the gelatin leaves in cold water. In a small bowl, using a stick blender, purée the mango with the coconut cream, lime juice, sugar, ginger, cardamom and vanilla. Squeeze the water from the gelatin, place in small bowl and heat in a microwave until dissolved, about 8 seconds, or melt in a small pan. Whisk into the mango mousse. Gently spoon into the corner base of each glass (see opposite). Chill until set.

To make the hibiscus gelée, soften the gelatin leaves in cold water. Dissolve as above, and stir into the cooled hibiscus immersion. Strain the flowers and set aside. (You can suspend them in the softly set gelée if you wish.) Remove the glasses from the fridge and place the glasses level. Carefully pour the hibiscus gelée equally into the glasses as shown. Chill until set.

For the coconut-lime mousse, soften, then dissolve the gelatin as above. Combine the coconut cream, lime juice and sugar to dissolve then whisk in the gelatin as above. Pour on top of the set hibiscus gelée and chill until set.

Garnish with toasted coconut shards to serve.

Note: If gold leaf gelatin (200 bloom) is unavailable, use the lower bloom strength silver (160) or bronze (140) but increase the amount you use. Use less platinum leaf as its set is stronger (250). All varieties are available online.

HEIRLOOM ORGANIC APPLE AND WALNUT GALETTE

If you love apples, you'll love not only eating but also making this galette: its simplicity itself with its free-form pastry, sliced apple halves and easy homemade apple butter and it can be chilled and ready to bake when you like! Rosemary is a surprising pairing with apples, walnuts and cinnamon, but it adds a distinctive pine-citrus aroma and is believed to have antioxidant and memory-strengthening benefits, too. You may not need to use all the apple butter for this galette, but it's also great on pork or yogurt or your favourite hot cereal!

SERVES 6

200g (7oz./1¾ cups) plain (all-purpose) flour

1 tsp granulated sugar

1 tbsp rosemary leaves, minced

2 tsp ground cinnamon

large pinch salt

115g (4oz./1 stick) cold butter, cut into small cubes

2 tbsp iced water

500g (1lb. 2oz.) mixed crisp organic eating apples (e.g. Granny Smith, Monty's Surprise, Canadien du Reinette)

30g (1oz./¼ cup) chopped walnuts, preferably organic

55g (2oz./½ stick) butter, melted and browned and mixed with ¼ tsp ground cinnamon

3 tbsp dark brown sugar, roughly chopped

1 egg, beaten, for glazing

1 tbsp cinnamon sugar (1 tbsp sugar, ½ tsp cinnamon, large pinch salt)

For the apple butter (makes 115g/4oz./½ cup):

2 tbsp salted butter

½ cinnamon stick, charred

leaves of 1 small rosemary sprig, or ¼ tsp dried rosemary

225g (8oz.) apples, peeled, cored and chopped

½ tsp lemon juice

1 tbsp caster (superfine) sugar

Whisk together the flour, sugar, rosemary and cinnamon with a big pinch of salt. Crumble in the cold butter using your fingertips or a pastry cutter until pea-sized. Drizzle in the iced water, tossing gently with a fork or your fingers to combine. If it doesn't hold, add a little more water, but don't overwork the dough.

Turn the dough out onto a lightly flour-dusted board and gather into a ball. Pat out and fold over twice. Wrap tightly in cling film (plastic wrap) and chill for an hour.

Make the apple butter. Melt the butter with the cinnamon and rosemary on medium heat in a 500ml (½-quart) pot. Simmer until you can smell the spices, about 3–4 minutes. Add the apples, lemon juice, sugar and 1 tablespoon of water, give it a stir, cover and cook until the apples are mushy, about 10–15 minutes. Remove the lid and cook down to a thick paste, stirring occasionally. Discard the cinnamon stick, then push the apples through a sieve until smooth. Cool the apple butter.

Cut the apples into quarters around the core then slice each chunk into thin slices, stacking together. Set aside.

Turn the dough out onto parchment paper then roll or pat out into a free-from tart about 5mm (¼in.) thick. Transfer to a baking tray, letting the paper edges hang over. Spread the apple butter onto the dough, leaving about 4cm (1½in.) around the edge. Add the apple stacks on top of the apple butter and fold the pastry edges over. Return to the fridge to chill. Preheat the oven to 190°C (375°F/gas mark 5).

Remove the galette from the fridge, sprinkle with the walnuts, then drizzle the brown cinnamon butter over all. Scatter the brown sugar on top. Glaze the crust with egg wash then sprinkle cinnamon sugar on the edges. Bake for 25–30 minutes until the crust is golden brown.

Energy spice

Energy is life: with it we swim; without it we sink. A big boost of these spices can help spark the system to strengthen and optimize the body's inherent stores of energy, whether for aiding digestion, increasing quality brain activity or stepping up physical exertion.

Energy Spice Health Heroes

Black Peppercorn ★ Coriander ★ Cocoa ★ Nutmeg ★ Tamarind

When systems in the body are in balance with proper nutrients – and not disturbed by too much stress, poor eating habits and lack of sleep – the body will be prompted to utilize its energetic vitality to best effect. However, when body and mind are out of sync, we become a reactive unthinking machine, turning to fast-working stimulants such as jam doughnuts or triple-shot lattes, which result in an instant sugar high or a caffeine buzz that soon has the body and brain feeling the consequences of those energy-crashing deficits.

These heroes are energy boosters for physical and mental activity, supporting body and mind for the challenges of a suduko puzzle or a successful workout! Peppercorn, the king of spice, is a super energy burner and may aid in weight loss with its ability to increase circulation. Coriander can help stimulate digestive energy, helping to ease gastric complaints and diseases of the digestive organs. Cocoa, full of long-staying nutrients, gives an energy boost during workouts and is a decadent heart-healthy treat. Nutmeg and mace stimulate the nervous system and focus the brain with their active compound myristicin and are thought to help eliminate toxins in the body through supporting liver and gallbladder functions. Tamarind, full of strong flavour and stronger benefit, contains a wealth of vitamins and minerals, including thiamine (B1) for energy and strength, energy-rich potassium and an active compound that may energetically inhibit fat formation.

Other energy spice heroes

Cinnamon A dash of cinnamon can help to keep your energy levels sure and steady because of the blood-sugar-balancing qualities it provides. It is also a primary ingredient in certain analgesic balms for external pain relief to warm and invigorate muscle tissue and increase blood flow to tired and aching muscles.

Clove These tiny dried flower buds boost energy through reducing inflammation and increasing circulation and have long been known and used as traditional medicine and an aphrodisiac to increase sex drive and libido. Clove has been studied for its natural energy-regulating properties, especially a concern for those with diabetic disease. The natural sweet-licorice flavour of the active compound eugenol adds a bit of sweet energy without the sugar.

Chili Pepper The active plant compound in chili pepper is capsaicin, which is good for the heart, arteries, blood and digestive system and also helps boost metabolism. Applied topically in an ointment, capsaicin rushes blood to the area and reduces pain by increasing blood circulation and stimulating endorphins.

Star Anise A hormonal stimulant for both men and women taken as a tea, star anise may increase sexual drive and may help lift the spirits when you're feeling tired or depressed. Star anise tea has a mild oestrogenic effect, so it may help regulate the menstrual cycle in women, too.

Mint A natural stimulant, mint clears 'brain fog', giving the brain a positive physical boost and enabling you to be more alert, retentive and focused. The scent of its essential oils is enough to recharge your energy levels, but whether mint is eaten, drunk or its diluted essential oil is applied to the skin, it can be enough to get your brain and body functioning on a high level again.

Horseradish Brimming with large amounts of vitamins, minerals and protein, horseradish has few calories and no fat. The proteins are immediately metabolized into useful energy and may help to fend off illness, disarm toxins and increase energy for physical activities. The sharp strong active compound in horseradish, sinigrin, may raise concentration levels to help you feel more intensely focused.

Black Peppercorn *The King Spice*

This most-used culinary spice, second only to salt, has been fought over for centuries on land and sea as the world's demand for this spice changed history.

The unassuming pepper plant (*Piper nigrum*) is a climbing vine that grows almost exclusively in equatorial tropical rainforests, primarily in India and Southeast Asia. Slow to mature, peppercorn clusters take years to appear. Peppercorns are actually a tiny fruit, of the drupe variety, a fruit with a single seed in the middle in tiny grape-like bunches. The tough woody vine and the clusters of tiny green peppercorns have no distinctive aroma (similar to the scentless fresh vanilla pod/bean) until dried, cured and processed, when they reveal their familiar pungent rich scent.

The finest black pepper, still grown on the Malabar Coast of India, contains the highest amount of piperine, the magic curative compound that many traditional folk healers, (Indian) Ayurvedic masters and modern-day Western medical professionals laud for its numerous healing properties. (It's this active compound in pepper that's the reason we sneeze when breathing the stuff!) It is believed to aid healing of a formidable number of diseases and complaints and is considered an energy booster and a possible weight-loss enabler. Piperine is considered and well-known as a thermogenic: it increases the body's metabolic stimulant rate, producing heat and therefore optimizing the body's ability to increase its calorie-burning capabilities.

However, pepper's most astonishing quality, drawing the most attention and analysis, is its ability to act as a bio-enabler or bio-enhancer: a substance that when paired with nutrients or even medicine can maximize absorption and longevity of the nutrients or medicine in the bloodstream. The centuries-old Indian healing art Ayurveda has often prescribed a spice mixture of pepper, long pepper and ginger called trikatu, thought to enhance the effects of medicines in this very way.

Green peppercorns are simply unripened black peppercorns. They have a more complex but milder, fresh taste and are most often purchased in little glass jars, preserved in brine or pickled. Firm but easily crushed or chopped, green peppercorns are added to salad dressings, stews and cocktails and give the pungent finish to a classic steak sauce (see page 121).

White peppercorns are one of the ingredients in the classic quatre épices spice mix. The peppercorns are allowed to ripen on the vine and picked when the skin of the berries turns red. The red berries are soaked in water to peel away the tough outer shell, revealing the tiny greyish white pepper 'corn'. Aromatic white pepper is generally sold as a finely ground powder and used in numerous classic dishes from white sauce to mashed potatoes and omelettes, as well as in Chinese and Scandinavian dishes.

Pink peppercorns are not true peppercorns but the ripe berries of a Brazilian peppertree and a member of the cashew family. Pink peppercorn has a milder taste and is encased in a bright-pink paper-like shell that is easily crushed between finger and thumb to release its delicate peppery aroma. True red peppercorns, which are picked at the same time as white ones, are very rarely available outside of their growing regions and are usually sold fresh so have a short shelf life. A recipe calling for red peppercorns usually means pink peppercorns.

' Black pepper, known as 'black gold' in ancient times, is one of the most important healing spices, which has been used for thousands of years. Its main ingredient is piperine, which gives it its spicy and hot properties. Piperine is a bio-availability enhancer, which means it helps to increase the properties of other spices such as turmeric. It has been found to increase anti-inflammatory cytokines in the body and improve lung and joint health as well as reduce pain. It has been used in Ayurveda medicine to enhance digestion and circulation and for its antimicrobial properties to treat diarrheal diseases, stomach and gut problems. It is shown to be useful in the prevention of obesity and studies are looking at its effect on weight reduction, dyslipidemia [an abnormal amount of lipids in the blood] and diabetes. Exciting new research sheds light on its ability to improve circulation to the brain and for the prevention and treatment of Alzheimer's disease. '

Eleni Tsiompanou, MD, PGDip, MSc Nutritional Medicine

Coriander *The Gentle Giant Spice*

How can a seed and a leaf from the same plant, which is related to parsley and carrot, taste so dramatically different? The leaves of *Coriandrum sativum* have been passionately argued about for years; as with Marmite, you either love or hate the taste, and many people even believe there is a coriander-leaf genetic predisposition (but that's for another book!). The leaf is not a spice but a soft herb and is used only fresh. Also known as cilantro or Chinese parsley, it is the must-have darling of Asian, Indian, Middle Eastern, South American, Mexican and Thai cuisine with its distinctive powerful love-it-or-leave-it smell. Used primarily as a garnish or added to a dish at the end of cooking, the coriander (cilantro) leaf has little to do with the traditional curative benefits of its spherical-shaped fruit-seed sister.

Coriander seed is one of the world's oldest spices, discovered in archaeological digs dating back to about 7000BC. It was also found in King Tut's tomb alongside other precious and medically valued spices of that period.

Coriander seed's remarkable gift of health is shrouded in its quiet and gentle scent. Its powerful antioxidants may help protect the liver from the damages wrought by fatty liver disease, chirrosis of the liver and hepatitis C. Its active phytonutrients stimulate the power of digestion and it is helpful in soothing complaints of flatulence, intestinal spasms and symptoms of irritable bowel syndrome. It is also being analysed as a protective agent against colon cancer and it has been noted that coriander extract could be beneficial in cases of lead exposure, due to its strong antioxidant compounds, as well as in stunting the common yeast infection *Candida albicans*. Further studies continue. The German official government agency 'Commission E', a government body composed of scientists, doctors, pharmacists and toxicologists tasked to study and report on more than 300 herbs and spices, has approved the seed of *Coriandrum sativum* for gastrointestinal complaints, including indigestion and loss of appetite and has stated no side effects, contraindications or drug interactions. All pretty remarkable for a little brown sweetly scented seed!

Coriander seed is an essential component of many spice blends, most notably India's garam masala, Ethiopan berbere, ras-el-hanout and baharat from Morocco and in European pickling spices, marinade mixes and gin. Its sweet, nutty, citrus flavour reminds me of my Nana's kitchen and it easily lends itself to the sweet side in dried- and fresh-fruit compotes, breads, cakes and cookies, as well as being perfect for popcorn (see page 114)! Coriander essential oil is used as a flavouring for the French Chartreuse and Benedictine liqueurs and makes a gently scented tea or tonic.

buecher.heilpflanzen-welt.de/BGA-Commission-E-Monographs/

---

6 "Coriander is hot and astringent; it stops heartburn, and when eaten last also causes sleep", wrote the father of medicine Hippocrates 2,500 years ago. Coriander is considered laxative, diuretic and good for the stomach in Ayurveda and traditional medicine. Modern science is interested in the bioactive constituents and pharmacological activities of coriander seeds and fresh herb. Studies have shown this spice to have diuretic, antibacterial, anti-inflammatory, anticancer, neuroprotective and other medicinal properties. The positive influence of coriander on the gut and its antimicrobial properties make it especially interesting in the 21st century, where research on gut microbiota and drug-resistant bacteria has opened up new avenues of understanding and treating illnesses. 9

Eleni Tsiompanou, MD, PGDip, MSc Nutritional Medicine

Cocoa *The Food of the Gods Spice*

Ahhh, lovely luxurious cocoa. It's all about the flavanols (naturally occurring antioxidants found in various types of plants and in significant amounts in cocoa beans): good for the heart, good for the soul. Don't confuse cocoa with sugary milky or white chocolate bars: choose chocolate that contains a minimum of 72 per cent cocoa solids. The higher the percentage, the darker and less sugary it is and the more flavanols it contains.

The 18th-century biologist and chocolate aficionado Carl Linnaeus named this favoured spice *Theobroma cacao*, the 'Food of the Gods'. Rich, decadent and packed full of antioxidants, cocoa also contains the feel-good amino acid tryptophan, used by the brain to make serotonin, which produces feelings of happiness. The naturally occurring chemical phenylethylalanine in chocolate is the 'love drug' and acts as an antidepressant in tandem with dopamine, one of the many brain balancers, plus the energy-giving theobromine, a stimulant that gives you that 'cocoa buzz'.

There are 22 species of cocoa trees, all indigenous to South and Central America, whose pods are picked and processed, and a growing percentage of which are being sold as single-origin chocolate. Only a handful – well actually a large bucketful, as the ripe colourful cocoa pods are the size of large oval footballs – grow on a single tree trunk per season. The 6–12m (20–40ft) tall cocoa tree must be grown in shade to thrive and is also vulnerable to fungi and pests, though new cross-bred resistant varieties are now being grown to slake the world's hunger for chocolate.

www.ncbi.nlm.nih.gov/pmc/articles/PMC4807961/

In the ancient Mayan culture, hot chocolate was never sweetened, instead this sacred and ceremonial drink was begun by roasting the bitter cocoa beans over the open fire, then boiling them in water and finally spicing them up with vanilla, cinnamon sticks and hellfire-hot chilies!

Since the 1930s, the British Royal Navy has been known for its traditional hot-cocoa beverage kye or kai, supposedly made from a massive block of unsweetened chocolate with the addition of boiling water from a below-deck steam pipe and either sweetened-condensed milk or custard powder. It was rigorously stirred and then supped during the late-night watches (with the occasional addition of Pusser's Rum!).

The terms for cocoa and cacao are interchangeable in today's chocolate market. Traditional cocoa is the powder left after the raw cocoa beans have been fermented and roasted (in a similar process to that for roasting coffee beans) and the cocoa butter has been extracted from the cocoa mass. Raw chocolate and cocoa is also made from fermented beans but left unroasted.

Raw chocolate and cocoa powder generally have a stronger and more astringent flavour and contain more of the active flavanol compounds than traditional chocolate, however there is still an enormous health benefit in adding unsweetened cocoa powder and dark (bittersweet) or semi-sweet chocolate to your day!

> While cocoa is now thought of as an indulgence, historically it was used as a medicine in the Mayan and Aztec civilizations, and still is used as such in many indigenous populations of Central and South America. Cocoa is especially rich in polyphenols, a group of protective antioxidant compounds found in many plant foods like red wine and tea, whose benefits for cardiovascular health have been extensively studied. These specific polyphenols make an important chemical called nitric oxide more available, which may explain the potential beneficial effects of cocoa on blood pressure, insulin resistance and blood lipids. An elixir indeed!

Geeta Maker-Clark, MD

Roberto Corti, MD; Andreas J. Flammer, MD; Norman K. Hollenberg, MD, PhD; Thomas F. Lüscher, MD, 'Cocoa and Cardiovascular Health', *Contemporary Reviews in Cardiovascular Medicine*

Nutmeg *The Golden Globe Spice*

This is the only tropical fruit that is the source of two different spices: the grey-brown woodlike nugget nutmeg and its elegant crimson-laced wrapping, mace.

A bit about the Spice Wars and a lot about nutmeg… To look at this tiny, globe-shaped (albeit fragrant) spice and read that almost an entire island-chain civilization was slain because of it truly boggles the mind, narcotic or not. In the Middle Ages, the wealthy and the royal in Europe knew about the medicinal properties of nutmeg. According to the Hippocratic-endorsed Greek medical theory of humours, which was still practised by European physicians of the day, nutmeg was a 'hot food'. It was believed that nutmeg could balance 'cold foods' like fish and vegetables and it was thought to cure the common cold. As the rumours spread of how nutmeg might prevent the deathly plague, for which there was no cure, the demand for nutmeg increased, and determined Portuguese traders plotted to wrench control from the Indian and Arab traders and profit from this nutmeg business at any cost. The diminutive nutmeg seed was worth its weight in gold. Portuguese and Bandans traded amicably for a century. However, another powerful country and company was in the race and was not going to play by the rules. By 1621, the Dutch East India Company had slaughtered nearly the entire Bandanese population and taken total control of the Banda Islands and the nutmeg trade, charging astonishingly over-inflated prices to deliver the precious nutmeg to Europe.

The British still occupied a little slice of the Bandanese Spice Islands when the Dutch seized control. Managing to escape with hundreds of nutmeg seedlings, the British took them to the Caribbean island of Grenada, then under British rule. The price of nutmeg and other precious tropical spices dived and so began the demise of the Dutch East India Company.

The nutmeg tree prefers living on the breezy oceans edge in rich volcanic soil. One male tree can pollinate up to 12 female trees, which will not begin bearing fruit for 10–15 years but will then continue fruiting for a further 30–40 years.

Sweetly scented nutmeg, in the US traditionally used extensively during winter holidays in eggnog, pumpkin pie and milk custards, is also included in an enormous array of savoury recipes. It pairs well with lamb, chicken and pork dishes, garam masala curry dishes, Northern European potato recipes and is always sprinkled on creamed spinach.

The active compound in nutmeg, myristicin, is a central nervous system stimulant, and on-going studies indicate that it increases sexual activity and eases anxiety and stress. Nutmeg is also considered stimulating to the brain and gives an energy boost to the body. An additional compound found in nutmeg could have benefit for anti-aging of the skin, as it appears to block the enzyme elastase, which breaks down the elastin protein strands that are a preventative for sagging skin.

> Nutmeg is the shelled, dried seed of the plant *Myristica fragrans*. Ground, it's an indispensable part of pumpkin-pie spice and also lends its distinct flavour to eggnog, béchamel sauce and the Moroccan spice mix ras-el-hanout.
>
> Taken orally, it has been used to treat a variety of gastrointestinal symptoms, including diarrhea, nausea, abdominal pain and intestinal gas. Nutmeg is also thought to have antimicrobial properties. It has also been used for treating cancer, kidney disease, insomnia and inducing miscarriage, though scientific evidence is lacking for these uses. Nutmeg oil has been used as a topical anaesthetic, including for mouth sores, toothache and joint pain.
>
> There are some safety concerns about using nutmeg medicinally. There have been case reports of both acute and chronic toxicity from nutmeg overuse. High doses, the equivalent of eating 5–20g of ground nutmeg or one to three whole seeds, might cause psychoactive effects including hallucinations. Long-term use of nutmeg in doses of 120mg or more daily has been linked to hallucinations and other mental side effects. Finally, nutmeg may interact with medications that are metabolized by cytochrome p450. However, all of these potential concerns occur at amounts far exceeding those that would be used in cooking and baking.

Linda Shiue, MD

Tamarind *The Sweet-Tart Spice*

The huge evergreen tamarind tree, native to tropical Africa, is prized for its edible pod-like fruit. Drought resistant and tolerant of high winds because of its extensive root system, but sensitive to frost, the regal tamarind, whose name is derived from the Arabic for 'Date of India', grows in nearly all the tropical and subtropical regions of the world. Clusters of long-fingered brown pods accumulate on branches and, when fully ripened, are harvested. One 40–75m (131–246ft) tree can yield up to 200kg (440lb.) of pods per year. The pods are peeled open, revealing the seeds surrounded by the sour-prune-like pulp, which is compressed into square 2.5cm (1in.) thick 'bricks' and allowed to firm up before being wrapped in cellophane and shipped all over the world. Tamarind is also available as a concentrate and a powder.

Tamarind's tart dark-brown pulp is liquefied in water (four parts water to one part tamarind pulp) to make tamarind water or juice. Tamarind syrup is made from sugar dissolved in tamarind juice and is used in the popular agua de fresca tamarindo in Mexico and in sweet-tart, refreshing tropical cocktails. Appropriately titled the 'lemon of the East', tamarind is used in numerous dishes of Malaysian, Indian, Thai, Indonesian and Central and South American cuisines, including curries, chutneys, hot-and-sour soup and dips for samosas. For a delicious breakfast, drizzle a spoonful or two of tamarind juice or jam atop creamy yogurt and sprinkle with pistachios and a handful of blueberries. It is also added as the surprise tangy ingredient in Worcestershire and brown sauces, barbecue and steak sauces and Angostura bitters. Its tart caramel-like flavour is a delicious change to the usual lemon juice and its healthy nutrients and flavour will get those creative juices flowing!

Tamarind mellows and sweetens with age but keeps indefinitely due to its high acid content. However, be warned that if it sits on the shelf too long, it will become a hard brick.

Rich in tartaric acid, which gives it its super sour flavour, tamarind contains a wealth of B-vitamins, especially thiamine for energy and strength, bone-building minerals, energy-rich potassium and vitamin K and its phytonutrient, one-two antioxidant punch! Its traditional health benefits include relief for dry eye and other optical conditions as well as for digestive and gastric conditions, due to its high fibre content, and is also said to offer relief to those suffering from bile-duct issues.

> Tamarind has a tradition of popularity for both its tangy yet sweet flavour profile and its properties as a digestive. Moreover, for centuries, people have found healthful uses for tamarind pulp to alleviate inflammation, sore throats and conjunctivitis. It contains a rich blend of minerals (potassium, calcium, magnesium, selenium, copper, iron and zinc) and vitamins (A, C, E, K, thiamin, riboflavin, niacin and folic acid).
>
> More recently, it has been celebrated for its dietary fibre, which features non-starch polysaccharides (NSP) that include natural gums, hemicelluloses, mucilage, pectin and tannins. The fibre also binds to toxins, which include cancer-promoting chemicals that may be in the food we eat. As a result, this reduces toxin exposure to the lining of the colon and its risk of causing cancer. In addition, tamarind fibre binds to bile salts and reduces their re-entry into the body via the colon. The significance of this is that bile salts are produced by cholesterol and thus their reduction in turn lowers LDL 'lousy' cholesterol, which can form plaques in blood vessels. Tamarind is rich in tartaric acid, which gives a sharply sour taste to food, in addition to its inherent activity as a powerful antioxidant.
>
> Malabar tamarind (*Garcinia gummi-gutta*) as dried fruit contains about 30 per cent hydroxycitric acid (HCA). Recent interest in HCA stems from its activity as a powerful inhibitor of fat formation in animal studies (it has not yet been studied effectively in humans). Also of interest is its demonstration in small-animal studies to reduce consumption of food. It is anticipated that more research will be focused on tamarind for healthy weight.
>
> (Safety note: Tamarind ought to be consumed in dietary amounts to avoid its laxative effect.)

Param Dedhia, MD

PEPPERCORN

CRUSHED AVOCADO AND PINK PEPPERCORN TOAST

A quick fun starter, hors d'oeuvre or appetizer for lunch. Crushing a creamy avocado on top of naturally fermented sourdough instead of wholemeal bread makes this recipe not only more flavourful but also more easily digestible as fermented foods contain naturally occurring probiotics to boost digestive health. It's paired here with quick-pickled radish plus black pepper, which helps increase nutrient absorption.

SERVES 2

2 or 3 radishes, trimmed and cut into matchsticks
3 tbsp rice wine vinegar
1 tbsp minced parsley
large pinch salt
large pinch sugar
2 or 3 slices sourdough bread

60ml (¼ cup) extra virgin olive oil, for brushing bread, plus extra to drizzle on top
1 avocado
40g (1½oz.) crumbled feta
squeeze of lemon juice
½ tsp each pink and black peppercorns, crushed

Put the radishes into a small bowl with the vinegar, parsley, salt and sugar. Mix together and set aside.

Using a knife or cookie cutter, cut the bread into shapes. Brush with olive oil on one side and crisp in a hot pan, or put in a preheated oven set at 180°C (350°F/gas mark 5), until golden brown and toasted.

Peel the avocado, remove the stone, then cut into eight pieces. Place one piece on each piece of toast and crush with a fork. Top with the pickled radishes and feta and sprinkle over a squeeze of lemon juice and some crushed peppercorns.

CORIANDER, PEPPERCORN, MINT

CUCUMBER AND CORIANDER FIZZ

Not your usual juice squeeze, this delicious combination of spices and fibre-rich veggies topped with fresh blackberries is packed with antioxidants and boosted with peppercorn. Omit the blackberries and add to spicy tomato juice and vodka for a quick and delicious Bloody Mary!

SERVES 2

350g (12oz.) hothouse or Persian cucumber, skin on
½ tsp black peppercorns, toasted and ground
2 tsp coriander seeds, toasted and ground
10g (¼oz./3 tbsp) chopped fresh coriander (cilantro)
15g (½oz.) piece fresh ginger, peeled and grated into a paste or minced (about ¼ cup minced)

4 mint sprigs
2 tbsp lime juice, or to taste
2 tbsp agave syrup or honey, to taste
soda water, to top up
ice cubes, to serve
6 blackberries, to garnish

Blend all the ingredients except the soda water, ice cubes and berries.

Equally divide between two ice-filled glasses and top up with soda water. Garnish with the blackberries.

CORIANDER, PEPPERCORN

SEEDED LAVASH BREADSTICKS

Neither crackers, nor biscuits, these crispy breadsticks are not the usual pizza-dough type but are packed full of flavourful healthy spice. Arrange in tall (well-cleaned) flower vases for a dramatic presentation and serve with your favourite veggie dips, hummus or the Jerusalem Artichoke Dip on page 70.

MAKES ABOUT 36

4 tsp olive oil	4 tsp cumin seeds
1 tsp dry yeast	1 tbsp black cumin (onion or nigella) seeds
1 tbsp mild honey	½ tsp celery seeds
500g (1lb. 2oz./4 cups) bread flour	½ tsp dried rosemary, crumbled
1 tsp kosher salt	olive oil, for brushing
1 tbsp coriander seeds, toasted and ground	sea salt flakes, for finishing
2 tsp peppercorns, toasted and ground	

Pour 300ml (1¼ cups) of warm water (38–50°C/100–120°F) into a stand mixer, or use a large metal bowl with a wooden spoon, add the oil, yeast and honey and mix well using a wooden spoon. Gradually add about one third of the flour, stirring with a dough hook or spoon for 1 minute. Sprinkle in the salt, coriander and pepper, then gradually add the remaining flour and the cumin, black cumin and celery seeds and rosemary, stopping occasionally to scrape down the sides of the bowl with a spatula. Add additional flour as needed if the dough is too sticky.

Knead using the dough hook, or turn the dough out onto a lightly floured wooden board and knead by hand, for a further 10 minutes until smooth and elastic. Place in an oiled container, cover and chill overnight.

The following day, preheat the oven to 200°C fan (400°F/gas mark 6). Punch down the dough and leave it to rest for 30 minutes.

Divide the dough into six pieces, keeping each one covered with cling film (plastic wrap) or a damp clean cloth. Roll out one piece, cover and let it rest as you roll out the others. When the dough is thin and has rested for about 5 minutes, brush with oil. Cut into 30cm (12in.) long breadsticks and leave to rest for a further 5 minutes. Roll out again and sprinkle on the salt flakes. Carefully lift the breadsticks and place them 1cm (½in.) apart on silicone- or parchment-paper-lined baking trays and bake in the oven until golden brown and crisp, about 10–15 minutes.

Cool on wire racks and store in a tightly covered tin layered with parchment paper.

HOT SMOKED LEAF AND CORN SALMON

Peppercorn is good for you. Once worth its weight in gold, and the flashpoint of bloody battles at sea, peppercorn is now quite common, inexpensive and is front and centre on the spice stage. Its active compounds, especially piperine, are enhanced when it is paired with other spices such as turmeric, suggesting that a grind of fresh peppercorn on nearly everything we consume will help the absorption of nutrients in our food. You'll also need wood chips for this recipe – we used manuka and rosemary – soaked in water to avoid fire. The kawakawa leaves used in the seasoning are pepper leaves from a piperine-related bush that grows prolifically in New Zealand. If you are unable to get hold of them, they can be substituted with 6–8 small wild pepper leaves (bai cha plu), available from Thai or Asian grocers.

SERVES 16 AS A CANAPÉ OR 8 AS A STARTER

1kg (2lb. 4oz.) salmon fillet, skin on, deboned

For the brine:

300g (10½oz./1½ cups) brown sugar

175g (6oz./¾ cups) kosher salt

For the seasoning/topping:

1 tbsp manuka honey

1 tsp each of dried whole pink, green, white and black peppercorns

1 tsp toasted fennel seeds, lightly crushed

grated zest 1 lemon

3–4 kawakawa leaves, torn into small pieces (see recipe intro)

a few grinds mixed peppercorns

In a bowl, mix together the ingredients for the brine. Place the salmon fillet, skin side down, in a large roasting dish. Cover the fillet completely in the brine mix and refrigerate for 4–8 hours. The brine mix will draw moisture out of the fillet and turn to liquid.

Wash the brine mix from the fillet under cold water and thoroughly dry using kitchen paper. Let the fish sit in the fridge for a further 1–2 hours. Remove the salmon from the fridge about 30 minutes before you are ready to smoke it to let the fish come to room temperature.

Preheat a hooded barbecue to 200°C (400°F/gas mark 6), placing a small tin bowl of water and the soaked wood chips in a large shallow foil dish on the lower cooking surface. Close the lid.

While the barbecue is heating up, place the salmon skin-side down on an oiled baking rack and, using a pastry brush or your hands, coat with the manuka honey. In a bowl, mix together the remaining seasoning/topping ingredients and sprinkle over the fish.

When the temperature is reached and the wood chips have started smoking, place the baking tray with the salmon on the upper rack of the barbecue. Close the lid and reduce the temperature to 140° (280°F/gas mark 1). Gently smoke for about 2–3 hours, checking every now and then that the wood chips are not burning – you may need to add a few more.

The salmon is ready when creamy spots appear on the outer flesh of the fillet. (This is cooked protein.) Depending on your barbecue, these spots may take less, or more, time to appear. Turn the barbecue off and, leaving the lid up, leave the salmon to cool. Carefully remove from the baking rack and transfer to a serving platter or tightly wrap in cling film (plastic wrap) and chill until needed.

TURKEY, FETA, STUFFING AND CRANBERRY SALAD

What to do with all the winter-holiday, family-gathering leftovers? After a day or two of feasting on family favourites, this is an easy, fun and healthy way to make a little space in the fridge. Instead of making them from scratch (though they are very easy), you could add a hydrated stock cube and a little oil to a cup of leftover stuffing to make the thin croutons that top this light salad, which is finished with spoonfuls of Cranberry Compote and drizzled with a cranberry and coriander seed and (cilantro) leaf vinaigrette.

SERVES 4

300g (10½oz.) rocket or cress and butter lettuce, torn

500g (1lb. 2oz.) cooked turkey, torn into shreds

100g (3½oz.) feta, cut into small cubes

200g (7oz.) Cranberry Compote (see below)

For the stuffing croutons:

40g (1½oz./⅔ cup) breadcrumbs

I tsp poultry seasoning

½ tsp each of garlic and onion powder

pinch each salt, sugar and cayenne pepper

1 tsp ground coriander

3 egg whites

½ chicken or vegetable stock cube, dissolved in ½ tsp hot water

4 tsp vegetable oil

For the vinaigrette (makes 300ml/1¼ cups):

120ml (½ cup) red wine vinegar

3 tbsp cranberry juice

1 garlic clove, minced

1½ tsp lemon juice

1½ tsp toasted ground coriander

1 tbsp minced coriander (cilantro) leaves, plus extra whole leaves to serve

1 tsp roughly chopped tarragon

1 tsp roughly chopped parsley

30g (1oz./¼ cup) dried cranberries

120ml (½ cup) extra virgin olive oil

To make the stuffing croutons, preheat the oven to 190°C (375°F/gas mark 5). Mix the breadcrumbs and seasonings together in a small bowl. In another small bowl, beat the egg whites and dissolved stock cube. Whisk in the oil then gently mix the breadcrumbs into the egg whites. Adjust seasonings. Using a small metal spatula, spread the stuffing batter into little circles or square shapes directly onto a silicone- or parchment-lined baking tray. Sprinkle with flake salt and bake for 10–12 minutes until crisp. To make the vinaigrette, put all the ingredients except oil into a blender with a tight-fitting lid and blend well. With the machine running, slowly drizzle in the oil so it will emulsify together. Season with salt to taste. To assemble, scatter the salad leaves on the plates and top with turkey, feta and teaspoonfuls of Cranberry Compote. Top with croutons. Drizzle the dressing over the top and scatter on a few coriander (cilantro) leaves to finish.

CRANBERRY COMPOTE

MAKES 2¼ CUPS

350g (12oz./3½ cups) cranberries

1 cinnamon stick, charred

200g (7oz./1 cup) granulated sugar

2 allspice berries

1 tangerine, sliced into 4 horizontally

¼ tsp white pepper

large pinch salt

Put all the ingredients into a pan with 240ml (1 cup) of water and bring to a gentle simmer. Cook for about 8 minutes then remove from the heat. Strain out the fruit and spices and set aside. Simmer the liquid until reduced by half.

Return the fruit and spices to the pan and stir to combine. Cool, then cover and chill until needed.

COCOA BUTTER ROASTED VEGGIE SALAD
WITH COCOA NIB VINAIGRETTE
Rachel Pol

'The first time I went to a cocoa farm in my native Panama I fell deeper in love with chocolate. It also made me feel responsible for the Native Indian communities who have abandoned cocoa farming because a fair price is not being met. Since then, we have been working with small growers to improve consistency and fair trade their cocoa beans, encouraging the new generation back into cocoa farming. Besides making our own chocolate from bean to bar with only two ingredients, cocoa nibs and raw sugar, we are constantly finding different ways to use it. Cocoa butter is a high stable fat with a long shelf life, rich in antioxidants. The cocoa nibs are packed with powerful nutrients, antioxidants and mood lifters that add a lovely crunch, with subtle notes of chocolate and a mild nutty flavor. This recipe draws inspiration from the Panamanian Rainforest, where cocoa is grown and root vegetables are widely available.' RP

SERVES 4

1 sweet potato, cut into small wedges
10 baby carrots, halved
20 pearl onions, peeled
1 turnip, cut into small wedges
1 parsnip, sliced diagonally 1cm (½ in.) thick
1 large potato, cut into small wedges
1 butternut squash, peeled and cut into 2.5cm (1in.) cubes
1 fennel bulb, cut into small wedges
1 tsp fennel seeds
1 tsp coriander seeds
1 tsp cumin seeds

3 tbsp cocoa butter, melted
1 tsp salt
55g (2oz./2 cups) fresh rocket (arugula), to serve
For the cocoa nib vinaigrette:
2 tbsp cocoa butter
2 tbsp cocoa nibs
4 tbsp olive oil
2 tbsp rice wine vinegar
½ tsp sugar
1 tsp salt

Preheat the oven to 200°C (400°F/gas mark 6). Spread out all the vegetables on a foil-lined baking tray.

Put the fennel, coriander and cumin seeds in small pan and heat over medium heat for 2 minutes, shaking occasionally. Transfer to a spice grinder and grind to a coarse powder.

Add the melted cocoa butter, spice mixture and salt to the veggies and toss well to coat thoroughly. Roast in the oven for 45 minutes until the veggies are tender and caramelized.

Make the cocoa nib vinaigrette. In a small pan over medium–high heat, melt the cocoa butter, add the nibs and sizzle for 30–45 seconds. Add the olive oil, rice wine vinegar, sugar and salt and take off the heat.

Serve the roast veggies on bed of rocket, drizzled with the cocoa nib vinaigrette.

SWISS RAINBOW CHARD AND FENNEL GRATIN

This is not your typical gratin: the rainbow chard variety 'Bright Lights' is full of pinks, reds, oranges and yellows, which makes a colourful presentation and a moreish way to eat more vegetables. The comforting scent of freshly grated nutmeg in this gratin will bring a smile to your face: nutmeg is thought to combat depression and wrinkles!

SERVES 4

600g (1lb. 5oz.) rainbow chard stems (keep leaves for another use)

2 tbsp grapeseed or vegetable oil

3 large (300g/10½oz.) red onions, chopped

1 tbsp thyme leaves

475ml (2 cups) full-fat (whole) milk

1 large fennel bulb, cored and sliced vertically into thin pieces

½ tsp fennel seeds, lightly toasted and ground

2 bay leaves, cut in quarters

3 garlic cloves, peeled and thinly sliced

2 tsp freshly grated nutmeg

1 tsp ground mace

3 tbsp butter or oil

3 tbsp flour

1 tsp ground white pepper

200g (7oz.) Havarti cheese, grated

50g (1¾oz.) hard cheese, e.g. Pecorino, Parmesan or mature Cheddar, grated

85g (3oz./1¼ cup) panko or dry breadcrumbs, seasoned with a pinch each salt, pepper, thyme leaves and paprika

juice of ½ lemon

paprika, for sprinkling on top

Preheat the oven to 180°C (350°F/gas mark 4). Remove the strings from the outer edges of the chard stems and trim the stems to about 15cm (6in.) in length, depending on the size of your baking dish. Add the stems to a large pan of boiling salted water and blanch until fork tender. Drain and set aside.

Heat the oil in a cast-iron or heavy pan on low heat and sauté the onion and thyme leaves until soft.

While the onions cook, gently warm the milk in a small saucepan and add the fennel bulb and seeds, bay leaf, garlic, nutmeg and mace. Poach the fennel until fork tender, then take off the heat. When cooled, strain the milk into a jug and reserve the fennel.

Melt the butter or oil over medium–low heat in a 1-litre (1-quart) pan and sprinkle in the flour and pepper. Whisk until it becomes a thick paste, then pour in one third of the seasoned milk. Add the remaining milk in stages, continuing to whisk for 2–3 minutes until smooth; the sauce will thicken as it cooks. Take off the heat and set aside.

To assemble the gratin, sprinkle a layer of seasoned breadcrumbs on the bottom of an oiled 30cm (12in.) square casserole, baking dish or loaf pan. Next arrange half the chard, side by side like matchsticks, spread over a layer of sauce, then a layer of onion followed by one of fennel, a squeeze of lemon juice and salt and pepper to taste and a layer of Havarti cheese. Repeat these layers, topping the final layer with breadcrumbs then the Parmesan. Sprinkle a little paprika over the top and place the casserole on a foil-lined baking tray and, with your hands, press the gratin down to compact the layers. Bake for 45 minutes until golden brown and bubbly. Remove from the oven and leave to settle for 30 minutes. Serve just warmed.

GREEN CHILLI PRAWN CEVICHE
WITH PALM-SUGAR POPCORN
Christine Manfield

'Coriander seeds are one of the most useful spices to have in the kitchen: they balance other more pungent spices and are a wonderful partner to myriad aromatic flavours. The harmonious fusion of flavours and textures in this ceviche preparation takes its inspiration from South America. Rather than using fresh corn, I have spiced up popcorn with ground coriander seeds and salt tossed through a palm sugar caramel to give the popcorn a real flavour boost and complement the green chili, lime juice and ginger in the tiger's milk dressing. Avoid using tiger prawns (shrimp) as the flesh is too firm for this recipe.' CM

SERVES 6

400g (14oz.) raw sashimi-grade shelled and deveined banana (or king) prawns (shrimp), sliced on the diagonal

½ avocado, diced

½ green (unripe) mango, peeled and julienne sliced

6 pomelo or grapefruit segments, broken into small pieces

½ small cucumber, peeled, seeded and julienne sliced

6 yellow grape tomatoes, quartered

1 small red onion, finely diced

½ long green chili, seeded and finely sliced

handful watercress leaves, stems removed

handful roughly chopped coriander (cilantro) leaves

1 punnet green shiso cress, snipped

For the tiger's milk dressing:

4 small green chilies, chopped

½ small fennel bulb, chopped

2 tsp chopped coriander (cilantro) roots

2 tbsp coriander (cilantro) leaves

1 small green tomato, chopped

2 small garlic cloves, chopped

1 golden shallot, chopped

2 tbsp chopped fresh ginger

zest of 1 lime

zest of ½ orange (or mandarin)

60ml (¼ cup) lime juice

1 tbsp caster (superfine) sugar

50ml (scant ¼ cup) extra virgin olive oil

For the palm-sugar popcorn:

3 tbsp grapeseed or vegetable oil

115g (4oz./½ cup) popping corn

85g (3oz./scant ½ cup) palm sugar

1 tsp coriander seeds, toasted and ground

1 tsp sea salt flakes

First make the tiger's milk dressing: process everything together in a blender until smooth. Keep refrigerated until ready to serve.

To prepare the popcorn, pour enough oil into a small saucepan to just cover the base and heat over low–medium heat. When hot, add the popcorn and cover with a lid. Shake the saucepan regularly until the corn has finished popping. Remove from heat and pour onto a flat tray.

Heat the palm sugar with 1 tablespoon of water in a saucepan and cook until caramel colour. Pour over the popcorn and stir with a chopstick to evenly coat. Sprinkle over the coriander and salt.

Put the prawns into a bowl, pour over the dressing and leave to marinate for 5 minutes. Add all the salad ingredients and mix gently with your hands.

Arrange the ceviche onto serving plates, scatter the palm-sugar popcorn over the top and serve.

WHOLE ROASTED FISH
WITH COCOA BUTTER AND TOMATO-ONION RELISH
François Kwaku-Dongo

'Every country has a street food that is typical of its region. In Abidjan, where I grew up, on the Ivory Coast in West Africa, everyone will tell you about 'poisson braisé avec attiéké'. It's a favourite childhood food memory and is basically fish braised on charcoal served with hot sauce and cassava grain. Cocoa butter, a major ingredient in chocolate making, can also be used in savoury dishes. Here, I use cocoa butter instead of butter or oil to roast my fish, which gives it a nutty aroma.' FKD

SERVES 4

4 x 550g (1lb. 4oz.) whole fish such as sea bream, striped bass or tilapia, scaled and gutted

140g (5oz./⅔ cup) melted cocoa butter

1 tsp kosher salt

1 tsp ground black pepper

½ bunch parsley, including stems

For the tomato-onion relish:

1 medium (140g/5oz.) yellow onion, quartered and thinly sliced

1 small (140g/5oz.) vine-ripe tomato, peeled and thinly sliced

1 tsp kosher salt

½ tsp ground black pepper

½ tsp bird's-eye chili, seeded and minced

60ml (¼ cup) white vinegar

3 tbsp vegetable oil

100g (3½oz./½ cup) melted cocoa butter

1½ bunches curly parsley, chopped

For the cassava grain:

275g (9¾oz./1½ cup) cassava grain or couscous

100g (3½oz./½ cup) melted cocoa butter

40g (1½oz./2 heaped tbsp) minced garlic

40g (1½oz./2 heaped tbsp) minced fresh ginger

1 spring onion (scallion), finely chopped

½ bunch curly parsley, finely chopped

1 tsp kosher salt

½ tsp ground black pepper

Preheat the oven to 190C° (375°F/gas mark 5). Set the fish in a large, shallow roasting pan, brush all over with the melted cocoa butter and season generously inside and out with salt and pepper. Stuff the cavity with the parsley.

Roast the fish in the centre of the oven for about 20 minutes, occasionally spooning the pan juices over the fish. The fish is done when the flesh is white throughout and an instant-read thermometer inserted into the thickest part near the head registers 57°C (135°F). Let the fish stand for 10 minutes, then carefully transfer it to a large platter and remove the parsley.

While the fish is roasting, prepare the relish. Toss all the ingredients together in a mixing bowl.

Prepare the cassava grain. Set up a double boiler. Put the cassava in a medium-sized bowl and cover with cling film (plastic wrap). Set the bowl on top of the boiling water and steam until soft, about 5 minutes. Set aside. (If using couscous, follow package directions.)

Meanwhile, heat the cocoa butter in a saucepan, add the garlic and ginger and cook until soft. Add the cassava grain and stir well. Cook for 3 minutes then remove from the heat and transfer to a mixing bowl. Stir in the spring onion (scallion) and parsley and season with salt and pepper.

To serve, spoon the relish over the fish and serve the cassava grain at room temperature on the side.

TAMARIND AND TAHITIAN LIME ROASTED DUCK
WITH GINGER-ONION CONFIT AND CRACKLING

This duck dish was originally created in 2001 for Cuisines of the Sun, a food and wine event in Hawaii. It was judged by the late, brilliant and formidable chef Jean-Louis Palladin as his favourite dish of the night. Packed with sweet tamarind, fragrant tropical spices, thin-skinned tropical limes and topped with warming ginger-onion confit, the duck is served with Crispy Cardamom Polenta (see page 157) and earthy roasted baby beetroot.

SERVES 6

1.5kg (3lb. 5oz.) duck legs and thighs, bone in, skin on

4 tbsp olive oil, plus a little for roasting the beetroot

4 tbsp dry sherry

475ml (2 cups) roasted duck or chicken stock

2 fresh or 4 dried kaffir lime leaves, bruised

5cm (2in.) piece fresh ginger, peeled

250g (9oz.) tamarind paste

6 small red, yellow or candycane baby beetroot, trimmed

1 tsp ground allspice

juice and zest of 2 Tahitian, Mexican or Italian limes

4 tbsp sweet chili sauce

1 tbsp kecap manis (Indonesian sweet soy sauce)

1 tbsp soy sauce

Crispy Cardamom Polenta (see page 157), to serve

1 small handful watercress, to garnish

1 small bunch chives, chopped, to garnish

For the spice mix:

½ star anise

2 allspice berries

½ cinnamon stick

For the ginger-onion confit:

100g (3½oz./¾ stick + 1 tbsp) butter

4 large onions, halved and thinly sliced

5cm (2in.) piece fresh ginger, peeled and finely chopped

Preheat the oven to 180°C (350°F/gas mark 4).

First make the spice mix. Heat a small pan over medium heat and toast all the spices until fragrant. Set aside.

To prepare the duck, trim off any excess skin from the meat and set aside in the fridge to make crackling later. Heat the oil in a large ovenproof pan over medium heat and fry the duck on all sides until the skin is crisp and golden brown. Drain the duck on kitchen paper and set aside. Return the pan to the heat and add the sherry. Cook for 2 minutes to deglaze the pan then remove from the heat. Add the prepared spice mix to the pan along with the stock, lime leaves, ginger, tamarind paste and duck legs and thighs. Stir everything to combine, cover with a tight-fitting lid and transfer to the oven to cook for 1½ hours or until fork tender.

Cut the baby beetroot vertically in half and place in a small roasting pan with a little oil and a sprinkle of salt and roast in the oven until soft, about 25 minutes. Cool and then peel and cut in half. Keep warm.

To make the crackling, slice the reserved duck skin into 5mm (¼in) pieces and place on a baking tray. Sprinkle with the ground allspice and roast in the oven with the duck for 30 minutes, until crispy and the duck fat is a clear yellow colour. Remove from the oven and drain on kitchen paper. Keep warm.

To make the ginger-onion confit, melt the butter in a frying pan (skillet) over medium heat, then add the onions and ginger. Cook slowly, stirring occasionally, until the onions are soft and golden. Season to taste and set aside.

When the duck is cooked, remove from the oven and lift the duck pieces out of the pan onto a chopping board. Shred the meat, discarding the skin and bones. Transfer the meat to a medium pan. Strain the cooking liquid then pour the liquid over the duck meat and stir in the lime zest and juice, chili sauce, kecap manis and soy sauce. Bring to a gentle simmer, season to taste, cover and keep warm.

To assemble the dish, place the polenta pieces in the centre of six serving plates and spoon over the duck. Spoon the ginger-onion confit around the duck and top with the roasted beetroot and duck-skin crackling. Serve garnished with watercress and chives.

FLEMISH PEPPERCORN RIB EYE STEAK
WITH CHILI-DUSTED TOBACCO ONIONS

This steak and its alluring peppercorn sauce brings back memories of moving as a teen to Europe – my backpack full of ballet slippers and a tiny Berlitz dictionary – where I landed a job with the Royal Ballet of Flanders in Belgium, somewhere I didn't understand the local language, but made fast friends with a neighbouring family of gourmet cooks. The tobacco onions, also called angry onions, have the hot kick from a pepper-paprika blend and are simple to prepare and cook and even easier to eat.

SERVES 4

4 x 225g (8oz.) rib-eye (or Scotch fillet) steaks

For the peppercorn sauce:

240ml (1 cup) demi-glace, veal or beef stock

120ml (½ cup) double (heavy) cream

60ml (¼ cup) cognac or brandy

60ml (¼ cup) Syrah, Zinfandel or other peppery red wine

4 thyme sprigs

3 tbsp green peppercorns in brine, drained, liquid reserved

2 tbsp unsalted butter

pinch brown sugar to taste

For the chili-dusted tobacco onions:

1 litre (1 quart) peanut (groundnut) or vegetable oil

125g (4½oz./1 cup) self-raising flour

1 tbsp fine polenta (cornmeal)

1 tsp salt

1 tsp sweet Hungarian paprika

½ tsp ground black pepper

½ tsp cayenne

½ tsp smoked paprika or chipotle powder

½ tsp ground cardamom

3 large (350g/12oz. total weight) yellow or sweet onions, thinly sliced into 3mm (⅛in.) rings

To make the sauce, whisk the demi-glace or stock, cream, cognac, wine and thyme together in a saucepan and bring to a simmer. Reduce by a third. Crush 1 tablespoon of the peppercorns, then add them all, with a little juice from the jar, to the pan. Whisk in the butter a little at a time using a wire whisk to thicken the sauce until it is smooth. Remove the thyme sprigs then season to taste with a pinch of brown sugar.

Make the chili-dusted tobacco onions. Heat the oven to 110°C (225°F/gas mark ¼). Line a baking tray with kitchen paper and set aside.

Heat the oil to 180° (350°F) on a food thermometer in a deep saucepan over medium heat. Whisk all the remaining ingredients except the onion rings in a medium-sized bowl. Add the onion rings and carefully toss to coat. Remove the onion from the flour mixture, shaking to remove excess, and spread out on a plate or tray. Fry the onions in the hot oil a few slices at a time for approximately 10 minutes or until crisp and golden brown, making sure you don't overcrowd the pan. Use a slotted spoon to remove the onions and drain immediately on kitchen paper. Repeat until all onions are fried. Keep them warm in the oven while you cook the steak.

Heat a barbecue or flattop grill to high or place a frying pan (skillet) over high heat until the pan is sizzling hot to sear the steaks. Pat the steaks dry, then brush them with oil on both sides and season with salt. Sear on the first side over high heat for about 3 minutes. Turn the steaks over and cook an additional 5–7 minutes for medium-rare. Remove the steaks from the grill, or the frying pan (skillet) from the heat, and leave to rest for 5 minutes.

To serve, spoon the peppercorn sauce over the steak (or on the side) and top with the onion rings. Serve with a luscious red wine or Belgian beer.

TOASTED PEPPER, LEMON AND STRAWBERRY SWIRL ICE CREAM

Black pepper is a surprising companion to sweet summer berries and here adds an addictively spicy base note to a creamy lemon- and strawberry-infused ice cream. Have fun with your guests when asking them to guess the flavour; they will be mystified when trying to settle on the secret ingredient but will be instantly converted to its aromatic charms.

SERVES 6

For the ice cream:	For the strawberry compote:
zest of 2 lemons	340g (12oz) strawberries
100g (3½oz/½ cup) caster (superfine) sugar	100g (3½oz./½ cup) caster (superfine) sugar
1½ tsp black peppercorns, toasted and ground	2 tsp limoncello
pinch salt	pinch salt
150ml (⅔ cup) freshly squeezed lemon juice	
480ml (2 cups) crème fraîche	

Put the lemon zest, sugar, peppercorns and salt into the bowl of a food processor or blender and process until the zest is fine and well combined. Add the lemon juice and blend until the sugar dissolves. With the motor running, add the crème fraîche. Cover and chill for 1–3 hours to allow the flavours to meld.

Wash, hull and slice the strawberries into a bowl. Add the sugar, limoncello and a pinch of salt and fold until the strawberries are coated. Lightly mash with a fork. Cover and let stand for an hour, stirring occasionally, then chill for 1–3 hours.

Freeze the lemon mixture in an ice-cream maker, following the manufacturer's instructions, or pour into a dish and freeze, stirring occasionally, until frozen.

Layer a third of the lemon ice cream into a freezer container, then add a third of the strawberry compote. Repeat these layers twice more, then cover and freeze.

PUMPKIN BREAD PUDDING

Nutmeg, and its webbed coral-red mace wrapper, has almost as strong an olfactory memory recall as the spice vanilla. It's also believed to help with memory, so go on, allow yourself another spoonful of this delicious dessert!

SERVES 6

375g (13oz./1½ cups) puréed roasted pumpkin or butternut squash

240ml (1 cup) double (heavy) cream

1 tsp sea salt

1 tbsp freshly grated ginger

1 tsp ground cinnamon

1 tsp freshly ground nutmeg

1 tsp ground mace

85g (3oz./¼ cup) molasses or treacle

210g (7½oz./⅔ cup) maple syrup

½ tbsp pure vanilla extract

1 tbsp brandy

4 large eggs

4 croissants, sliced horizontally and toasted

250g (9oz.) pitted prunes, cut into small dice

60g (2¼oz./scant ½ cup) crystallized ginger, chopped

300g (10½oz./scant 1 cup) Cranberry Compote (see page 108)

butter, for buttering the dish

nutmeg-dusted whipped cream or vanilla ice cream, to serve (optional)

In a large bowl, combine the puréed pumpkin, cream, salt, ginger, cinnamon, nutmeg, mace, molasses, maple syrup, vanilla, brandy and eggs and beat well.

Add the toasted croissant slices and gently turn over in the custard mixture until they are thoroughly coated. (You might want to wear gloves as it's really gooey!) Using your hands or a large spoon, layer the croissants into the prepared dish, sprinkling with the chopped prunes, crystallized ginger and Cranberry Compote (see page 106) between each layer and finishing with a layer of croissant. Tightly cover the dish with cling film (plastic wrap) then foil. Refrigerate and allow to soak for at least 1 hour or preferably overnight.

Preheat the oven to 160°C (325°F/gas mark 3). Butter a deep casserole dish.

Bake in the oven for about 1 hour (a knife inserted in the centre should come out clean). Remove the cling film (plastic wrap) and foil and bake for an additional 15 minutes to lightly brown the top. Remove from the oven and let cool to room temperature.

To serve, cut into slices, gently heat in the oven or microwave and serve with a spoonful of nutmeg-dusted whipped cream or vanilla ice cream.

COCOA

COCOA NIB, SEED AND CHERRY BARS

Lovely, luxurious, crunchy cocoa nibs not only taste delicious but they're also good for the heart, thanks to the flavanols. These easy-to-make-and-take bars are full of them, as well as those 'happy-brain' cherry anthocyanins.

MAKES ABOUT 16 SQUARES

115g (4oz./1¼ cups) rolled oats, toasted (do not use quick-cooking oats)

100g (3½oz./¾ cup) Brazil nuts, roughly chopped

2 tbsp chia seeds

30g (1oz./¼ cup) sunflower seeds

3 tbsp cocoa nibs

90g (3¼oz./¾ cup) dried cherries or cranberries

55g (2oz./scant ⅓ cup) crystallized ginger

40g (1½oz./½ cup) unsweetened coconut flakes (chips)

6 tbsp (90ml/⅓ cup) runny honey or date syrup

125g (4½oz./½ cup) sunflower or nut butter (such as peanut or almond butter)

Preheat oven to 160°C (325°F/gas mark 3).

In a food processor, pulse the oats, Brazil nuts, chia and sunflower seeds, cocoa nibs, dried cherries or cranberries and ginger until finely chopped. Fold in the coconut flakes (chips) then add the honey and sunflower or nut butter, mixing to combine. Pour the mixture into a 23cm (9in.) square (or small rectangular) pan. Press to flatten and level the top and bake for 20 minutes. Cool and cut into bite-sized squares or bars.

COCOA, CINNAMON

SPICED COCOA NIB COFFEE

What better way to enjoy a bit of good-for-you cocoa? Teamed up with some more favourite spices, this is a warm comfortable way to get your daily dose of flavanols.

SERVES 2

115g (4oz./1 cup) cocoa nibs

⅛ tsp cardamom seeds

1 allspice berry

½ cinnamon stick, broken into chips

½ vanilla pod (bean), chopped

whole milk, coconut or almond milk and sweetener to serve (optional)

Put the cocoa nibs, cardamom, allspice and cinnamon in a sauté pan and toast over low heat for about 10 minutes, until fragrant, swirling the pan to prevent the spices burning.

Grind the toasted spices with the chopped vanilla in a spice grinder until the mixture resembles coffee grounds. This will make more than you need, so store tightly sealed in a jar or tin to save for another day.

Spoon 7 tablespoons of the cocoa blend into a French press. Pour in 475ml (2 cups) of filtered boiling water, cover with a cloth or cozy to keep warm and steep for 7–10 minutes. Press the plunger down and pour into two cups or mugs. Serve with your favourite kind of warmed milk and sweetener if you wish.

COCOA, CINNAMON

VALENCIA SMOOTHIE

The winning combination of orange, cocoa powder and cold-brew coffee is a natural low-sugar pick-me-up.

SERVES 1

3 tbsp oats	juice and zest of ½ orange
35g (1¼oz./¼ cup) raw cashew nuts	1 banana, sliced
1 tbsp cocoa powder	2 pitted dates, chopped
pinch kosher salt	120ml (½ cup) cold-brew coffee
generous pinch cardamom	4 cracked ice cubes
¼ tsp cinnamon	

Soak the oats and cashew nuts in 60ml (¼ cup) water overnight.

Drain the oats and cashew nuts and put in a single-serve juicer-blender with all the remaining ingredients and blend until smooth.

Pour into a tall glass and serve immediately.

TAMARIND, NUTMEG, STAR ANISE

TAMARIND SMOOTHIE

Tamarind looks like a dusty brown flavourless legume, but the pod hides a wealth of rich flavours, ancient remedies and promising and unusual talents, from alleviating dry-eye syndrome to counteracting kidney stones. The tamarind spice purée can be made two days ahead of time and can be doubled easily.

SERVES 1

1 heaped tbsp tamarind paste	1 tsp lemon juice
¼ tsp ground cinnamon	sprinkle of lemon zest
¼ star anise (⅛ tsp ground)	240ml (1 cup) coconut milk
½ vanilla pod (bean) or ¼ tsp ground vanilla powder or pure vanilla extract	ice cubes, to finish (optional)
	freshly grated nutmeg, to serve
1 tbsp coconut sugar, or to taste	
1 medium-sized apple, cored and sliced into quarters	

Put the tamarind paste into a pan with 175ml (¾ cup) of water and boil until smooth. Strain the juice back into the pan and discard the tamarind seed.

Bring the juice back to the boil, add the cinnamon, star anise, vanilla and coconut sugar. Remove from the heat and leave to cool. Once cool, remove the vanilla pod (bean) and star anise, or leave the star anise to blend into the smoothie.

Put the tamarind juice into a blender and add the apple and lemon juice and zest. Blend in the coconut milk, adding ice cubes to thicken. (For a thicker smoothie, freeze the coconut milk into cubes.) Dust with freshly grated nutmeg and serve.

Warming spice

When there's a chill in the air, these spices will provide warmth to body and soul,
leaving you with a healthy glow from their alleged ability to increase circulation,
open pores and sinuses and stimulate the body's defence mechanisms
to stave off chills, aches, pains and disease.

Warming Spice Health Heroes

Chili Pepper ★ Ginger ★ Mustard Seed ★ Horseradish ★ Wasabi

An infusion of warming spices ground and blended together – spicy, sweet, brain-fog-clearing ginger; tangy, sharp, pulmonary-clearing cardamom; tummy-soothing, maple-scented fenugreek; a grating of digestive-easing nutmeg; and the toasty bio-enabler peppercorn – is a recipe that will warm your insides with phytonutrients and power-packed vitamins. But whether you include them in a spice-infused tisane; a toddy of cold-fighting garlic, honey, lemon and ginger; or a rich, spice-rubbed roast dinner, the comforting, healing aromas and flavours of these spices will provide a rush of health-protective and feel-good endorphins that will push away the winter blues.

Chili peppers cause our pain sensors to rapidly release fight-or-flight endorphins that flood the taste buds and the brain then rush to the circulatory and digestive systems with warming-to-the-bone capsaicin. Horseradish is a circulatory-system star, a super antiseptic and a strong decongestant that helps open blocked respiratory passages. Ginger is said to improve circulation and is recognized as a spice with a talent for warming the body. It has been used for hundreds of years in traditional medicine as a diaphoretic to open the pores and induce sweating, increasing circulation and heat. Mustard seed may support the circulatory system with its large number of minerals, including iron, manganese and copper, which team together with active isothiocyanates (disease-preventing compounds) to warm and strengthen the body. Wasabi has similar attributes to horseradish and also contains warming isothiocyanate compounds and circulation-boosting properties.

Other warming spice heroes

Garlic This super-warming and stimulating antioxidant and antimicrobial hero of ancient Greek and Chinese medicine was fed to Egyptian slaves to give them good health and long-lasting strength. Its heating and stimulating effects have been recognized for thousands of years and it has been used as a remedy to treat everything from the common cold to contagious diseases.

Cardamom A fragrant pungent and warming spice used in chai tea, cardamom helps to lower blood pressure. Its most active oil, cineole, impressively both antibacterial and an antioxidant, has been recently trialled as an aid for asthma and other respiratory ailments, showing great promise.

Cumin The divine aroma of cumin seeds roasting in a pan will stimulate your taste buds, which is the first step towards good digestion. Cumin is considered a warming spice as it boosts blood circulation, improves the flow of oxygen through your cells, aids digestion and staves off the effects of food poisoning in the digestive system with its antibacterial power. It also helps to loosen phlegm and is a powerful expectorant. Black cumin, or nigella, has appetite-stimulating characteristics and is a natural thermogenic (heat-producer).

Black Peppercorn These pungent balls act as a warming bio-enabler, increasing blood flow and maximizing absorption and benefit of other nutrients. They are also good for easing discomfort in the digestive tract, reducing gas while increasing hydrochloric acid in the stomach, which helps to reduce stomach distress and fight bacterial growth in the intestines.

Fenugreek One of the earliest plants known to have been used medicinally, fenugreek may improve liver function and reduces pain with its warming, diaphoretic (perspiration-inducing) attributes. The raw seeds, softened by soaking in warm water, have traditionally been used to treat sluggish digestion. Fenugreek also relieves muscle and joint pain by increasing blood flow and reducing inflammation.

Nutmeg Said to help eliminate toxins in the body through supporting liver and gallbladder functions, nutmeg is thought to be especially beneficial to those suffering from liver disease. Nutmeg oil can warm and ease stomachaches by removing the excess gas from your intestines and is also thought to increase appetite.

Chili Pepper *The Endorphin Spice*

Known and grown around the world, chili peppers are native to the Americas, where they have been consumed since 6000BC. The Mayans had a great idea: I'm hooked on lattes boosted with a spoonful of raw cocoa powder, toasted Ceylon cinnamon and just a dash of hot chili powder (though the authentic version is a little extreme on the Scoville heat scale for me)!

Christopher Columbus is credited for having 'discovered' capsicums (family members include the heatless green bell pepper, the scorchingly hot scotch bonnet and some 3,000 other relatives) while searching, unsuccessfully, for black pepper. Soon thereafter, chili seeds travelled aboard Spanish and Portuguese galleons and were soon scattered into the far reaches of India, China, Indonesia, Africa and Europe.

Several studies have demonstrated the antioxidant properties in chili and its ability to scavenge free radicals, reduce antioxidative stress and promote cellular integrity. It turns out that chili-consuming countries generally have lower rates of cardiovascular disease than populations that eat a bland diet.

The hotter the chili pepper, the more capsaicin it contains, the highest levels of this alkaloid being found in the chili seeds and inner 'rib' membrane, accounting for the hot spicy sensation one experiences and that 'chili heads' crave to distraction. When you eat a capsaicin-laden chili, your body's pain receptors react immediately: Ouch! That's really hot! Then the body releases endorphins, natural morphine-like compounds that flood the body in immediate response to pain and are thought to be one of the strongest drugs produced in the body. There may be an instant welling of tears, but soon after, you get an exultant whoosh, a runner's high – a chili rush of pain, then chili pleasure. Incidentally, chili is considered an aphrodisiac for that very reason. It has also been credited with inducing a euphoric sense of wellbeing and enhancing mood, alertness and improved physical coordination.

Another good reason to eat chilies is, of course, their flavour: they simply make food taste better, from South African piri piri chicken, to Mexican Pork Chile Verde (see Anne Conness's version on page 40) and from Chinese kung pao chicken to India's vegetarian vindaloo curries. Mexican culture has two names for nearly every one of the country's 150 varieties of chili: a fresh green jalapeño, for instance, becomes a rich dark-red chipotle when dried. Dried chilies have a concentrated, complex and sweeter flavour, lasting an indeterminate amount of time as long as kept covered and dry. Fresh chilies come in shades of green, yellow, orange, red, purple and black and have a freshness and hydrating bite of heat, perfect for fresh salsas, sauces, gazpacho (see pages 144–5) and vegetarian dishes.

When buying fresh chilies, feel for firmness and look for ones that have shiny dry skin and are heavy for their size. Stored loosely and dry in the fridge, they will keep for about two weeks. They will also freeze well if tightly wrapped.

' It's the capsaicin in chilies (concentrated most of all in the seed pod, then the ribs, then the seeds and a modest amount, comparatively, in the flesh) that makes your nose run and your palate tingle. That tingle, a jangling of the seventh cranial nerve and not one of the five or six flavours, depending on who you believe, is good for you: it has helped people with cluster headaches, diabetic neuropathic pain and irritable bowel syndrome. Capsaicin has been commercialized: it's in patches, capsules, creams and nasal sprays, and available over the pharmacy counter.

Capsaicin works by depleting the body's nerve fibres of substance P, a neurotransmitter the body employs to transmit pain from one place to another. Capsaicin also desensitizes the GI tract to pain in those who already have pain. Hotter chilies seem to have more benefits, including an improved ability to clear insulin from the bloodstream. By the way, a chili's excessive heat can be turned down by rinsing your mouth with something cold (5 degrees C) – it does not have to be milk or something sugary, though both of those cold solutions work. Sadly, beer does not work better than water. '

John La Puma, MD

http://www.ncbi.nlm.nih.gov/pubmed/7708405 cluster ha; http://www.ncbi.nlm.nih.gov/pubmed/21573941 IBD; http://www.ncbi.nlm.nih.govpubmed/24867591 IBD-more; http://www.ncbi.nlm.nih.gov/pubmed/2385629

Ginger *The Balancing Spice*

My partner, mother and siblings are all comfortable and relaxed gliding along in a sailing boat. I love the gentle ocean breezes, monitoring the anchor, making simple meals in the galley and working the winches for the sails to securely hold the wind, but when the sea surface becomes like the inside of a washing machine, it's time to reach for that bit of ginger in hope that my queasy tummy will subside as my ballet brain fights for equilibrium to balance that salty sea foundation.

Ginger, a rhizome that most likely originated in Southern China or Northern India, has been grown since ancient times and used ever since to ease digestion and nausea. The pungent spicy-hot taste of fresh ginger is due to gingerols, the dominant compound, which is converted to a gentler sweeter essence, zingerone, when cooked. Dry ground ginger is more pungent than fresh because gingerol converts to the concentrated form, shogaol. Candied or crystallized ginger is made by simmering fresh ginger pieces in sugar syrup, dredging in granulated sugar and drying them. Pink sushi ginger or nori, which is used as a sushi garnish, is thinly sliced ginger, pickled with sugar, rice wine vinegar and salt. Ginger is also bottled and fermented to make ginger beer and made into ginger oil to flavour food and drink or use as medicine.

Ginger (*Zingiber officinale*) is also a potential brain tonic and super food: a large test-study of middle-aged and elderly women showed that ginger can improve brain function in such tasks as singular focused thinking, cognitive skills and memory and can protect against age-related damage to the brain, with no obvious side effects. Ginger's antibacterial chemistry is also effective against gum disease such as gingivitis and periodontitis.

Current pharmacological research indicates the urgent need for the development of new, safe and efficacious drugs to help reduce the global burden of tuberculosis, on which current-day antibiotics have little effect and are impossibly difficult to logistically distribute to the millions of people in need, the majority of whom live in remote villages. Natural products, especially those from the phytogenetic (plant-based) environment have been less intensively researched, even though they are known to contain structurally diverse active compounds and have been used as traditional cures for centuries. A medical research team has been investigating Ghanaian medicinal plants that include *Zingiber officinale* for their antituberculosis activity. Traditionally used by Ghanaian communities to treat coughs and other disease conditions with symptoms of tuberculosis, this handful of plant life is being studied as a possible channel towards prevention or cure of this most infectious and deadly disease.

Galangal (the word is derived from the Chinese for ginger) is likewise a rhizome. Used in Thai, Malay and Indonesian cuisine, galangal has a thinner, lighter pinkish skin and a hotter but more delicate taste and is grown almost exclusively in India and Eastern and Southeastern countries. Lesser galangal is the type most used for traditional medicinal purposes. Rich in iron, sodium and vitamins A and C, it is used in similar traditional cures to ginger.

www.ncbi.nlm.nih.gov/pmc/articles/PMC4801013/

' The underground stem or rhizome of *Zingiber officinale*, edible yellow ginger is a super spice. Fresh ginger juice is used for treating burns, and the essential oils have been used to relieve pain. Ginger can slow inflammation in the body, protect DNA, quell nausea (especially in pregnancy), treat motion sickness and indigestion and even migraine. Migraine? Barely an eighth of a teaspoon (540mg) of powdered ginger, dissolved in water, was tested against sumatriptan, a potent, approved, injectable migraine drug, and found to be equivalent when given at the very start of the headache: similar pain relief within two hours. How might ginger work to help headaches? It may stop the production of chemicals called prostaglandins, which mediate inflammation in the body and cause muscle contractions. I like to have people use food instead of extracts when they can... and ginger comes crystalized, in lollipops and syrups.

Note: there is mixed data about an interaction between ginger and the anticoagulant medication Coumadin, so if you are taking the latter, talk to your doctor about both. '

John La Puma, MD

http://www.ncbi.nlm.nih.gov/pubmed/23657930; http://www.ncbi.nlm.nih.gov/pubmed/26488162

Mustard Seed *The Prevention Spice*

The tiny mustard seed, a member of the brassica genus (which includes broccoli, Brussels sprouts and kale), is full of goodness and promising disease-prevention properties. These little seeds initially have no aroma, but when activated with the addition of liquid, such as water or vinegar, they release enzymes that create an intensely strong nose-running flavour, full of minerals and vitamins, including selenium, magnesium, B-complex vitamins and antioxidants A, C and K. Mustard seed will keep indefinitely.

Mustard may improve immunity and contains a large number of minerals that support the circulatory system (iron, manganese and copper), which team up with the warming properties of active isothiocyanates (sulphur phytochemicals, disease-preventative compounds that also gives cruciferous vegetables their memorable taste) to strengthen the body.

There are many species of mustard, but the most commonly used for food and food medicines are the oily mustard seeds, called condiment mustard. Mustard has always been of importance in Europe as it is one of the few spices that grows locally and quite prolifically so is inexpensive to acquire. The common white or yellow mustard, *Sinapas alba* is often 'prepared' with the addition of vinegar, turmeric, salt and 'secret seasonings', usually sold in squeezy bottles and extensively used in the US to top hamburgers and hot dogs. In Britain, water is added to dried yellow mustard powder and served as a nose-tingling addition to hot and cold roasts, or cooked with vegetables and vinegar to make the bright yellow condiment piccalilli. The sweet-and-spicy Italian version, mostarda di frutta, is traditionally made with powdered mustard, quince and fresh fruits. Both are favourites with cheese boards or served alongside cooked cold chicken and meats.

Brown (also called Chinese) mustard, *Brassica juncea*, was traditionally made with grape must 'mustard' or wine plus vinegar, salt and honey (see Vanilla Honey Mustard, page 164) and both whole-grain and ground prepared mustard is popular all over Europe. In France, three main types of mustard are treasured: Bordeaux mustard, mild and brown, contains vinegar, sugar and often tarragon or other soft herbs; Dijon is creamy yellow and strongly flavoured; moutarde à l'ancienne, made of crushed mustard seeds, has a mild taste. Germany has its own mustard, similar to the Bordeaux style, sometimes including beer, which is served with its world-famous sausages. Mustard is also an important ingredient in traditional sauerkraut and other naturally fermented vegetables.

The tiny black mustard seed (*Brassica nigra*) contains considerably more heat and is used almost exclusively in Indian and Eastern cuisine. The seeds are fried in hot oil to tame the pungent heat and impart a nutty flavour.

Mustard oil is made from brown mustard seed and other mustard species. It is used in Eastern cuisine and has strong preserving qualities so is added to pickles and chutneys. Mustard oil is also used, surprisingly, as a traditional topical treatment to stimulate hair growth.

'The seeds of the cruciferous mustard plant, which come in yellow, brown and black varieties, have been used both medicinally and in cuisine since ancient times. In fact, Hippocrates, the father of Western medicine, used mustard seed in his practice. Crushing or exposing the seeds to water activates enzymes, which give mustard its characteristic sharp, hot taste as well as releases its medical properties.

Medicinally, mustard has been used traditionally in a topical form, for body aches and as a poultice to ease respiratory congestion. It has also been used as both a laxative and an emetic [to cause vomiting].

Like other members of the brassica genus, mustard seeds contain antioxidants, including isothiocyanates. The isothiocyanates in mustard seed (and other brassicas) have been repeatedly studied for their anticancer effects. In animal studies – and particularly in studies involving the gastrointestinal tract and colorectal cancer – intake of isothiocyanates has been shown to inhibit formation of cancer cells and growth of existing cancer. Finally, mustard seeds are good sources of selenium and magnesium, two minerals that have multiple health benefits, including in moderating blood pressure, managing migraines and menopause. (Note: using mustard topically can cause skin irritation, including burns and ulcers, with prolonged use.)'

Linda Shiue, MD

Horseradish *The Antibiotic Spice*

This relative of mustard and cabbage has been growing in English fields since the 15th century. In fact, it has nothing to do with either horses or radishes (it looks more like a gangly white carrot to me), but a lot to do with food and medicine. Unlike chili pepper, which is hot on the tongue, the tingling heat from crucifers, such as mustard, wasabi and horseradish, is inhaled – a much faster delivery system!

This perennial cruciferous root with taupe-coloured skin and white flesh has no scent when picked or purchased, but once the skin is broken, the volatile oil sinigrin breaks down into an enzyme called allyl isothiocyanate, which has a scent similar to mustard oil. This enzyme is a natural and powerful antibiotic. Loaded with healing phytochemicals, horseradish contains an abundance of energetic compounds that are actively being tested to aid the lungs, digestion, joints, muscles and the immune system. Indeed, there is on-going anticancer research on these horseradish compounds.

Horseradish has been popular for centuries all over Europe. In the US in the 1800s, a young entrepreneur named Henry John Heinz made horseradish in vinegar and sold it in little jars: America's first convenience food. The H. J. Heinz Company, commonly known simply as Heinz, later paired bottled horseradish with tomato ketchup to invent cocktail sauce to spoon atop boiled shrimp and seafood with a lemon-wedge garnish. Horseradish is also popular infused in vodka in a Bloody Mary, mixed with sour cream for a jacket potato and served with a slice of prime rib, or with poached salmon, blended with mustard, cream and a squeeze of lemon and fresh dill.

Germany takes top honours not only for its medical research into horseradish but also for its horseradish-focused sauces, often serving this pungent nose-opening condiment simply peeled and grated with meals.

Note that grated and peeled horseradish needs to be used immediately, or preserved in vinegar, as it loses its flavour and oxidizes once prepared. Most horseradish preparations require little or no heat but when cooked become milder, so I recommend adding horseradish at the end to taste. If you are preparing horseradish at home, make sure your kitchen is well ventilated and all ingredients are at hand.

'Horseradish, a member of the brassica or cruciferous vegetable genus, is a long root native to the Mediterranean. It has an easily recognizable sharp taste when grated, which complements beef as well as smoked fish.

The sharpness characteristic of horseradish comes from the release of volatile compounds. Medicinally, these volatile compounds have long been used to ease respiratory congestion, and also to treat sinusitis and bronchitis. Their efficacy in treating these ailments is due to the fact that horseradish is a great source of vitamin C, higher than in oranges and lemons. In addition, the volatile compounds in horseradish have antimicrobial activity. Traditionally, people have considered horseradish to have diuretic properties and have used it to treat urinary tract infections, kidney stones and fluid retention. It has also been used to treat joint pain, gallbladder disorders, sciatic nerve pain, gout, colic and intestinal worms in children, though scientific data are lacking for these.

There is a potential concern that eating large amounts of horseradish or other cruciferous vegetables can decrease thyroid function, however this has only been shown in animal studies and would not be a concern at normal levels of consumption of these nutritious vegetables. '

Linda Shiue, MD

Wasabi *The Mountain Brook Spice*

Most sashimi aficionados have never seen true wasabi: in fact, there is very little real wasabi on the world market as most is made from horseradish – commonly referred to as 'wasabi Japanese horseradish'. Most powdered wasabi is bitter, and often not made from true wasabi rhizomes, and, most surprisingly, the wasabi horseradish most consumed by Americans is in a pill capsule, not on sushi. The powder used in sushi bars is 99 per cent horseradish. This is not to say, of course, that horseradish is inferior: as we've seen, it has a plethora of exciting uses for food and health. But where's the real wasabi and how does it differ?

Initially known as 'wild ginger', wasabi has similar attributes to ginger and a flavour palette similar to horseradish, to which it is only distantly related. Horseradish and wasabi also share the brain-clearing heat rush of a similar type of enzyme. But wasabi can thrive only in restrictive conditions and it takes many years for the crucifers to mature. Most of the world's true wasabi (*Eutrema wasabi* or *Wasabia japonica*) is native to Japan, where it is grown from a total of 17 wasabi cultivars, forms an integral component of the national cuisine and has been recognized since the 10th century for its medicinal properties. It is now successfully grown in other countries, too, including Canada, Brazil, Israel, the US state of Oregon and the pristine mountain regions of New Zealand. In Japan, this perennial pale-green-fleshed rhizome has been cultivated on the banks of bubbling mountain brooks for over 1,000 years. Commercial wasabi growing is based on two growing methods: the upland or soil-grown wasabi and the 'flooded-field' or water-stream-grown wasabi. The latter yields a superior rhizome-to-leaf ratio and, as the rhizome is the part of wasabi most popularly consumed, this is the most profitable method.

Nutritionally and for wellbeing, what sets wasabi apart from mustard and horseradish is its promising anticancer properties. There is evidence that its active isothiocyanate (ITC) compounds may have a chemopreventive effect on cancer, including of the lung, breast, liver, oesophagus, bladder, pancreas, colon and prostate. Promising studies continue.

Agriculturally, there is on-going research to develop a natural fungicide using natural phytogenetic wasabi extracts to prevent fungal damage to oilseed, rapeseed and canola crops.

If using a tin of 'wasabi' powder, check the ingredients to ensure it contains wasabi rather than horseradish, mustard and green food colouring. Add just enough water to hydrate and enjoy with your sushi. You can also add it to salad dressings, mashed potatoes, a seafood sauce or even ice cream!

'Also known as Japanese horseradish, wasabi (*Wasabia japonica*) is a distinct herb from horseradish, native to Japan. Its stem is freshly ground to produce a condiment that accompanies raw fish, though in Western sushi restaurants, the bright green paste that comes alongside your sushi is more likely to be food-colouring-enhanced horseradish combined with mustard.

Wasabi is thought to have many health benefits, including antimicrobial, potential anticancer (being rich in antioxidants), anti-inflammatory and also blood-thinning properties (specifically, decreasing platelet aggregation). Japanese manuscripts dating as far back as the eighth century mention wasabi, when it was used more as a medicinal herb than as food.

Wasabi is a source of fibre, protein and many micronutrients, including vitamins A, C and many B vitamins. It is a good source of many minerals, including calcium, iron, magnesium, phosphorus, potassium, sodium and zinc. Wasabi also has high levels of antioxidants, the isothiocyanates. In a recent study of the antibacterial properties of various foods, wasabi ranked as the most potent antibacterial against *E. coli* and *Staphylococcus aureus*. This means that the wasabi you eat with your raw fish may not only enhance the flavour, but may also help prevent food poisoning. It has also been shown to be effective against respiratory pathogens, and may also help prevent sinusitis by acting as a decongestant, which diners will notice immediately when eating too much wasabi at once.'

Linda Shiue, MD

CHILI, PEPPERCORN, CUMIN

HERB AND HARISSA GAZPACHO
WITH CRISPY CHICKPEAS

This traditional Spanish late-summer chilled tomato soup gets an international twist with a protein-rich, gluten-free, spicy, harissa-crusted chickpea topping in place of toasted bread croutons. Use soft, over-handled, 'well-loved' tomatoes for this, but make sure that they are still fresh and not mouldy or fermented.

SERVES 4

1.3kg (3lb.) fresh soft 'well-loved' tomatoes

7 celery sticks, strings peeled

2–3 cucumbers (550g/1lb. 4oz.), peeled and seeded

½ onion or 2 shallots

handful (10g/¼oz.) chopped soft fresh herbs, e.g. basil and parsley

1 tbsp Gazpacho Harissa Paste (see opposite)

juice of 3 lemons

1 litre (4¼ cups) low-sodium vegetable juice

3 tbsp olive oil, plus extra for drizzling

1–2 tsp fine sea salt

1 firm ripe avocado

Crispy Chickpeas (see opposite), to serve

Bring about 10cm (4in.) of water to the boil in a large pan. While the water is heating, turn each tomato upside down and make a small 'X' at the base just to pierce the skin. Have a medium bowl half filled with ice and water and a slotted spoon at the ready. Add the tomatoes to the boiling water, leave for a couple of minutes, then remove and plunge them into the iced water. Peel off the skins and cut out the core. Pour out the water and use the bowl to build your gazpacho.

Roughly chop the tomatoes, celery, cucumbers and onion and add to the bowl. Add the herbs, harissa paste, lemon juice, vegetable juice and olive oil.

Use a stick (or bar) blender to mix the soup, leaving some small chunks. Season with salt and additional harissa to taste. Chill until icy cold.

Peel and stone the avocado and cut the flesh into small pieces. Ladle the gazpacho into chilled soup bowls, top with a spoonful of avocado and garnish with a drizzle of olive oil, then scatter over the crispy chickpeas.

GAZPACHO HARISSA PASTE

MAKES ABOUT ⅔ CUP

2 tsp black peppercorns

2 tsp coriander seeds

1 tsp cumin seeds

1 tsp fennel seeds

2 tsp chopped garlic (or to taste)

½ green chili, seeded and minced

zest of ½ lemon

1 tbsp olive oil

1 tbsp ground chipotle powder or smoked paprika powder

½ tsp ground cayenne

2 tbsp ground sweet Hungarian paprika

Toast then finely grind the peppercorns and the coriander, cumin and fennel seeds.

Using a mortar and pestle, grind the garlic, chili and lemon zest. Add the toasted ground spices and the olive oil. Add the remaining spices and grind into a paste, using more oil if needed.

Stored tightly sealed and chilled, the paste will keep for several months.

CRISPY CHICKPEAS

MAKES ABOUT 3 CUPS

200g (7oz./1 cup) dried chickpeas (or 3 cups canned, drained and air-dried)

1 tsp baking soda

250ml (1 cup) grapeseed or vegetable oil

1 tbsp Gazpacho Harissa Paste (see above)

¼ tsp garlic powder

Put the dried chickpeas and baking soda in a 1-litre (1-quart) pan and pour over enough water to cover. Cover the pan and leave to soak for 8 hours.

Strain, rinse and return the chickpeas to the pan. Cover with water and bring to the boil, then reduce to a simmer and cook for 2 hours, or until fork tender. Cool on a large baking tray to let the chickpeas dry.

Mix the harissa blend and garlic powder in a medium-sized bowl and set aside.

Heat the oil in a large frying pan (skillet) to about 180°C (350°F). Test a chickpea: if the oil bubbles around it, it is ready to fry. Cook the chickpeas in batches, making sure the pan does not become overcrowded, for about 3–4 minutes, until crispy.

Drain on kitchen paper, then quickly toss in the bowl of spices.

Sprinkle on top of the gazpacho.

Illustrated on pages 142–3

COUNTRY ONION MUSHROOM SOUP

This is a quick and simple, thick, potage-style soup that I created as executive chef of Bridge Street restaurant in Bigfork, Montana, owned by the award-winning Chateau Montelena Winery in Napa, California. The restaurant was surrounded by a lovely herb and veggie garden, where I grew the horseradish used in this dish. When the time came to make it, the entire kitchen crew would back away as this fresh spice is odourless when uprooted, but once you break the skin, the smell is pungent! The volatile oil it contains is a powerful natural antibiotic but it can make you swoon and your eyes fill with tears!

SERVES 2–4

1 head garlic	50ml (scant ¼ cup) port
1 tbsp olive oil	475ml (2 cups) vegetable stock
1 tbsp grapeseed oil	200g (7oz./1 cup) mashed potato
250g (9oz.) mushrooms	1–2 tsp lemon juice
⅛ tsp (large pinch) nutmeg	2 tsp pure horseradish, fresh or from a jar, to taste
1 tbsp fresh thyme leaves	⅛ tsp freshly grated nutmeg, to garnish
125g (4½oz./½ cup) Turmeric Melted Onions (see below)	garlic bread, to serve (optional)

Preheat the oven to 180°C (350°F/gas mark 4). Cut the top off the garlic head to expose the cloves, then peel away just the outer layers of the garlic-bulb skin, leaving the skins of the individual cloves. Wrap loosely in foil and drizzle a tablespoon of oil over the garlic. Close the foil at the top, place on a baking tray and roast in the oven for about 30–35 minutes until soft and golden brown.

While the garlic is roasting, make the Turmeric Melted Onions (see below.)

Heat the grapeseed oil and sauté the mushrooms with the nutmeg and thyme leaves in a 2-litre (2-quart) pot until almost dry over medium heat, about 5 minutes.

Reduce the heat to low, add the Turmeric Melted Onions and half the roasted garlic (keep the other half for other use; it will keep for about 2 weeks refrigerated) and mix well. Add the port and reduce for 2 minutes or so. Add the stock and simmer for 3–5 minutes.

Stir in the mashed potato, lemon juice and horseradish and season to taste with salt and pepper.

Serve warmed in big bowls, topped with a sprinkle of freshly grated nutmeg, accompanied by your favourite garlic bread, if wished.

TURMERIC MELTED ONIONS

MAKES 2 CUPS

50g (1¾oz./½ stick) butter	4 medium brown onions (450g/1lb.), halved and thinly sliced
60ml (¼ cup) grapeseed or vegetable oil	10 grinds black pepper (optional)
1 tsp ground turmeric	

Heat the oil and melt the butter in a pan over medium–high heat, stir in the turmeric and cook for 1 minute. (Adding turmeric to the sizzling oil intensifies the flavour and nutrients; the pepper adds even more goodness.)

Add the onions and when they begin to let off steam, turn the heat down to medium–low and cook for 20–30 minutes, stirring occasionally, until translucent, melted and light-yellow-brown in colour.

Add the pepper and stir for a few minutes.

Remove from heat, cool, then cover and chill until needed.

CHILI, GINGER, CUMIN

KULI KULI PEANUT CAKES
WITH QUICK CHILI-PICKLED ONIONS AND TOASTED BLACK CUMIN SEEDS

Inspired by the age-old Nigerian snack, kuli kuli is packed full of protein and this version has an added chili kick, layered with the subtle sweetness of cinnamon. It is good for the circulation and makes a great gluten- and dairy-free vegan two-bite hors d'oeuvre.

MAKES 24 (4cm/1½ in.) CAKES

200g (7oz./2 cups) blanched lightly oven-toasted peanuts (groundnuts)

4 tsp freshly grated ginger

12 drops hot chili sauce (Tabasco), or to taste

2 tsp soft brown sugar

1 tsp cinnamon, ground

¼ tsp flaked salt, or to taste

peanut (groundnut) oil, for frying

½ cinnamon stick (optional)

chervil or parsley leaves, to garnish

For the chili-pickled onions:

1 small red onion (about 100g/3½oz.), halved and thinly sliced

½ fresh hot red chili, e.g. jalapeño, Anaheim or Serrano, sliced into thin rings

zest of 1 lime and juice of ½

60ml (¼ cup) rice wine vinegar

1 tsp minced parsley

1 tbsp black cumin seeds (nigella or onion seeds), plus extra for garnishing

First make the chili-pickled onions. Mix all the ingredients together in a small bowl, cover and chill until ready to use.

Using a food processor, or by hand with a mortar and pestle, grind the peanuts (groundnuts) and ginger together until sesame-seed size. Add a little peanut oil if the nuts are too dry but don't allow it to turn into peanut butter.

Blitz in the hot chili sauce, sugar, cinnamon and salt. Tightly squeeze a bit in your hand to make sure the kuli kuli isn't too oily or it won't be crispy when you cook it. Use up to 4 teaspoons of water to help the mixture hold together. Shape into 4cm (1½in.) sized cakes (about 15g/½oz.) and place on a tray.

Pour peanut (groundnut) oil into a frying pan (skillet) to a depth of 4cm (1½in.), add the half cinnamon stick (if using) and heat to 165°C (325°F).

Fry the cakes in batches until golden brown, about 2 minutes each side. Drain on kitchen paper. If your kuli kuli turn out soft rather than crispy, pop them into a low oven (110°C/225°F/gas mark ¼) to dry out and harden without burning.

To serve, mound a large pinch of chili-pickled onions on top of the kuli kuli and garnish with a chervil or parsley leaf and a sprinkle of black cumin seeds.

TURKISH EGGS

Peter Gordon

'These are known as çılbır in Turkey, (pronounced chil-bir) and they always have raw garlic mixed into the yogurt. At The Providores, where they are our biggest-selling brunch dish, and also very popular on the all-day menu, we don't add the garlic as our customers find it too confronting. Like Turkish cooks, I use a generous amount of a mild and seedless but truly tasty chili flake called kirmizi biber, which is also known as Aleppo chili. I have also made it using Korean chili flakes, which likewise give the buttery oil a delicious red hue. We always serve this with toasted sourdough.' PG

SERVES 4 (ALLOW 2 EGGS PER PERSON)

300g (10½oz./1¼ cups) thick plain yogurt

1 garlic clove, finely crushed

½ tsp flaky salt

50ml (scant ¼ cup) extra virgin olive oil

50g (1¾oz./½ stick) unsalted butter

1 tsp dried chili flakes (more or less to taste)

1 tbsp snipped dill or flat parsley

8 eggs

100ml (scant ½ cup) white vinegar (this may seem excessive, but it isn't!)

Whisk the yogurt, garlic and salt with half the olive oil for 15 seconds then put to one side (it's best served at room temperature).

In a small pan, cook the butter until pale nut brown (beurre noisette). Remove from the heat and add the chili flakes, then swirl the pan gently to allow them to sizzle for 20 seconds. Add the remaining olive oil and dill and put the mixture to one side, keeping it warm.

Add the vinegar to 1½ litres (1½ quarts) of simmering water in a medium-sized, deep pan and poach the eggs. Never add salt to the water when poaching eggs as it causes them to break up.

To serve, divide three quarters of the yogurt among four warmed bowls. Place two drained poached eggs in each bowl then spoon on the remaining yogurt. Drizzle the chili butter on top and eat straight away.

WASABI

WILD RICE SALAD
WITH ASIAN ORANGE VINAIGRETTE

The most commonly eaten food in the world, rice is paired with hundreds of ingredients and here is one of my favourites: a rice salad with wasabi and orange. From the brassica genus (like broccoli and Brussels sprouts), wasabi has an undeniable heat and, as well as quickly clearing the sinuses, is being studied for its possible anticancer benefits.

SERVES 4 AS A MAIN OR 6 AS A STARTER

175g (6oz./1 cup) brown rice

175g (6oz./1 cup) white rice

175g (6oz./1 cup) wild rice

120ml (½ cup) orange juice

200g (7oz./2 cups) dried apricots, sliced

70g (2½oz./½ cup) crystallized ginger, minced

225g (8oz.) fresh water chestnuts (or 1 small can, drained)

160g (5¾oz./1½ cups) toasted pecans, roughly chopped,

½ bunch chives, snipped

For the Asian orange vinaigrette:

240ml (1 cup) seasoned rice vinegar

240ml (1 cup) grapeseed or canola oil

2 tbsp toasted sesame oil

2 tbsp soy sauce

juice of 1 or 2 limes plus zest of 1

120ml (½ cup) orange juice (from poached apricots, see above)

2 tsp freshly grated wasabi, or 1 tbsp wasabi mustard powder, mixed with water to make a thick paste

Cook the different types of rice according to package directions. Drain and chill.

Heat the orange juice, add the apricots and ginger and simmer for 10 minutes. Remove from heat and leave to cool. Drain and reserve the juice for the vinaigrette.

To make the vinaigrette, combine all the ingredients in a bowl and mix well.

Toss the rice, water chestnuts, pecans and chives in a large bowl. Add the drained apricots and ginger. Pour over the dressing and mix well.

Chill, covered in the fridge, for at least 2 hours and up to a day.

BANANA-LEAF-WRAPPED SNAPPER
WITH BANANA CORIANDER SALSA AND CREAMY CARDAMOM POLENTA

This Thai-tropics-inspired dish is perfect to cook and share out of doors on a summer's day. Galangal, which is similar to ginger and has a smooth pungent flavour when cooked, was used in ancient Indonesia — and indeed is still used today in traditional Indonesian medicine — to help joint pain and inflammation. Its warming qualities provide a perfect balance to this warm, sunny dish.

SERVES 4

	For the banana coriander (cilantro) salsa:
1 large banana leaf	1 green-tipped banana
4 x 175g (6oz.) boneless snapper fillets	2–3 tbsp coconut milk
115g (4oz.) fresh galangal (or ginger), grated	zest and juice of 2 limes
1 large red (bell) pepper, thinly sliced	2 tsp sweet chili sauce
1 large green (bell) pepper, thinly sliced	dash fish sauce
1 large yellow (bell) pepper, thinly sliced	2 tsp grated fresh galangal (or ginger)
8 fresh kaffir lime leaves, half chopped	¼ tsp ground cardamom
3 shallots, sliced in rings	55g (2oz.) palm hearts or bamboo shoots, diced
3 tbsp butter, softened	30g (1oz./3 tbsp) diced red onion
2 tbsp rice wine vinegar	⅓ bunch coriander (cilantro), or to taste
¼ tsp salt	¼ bunch Thai basil, or to taste
fresh ground pepper, to taste	
1 tbsp grapeseed or vegetable oil, for brushing	

Make the Creamy Cardamom Polenta and Crispy Shallots (see opposite).

Preheat the oven to 180°C (350°C/gas mark 4) or heat a barbecue.

Wave the banana leaf over a gas flame, or use a blowtorch or candle, for a few seconds until the leaf is shiny and supple. Cut into four hearts about 5cm (2in.) longer and wider than the fish. (If you can't get hold of bamboo leaf, simply use parchment paper.) Rinse the fish fillets and gently pat dry.

Combine the galangal or ginger, (bell) peppers, chopped kaffir lime leaves and a third of the shallots in a saucepan with 1 tablespoon of the butter and sweat until soft.

Brush one side of each banana leaf heart with oil and scatter over the (bell) pepper-onion mixture, then place one fillet on top of each. Top each with 1 kaffir lime leaf. Fold over the banana leaf like an envelope and secure with kitchen twine or toothpicks. Cook on a stovetop grill plate or on the barbecue for about 15 minutes, turning once halfway through.

Make the sauce while the fish cooks. Melt 1 tablespoon of the butter in a small saucepan with the remaining shallot. Stir for 2 minutes then add the vinegar and 2 tablespoons of water. Simmer until reduced by a quarter. Slowly whisk in the remaining butter until it begins to emulsify/thicken. Set aside until ready to serve.

Make the banana coriander (cilantro) salsa. Peel and cut the banana into small dice and set aside. Whisk together the coconut milk, lime juice and zest, chili sauce, fish sauce, galangal or ginger and cardamom. Add the palm hearts, onion, Thai basil and coriander (cilantro). Season to taste.

To serve, cut the twine or remove the toothpicks and open the banana leaf. Carefully arrange the fish on the polenta. Scatter the peppers around the fish. Spoon the sauce over the fish and top with crispy shallots. Serve with the banana coriander (cilantro) salsa.

CREAMY CARDAMOM POLENTA

Coconut milk adds a tropical healthy richness to polenta. Stirring it as suggested makes a creamy texture infused with the alluring taste of cardamom. This also makes a nourishing breakfast bowl topped with fresh fruit and sprinkled with coconut sugar.

SERVES 4

500ml (2 cups + 2 tbsp) coconut milk and 500ml (2 cups + 2 tbsp) water

I tbsp brown sugar

1 tsp salt

140g (5oz./1 cup) polenta (not quick cooking) or fine yellow cornmeal

85g (3oz./⅓ cup) Greek-style or coconut yogurt, to finish

1 tsp black (or green) cardamom seeds, toasted and ground

Bring the coconut milk and water to a boil with the sugar and salt in a heavy 2-litre (2-quart) pan. Add the polenta in a thin stream, stirring constantly with a wooden spoon. Cook over moderate heat, stirring constantly, for 3 minutes.

Reduce the heat to low and simmer the polenta, covered, stirring for 1 minute after every 10 minutes of cooking, for about 30–35 minutes in total.

Remove from the heat and stir in the yogurt until combined. Spoon onto plates or into a serving bowl and sprinkle a pinch of cardamom on top.

The polenta can be made 30 minutes ahead and kept covered at room temperature (do not let it stand longer or it will solidify). Just before you serve, reheat it over low heat – you may need to add a bit more warmed liquid if it's too thick – then stir in the yogurt until thoroughly blended.

VARIATION: CRISPY CARDAMOM POLENTA

If making polenta for the duck recipe on page 118, reduce the liquid of your choice to 700ml (3 cups) and add 2 tablespoons of butter or oil. Cook as directed above, then pour the polenta into an oiled baking tray and smooth the top. Cool and cut into shapes. Fry in a pan over medium heat with a little butter or oil on both sides until golden brown and crispy.

CRISPY SHALLOTS

3 shallots, cut and separated into thin rings

rice flour, to coat

oil, for deep frying

flake salt

Toss the shallot rings in rice flour.

Pour the oil into a small pan to a depth of about 2.5cm (1in.) and heat to 180°C (350°F).

Shake the flour from the shallot rings and fry in batches, until golden and crispy. Drain on kitchen paper then sprinkle with flake salt.

Illustrated on pages 154–5

★

MUSTARD, GINGER, GARLIC, CARDAMOM

TONGA CHILI-LIME CHICKEN

Created at a Tongan vanilla plantation using ingredients available on the plantation, including passion fruit, freshly juiced limes, fresh ginger and vanilla, which I made into a mustard, this dish easily adapts for parties by substituting the thighs and drumsticks with the same amount of chicken wings.

SERVES 6

750g (1lb. 10oz.) chicken thighs and/or drumsticks, bone in, skin on

1 small handful coriander (cilantro) leaves, for garnishing

For the marinade:

2 garlic cloves, chopped

1 tbsp freshly grated ginger

1 tsp coriander seeds, toasted

½ tsp cardamom seeds, toasted

240ml (1 cup) grapeseed or vegetable oil

60ml (¼ cup) lime juice

½ medium onion (100g/3½oz.), chopped

120ml (½ cup) passion fruit juice (or fresh pineapple juice), or 4 passion fruit, pulped and seeded

1 tbsp coconut or brown sugar

¼ tsp salt

120ml (½ cup) seasoned rice wine vinegar

2 tsp Dijon mustard, or Vanilla Honey Mustard (see page 164)

large pinch nutmeg

30g (1oz./½ cup) fresh coriander (cilantro) leaves, chopped

2 fresh red chilies, thinly sliced

Cut any excess fat off the chicken pieces and discard, then transfer the chicken to a medium-sized bowl or casserole dish. Using a mortar and pestle, grind the garlic, ginger and coriander and cardamom seeds to make a paste. Transfer this paste to a food processor (or use a stick blender), add all the remaining marinade ingredients except the chilies, and whizz until smooth. Stir in the sliced chilies then pour the marinade over the chicken to coat. Cover the dish, or put everything into a zip-sealing bag, and chill for 2–8 hours.

Preheat the oven to 180°C (350°F/gas mark 4).

Drain the chicken from the marinade and set aside. Bake the chicken pieces for 25 minutes, or until juices run clear. Remove from the oven, transfer onto a serving plate, cover and let rest for 10 minutes.

To serve, reduce the leftover marinade and drizzle it over the chicken, then scatter the coriander (cilantro) leaves, and the chilies from the reduced marinade over all and serve immediately.

'THE THATCHED COTTAGE' COTTAGE PIE

I first sampled this classic British comfort food at The Thatched Cottage far from the London lights. The Thatched Cottage version has a secret nose-running spice in the minced beef with mashed potato topping. I watched as fresh horseradish root was pulled from an old wooden barrel planter, then brushed, peeled, chopped, quickly blanched (to retain the bright white colour) and the pieces tossed in a blender with warmed white vinegar. We all held our breaths as the lid was removed and the coarse pungent root was quickly packed into a glass jar and the lid hastily sealed in place. Horseradish makes the perfect counterpoint to creamy soothing potato mash, and current German studies indicate that it contains enormous amounts of natural antibiotic, helping to counteract respiratory infections and diseases such as bronchitis, pneumonia and strep throat.

SERVES 4

2 tbsp oil

500g (1lb. 2oz.) minced (ground) beef

2 onions, chopped

2 carrots, peeled and chopped

2 garlic cloves, minced

1 tbsp dried mixed herbs

1 tbsp Worcestershire sauce

1 beef stock cube

240ml (1 cup) dry white wine

10g (¼oz./¼ cup) parsley leaves, chopped

3 tbsp HP sauce

2 tbsp tamarind paste

Worcestershire sauce and extra horseradish, to serve

For the horseradish mash:

1 kg (2lbs. 4oz.) floury baking potatoes (e.g. Maris Piper, King, Russet), peeled and cut in half

½ tsp sea salt, or to taste

120ml (½ cup) milk

55g (2oz./½ stick) salted butter

2 tbsp fresh or jarred pure horseradish (not creamed)

Preheat the oven to 180°C (350°F/gas mark 4).

Heat a large frying pan (skillet) and add the oil. Sauté the beef over low heat, stirring with a wooden spoon to break up any lumps. Add the onion, carrot, garlic and dried mixed herbs, stirring well. Add the Worcestershire sauce, stock cube and 500ml (2 cups) of water. Cover and simmer for 10 minutes.

Add the wine, parsley, HP sauce and tamarind paste, then simmer and reduce to thicken. Season to taste.

For the mash, put the potatoes in a pan with the salt and pour in enough water to cover. Bring to the boil then turn down the heat to a simmer and cook until the potatoes are fork tender.

Drain and mash using a ricer or potato masher. Mash in the milk, butter and horseradish, adjusting seasoning to taste, until smooth.

Spoon the beef into four individual ovenproof dishes or one large baking or casserole dish. Spoon or pipe the mashed potatoes on top, covering the beef filling completely, and using the back of a fork, make a decorative pattern on top. Place the dish or dishes on a foil-lined baking tray and bake until bubbly, about 20 minutes for individual dishes or 30 minutes for a large one. If you wish, you can place it under the grill (broiler) for an additional 10 minutes to brown the top.

Serve with Worcestershire sauce and extra horseradish.

SAZON RUB BEEF ROAST
WITH CHIMICHURRI ARGENTINA

A popular cut of beef known in South America as 'cuadril' and elsewhere as rump roast or tri-tip, this is a shoulder of beef with the fat cap intact. This spice crust is inspired by the hugely popular South American dry spice blend sazon. This blend is packed full of fresh oregano, garlic and spices. You can apply the rub to the beef up to two days ahead and the sauce, too, can be made a day in advance. Chimichurri Argentina is a parsley- and oregano-packed, pesto-type sauce, bright with vinegar and hot with chilies.

SERVES 4–6

1kg (2lb. 4oz.) piece of beef rump cap (aged 3 months is ideal)

For the sazon rub:

1 tbsp grapeseed oil, plus extra for brushing

1 tbsp lime juice

1 tbsp coriander seeds, crushed

1 tbsp cumin seeds

1 tbsp salt

2 tsp fresh oregano

2 tsp chipotle powder

1 tsp freshly grated ginger

1 tsp black peppercorns

1 tsp chili flakes

1 tsp dried mint

½ tsp ground turmeric

For the chimichurri Argentina:

2 bunches (60g/2¼oz.) fresh parsley

1 bunch (25g/1oz.) fresh oregano

4 garlic cloves, peeled

120ml (½ cup) apple cider (or juice)

½ apple, peeled, cored and chopped

1 tbsp apple cider vinegar

1 whole fresh red jalapeño or other chili pepper, seeded and chopped

120ml (½ cup) extra virgin olive oil

Combine the rub ingredients together in a small bowl.

Pat the beef dry using kitchen paper. Score the fat, making incisions about 1cm (½in.) deep 5mm (¼in.) apart. Brush with oil to coat. Pack the rub into the fat on top of the beef, then cover and chill for 2 hours. Remove the beef from the fridge at least an hour before cooking to let it come to room temperature.

Make the chimichurri Argentina. Put all the ingredients except the oil in a food processor, or small blender, and pulse until coarsely chopped. Slowly drizzle in the oil until combined, adding more if you wish. Spoon into a serving bowl, cover and chill until needed.

Turn on the extractor fan, then heat a stovetop grill pan/plate or barbecue to medium–high, place the beef on it, fat-side up, and cook for about 6 minutes, then carefully turn it over and cook fat-side down for an additional 6–8 minutes. Test for doneness with a thermometer if you like (it should have reached 55°C /130°F for rare/medium–rare).

Remove from heat and transfer to a carving board. Loosely cover with foil and let rest for 15–20 minutes. Thinly slice the beef across the grain and serve with the chimichurri Argentina.

MUSTARD, PEPPERCORN

BREAD AND BUTTER PERSIAN PICKLES

This tangy but slightly sweet pickle is delicious and is made with Persian (also known as Lebanese) cucumbers, which have a slightly thicker skin than hothouse ones, and few if any seeds.

MAKES 3 MEDIUM-SIZED JARS

900g (2lb.) Persian cucumbers, thinly sliced

450g (1lb.) white onions, thinly sliced into half moons

2 large (bell) peppers (red and yellow), seeded and cut into thin strips

2 tbsp sea salt

140g (5oz./1 cup unpacked) brown sugar

140g (5oz./¾ cup) granulated sugar

1 tbsp turmeric

2 tsp black peppercorns, toasted

1 tsp each yellow and black mustard seeds

1 tsp each celery, fennel and ajwain seeds, toasted

¼ tsp whole cloves

1 litre (4¼ cups) white vinegar

Layer the vegetables into a strainer and gently toss with the salt. Cover with a clean cloth and leave for 3 hours. Drain the vegetables, rinse thoroughly and drain again.

Put the sugars, spices and vinegar in a large stainless-steel or enamel pan (remember that turmeric stains!) and bring to the boil. Add the vegetables and return to the boil for 1 minute. Turn off the heat and spoon the vegetables into sterilized jars, then pour the liquid over all. Seal the jars, rinse under running water and cool on the work surface.

Store in a dark pantry and keep refrigerated once opened.

MUSTARD, HORSERADISH

VANILLA HONEY MUSTARD

I originally created this for my first book, Vanilla Table, *but kept it aside as I was interested in researching and creating a line of condiments, preserves and fermented vegetables. As vanilla and mustard are actually both naturally bitter, pairing them together with a dash of honey and vinegar and a bit of horseradish heat makes for a sweet, hot and aromatic combination that is just the thing for adding a bit of chutzpah to a plain-tasting dish.*

MAKES ABOUT 500ml (2 CUPS)

115g (4oz./¾ cup) yellow mustard seeds

55g (2oz./6 tbsp) black mustard seeds

325ml (1⅓ cups) white wine vinegar, plus more if needed

2½ tbsp mild-flavoured runny honey

1 tsp grated horseradish, fresh or from a jar

½ tsp dried tarragon

1 tbsp sea salt

1 vanilla pod (bean) split, scraped and cut into 6 pieces, or 1 tsp vanilla paste

Grind the yellow mustard seeds in a spice grinder or mortar and pestle to the desired texture, but leave the black seeds whole. Mix together in a bowl and stir in half the vinegar. Let stand for 15 minutes, then add the remaining ingredients, combining well and adding additional vinegar if too dry. Cover with a clean cloth and leave to stand overnight.

Spoon the mustard into sterilized jars and seal. It will be ready to use in 4 weeks and will keep, stored in a cool dark place, for up to 12 months.

PEAR AND BARLEY TART
WITH GINGER MILK SHERBET

Sarah Johnson

'This dessert is truly a sum of all its parts. The nuttiness of the barley adds depth to the subtle, floral notes of the pear. And while warm crumble and ice cream are a classic match, the clean coolness of the sherbet gives way to the heat of the ginger, calling you back for another bite. It is worth seeking out ripe pears for this dish. When selecting the pears, press the bottom of the fruit gently with your thumb. The flesh should give ever so slightly. Avoid overly soft pears that will fall apart when cooked and put aside under-ripe fruits that have yet to develop flavour. Ginger has become one of my favourite ingredients to cook with. In this milk sherbet, I enjoy the lighter texture over more traditional ice creams as I find it brings out the fresh lemony flavours of the ginger that would otherwise be lost in the richness of an ice cream. While this dessert has an autumnal feel, the sherbet pairs well with fruits from other seasons, too. Try this tart with rhubarb and strawberries in spring, or blackberries and peaches in summer. In winter, serve the ginger ice milk in a bowl with clementines and kumquats and a scattering of the toasted barley crumble over the top.' SJ

SERVES 6–8

For the ginger milk sherbet:

500ml (2 cups + 2 tbsp) whole milk

70g (2½oz.) fresh ginger, peeled and sliced into thin disks

1 small egg white

55g (2oz./¼ cup) sugar

1 tsp freshly grated ginger

For the barley crisp topping:

85g (3oz./generous ½ cup) barley flour

40g (1½oz./⅓ cup) plain (all-purpose) flour

3 tbsp demerara sugar

2 tbsp granulated sugar

pinch salt

85g (3oz./¾ stick) unsalted butter, at room temperature, diced

10g (¼oz./1½ tbsp) barley flakes

For the barley shortcrust pastry:

175g (6oz./1½ sticks) butter, at room temperature

115g (4oz./generous ½ cup) caster (superfine) sugar

45g (1½oz./⅓ cup) icing (confectioner's) sugar

2 egg yolks

85g (3oz./generous ½ cup) barley flour

160g (5¾oz./1¼ cups) plain (all-purpose) flour

For the pear filling:

about 1kg (2lb. 4oz./about 5 or 6) ripe pears, cored but not peeled, cut into bite-sized pieces

100g (3½oz./½ cup) sugar, plus more to taste

juice and zest of ½ lemon

½ tsp freshly grated ginger

To make the ginger milk sherbet, put the milk and sliced ginger in a pan and bring to the boil. Immediately remove from the heat and cool to room temperature. Cover and chill. (This part can be done a day in advance and stored overnight.)

When cooled, strain the milk through a fine mesh sieve, discarding the ginger. Using an electric mixer, or by hand, whisk the egg white until light and frothy. Slowly add the sugar while continuing to whisk your meringue until soft peaks form. Add the freshly grated ginger to the milk, then gently fold in the meringue. Don't worry about incorporating the meringue entirely; the mixture will look separated, but will come together once it is churned. Churn immediately in an ice-cream maker according to the manufacturer's instructions. Transfer the milk sherbet to the freezer and continue to chill. This sherbet is best enjoyed the same day but will keep for several days.

To make the crispy topping, combine the flours, sugars and salt into a large bowl. Add the chilled butter and toss to coat. Rub the butter between your fingers into the dry ingredients until it resembles coarse breadcrumbs.

Add the barley flakes and mix until the mixture holds together when squeezed in your hands. Take care not to overwork the flour or the mixture will lose the crumbly tender texture when baked. Cover and place in the fridge until you are ready to use. (The topping can be prepared up to a week in advance.)

To make the pastry, in a mixer with a paddle, beat the butter until smooth. Stop, scrape down the side of the bowl, then add both sugars, mixing on medium speed until incorporated. Stop, scrape down the side of the bowl, then, with the mixer running, add the eggs one at a time, ensuring each egg is emulsified, scraping after each egg. Add the flours and salt, pulsing until just combined.

Turn the pastry dough out onto a work surface and gently bring together to a ball (you should not have to knead.) Wrap in cling film (plastic wrap), rest and chill in the fridge for at least 30 minutes. Preheat the oven to 160°C (325°F/gas mark 3).

Remove the pastry from the fridge and allow to come to room temperature. While the dough is softening, butter a 28cm (10in.) tart tin and line the base with parchment paper.

Roll the dough out onto a piece of parchment paper, using the rolling pin to transfer the dough to the tart tin. Trim off the excess to the edge of tin. Leave to rest in the fridge for another 30 minutes.

Remove the pastry from the fridge, prick the bottom of the tart shell with a fork and bake for 15–20 minutes until slightly golden. Remove from the oven and cool completely before filling the tart.

Put the pears into a bowl and sprinkle with the sugar, lemon zest, juice and ginger. Gently toss to coat. Let sit for at least 10 minutes. Taste the fruit and add more sugar if desired. Spoon the pears into the prebaked pastry case, adding any leftover sugar or juice clinging to the bowl. Sprinkle over the crisp topping, carefully pressing it into the fruit. Bake for 25–35 minutes, until golden and bubbly.

Remove from the oven and leave to rest for 20–30 minutes. Serve warm with a generous scoop of the ginger milk sherbet.

Illustrated on pages 166–7

GREAT GRANDMA TUPPER'S TRADITIONAL MOLASSES COOKIES

Molasses and ginger are a great mineral boost combination and what better way to enjoy them than in these soft and chewy moreish treats, full of mineral-rich iron, calcium, magnesium and copper. The recipe for them dates back to the 1930s; while I have added a bit more ginger than Grandma Tupper, the dusting of granulated sugar on top, and tasting the sugar crunch when biting into this sweet but healthy treat, is timeless.

MAKES ABOUT 20

225g (8oz./1 cup) granulated sugar, plus extra for sprinkling

1 tsp salt

2½ tsp ground ginger

2 tsp ground cinnamon

¼ tsp ground cloves

325g (11½oz./1 cup) molasses or treacle

1½ tsp baking soda

2 large eggs, beaten

225g (8oz./2 sticks) vegetable shortening or unsalted butter

2 tsp freshly grated ginger

550g (1lb. 4oz./4½ cups) plain (all-purpose) flour, plus extra for flouring the board

150g (5½oz./1 cup) raisins

35g (1¼oz./¼ cup) crystallized ginger, chopped

Stir the sugar, salt and spices together in a large bowl.

In a separate bowl, beat the molasses and soda.

Add the beaten eggs, shortening or butter and grated ginger to the sugar and spice mixture and beat well, then beat in the molasses.

Sift in the flour, add the raisins and crystallized ginger and mix well. The dough should be soft and sticky; if it is a humid day, you may need to add a little more flour. Divide the dough into three, shaping into discs, and wrap each piece in cling film (plastic wrap) and chill for 1–2 hours.

Preheat the oven to 160° (325°F/gas mark 3). Flour a board well and pat out the dough about 5mm (¼in.) thick and cut into shapes using a floured knife or a round cookie cutter.

Sprinkle the tops with granulated sugar, transfer to a baking tray and bake for 15 minutes.

Leave to cool for a few minutes on the baking tray then transfer to a wire rack and cool completely.

Stored sealed in a tin or jar, the cookies will keep for 3 weeks – if they last that long!

Restorative spice

When you are challenged with an overabundance of decisions to make and more on your to-do list than there are minutes in the day, a restorative spice in a smoothie, dinner dish or a simple cuppa will help your body reboot, restoring health, radiance, strength and balance.

Restorative Spice Health Heroes

Garlic ★ Cardamom ★ Pomegranate ★ Fenugreek ★ Thyme

The potent and abundant active compounds contained in these spices show promise in restoring health and rebalancing the body by assisting our automatic natural functions to heal and reset with renewed strength, vitality and balance to better enable the body to regulate itself.

Garlic, with its long-standing reputation as a heroic natural antibiotic and its ability to reduce nitrosamines (chemical carcinogens), has many talents and works its curative, restorative magic to repel colds, flus and inflammatory diseases. Cardamom's active cineole healing compounds, contained in its tiny pungent seeds, are packed full of antibacterial, antioxidant and antiseptic power. Fenugreek restores and rebalances blood sugar with its active bio-identical compound diosgenin, which helps to restore insulin and triglyceride levels. It also contains high amounts of fibre to aid in restoring proper digestion. Thyme helps restore healthy respiration and balanced pulmonary function. Rich in volatile compounds, including thymol, thyme's many talents include disabling bacterial infection and contagious diseases and lessening the effects of damage from over-indulgence in alcoholic beverages. Pomegranate, and its active polyphenol compound, ellagic acid, shows promising results as a restorative for its anti-wrinkle effects: it is used as a treatment to fight the collagen degradation that causes skin aging. Pomegranate may also help in fast-tracking immediate strength recovery after vigorous exercise and may benefit the restoration of sperm quality and quantity and the increase in testertone levels in men.

Other restorative spice heroes

Lemongrass A cup of soothing lemongrass tea will help restore your body and mind thanks to its powerful antioxidant citral, which activates key detoxifying enzymes that can defend cells from damage by free radicals. It is being tested as a treatment for oral thrush and vaginal yeast infections. Lemongrass shows great promise in anticancer activity: citral is thought to help protect, restore and rebuild damaged cells.

Bay Leaf Laurel bay oil, cineole, is known as a strong antioxidant. More powerful than other plant-derived phytochemicals such as vitamin C, the antioxidant compounds in bay leaves are released in cooking as the scent of bay infuses your food. Encouraging studies indicate that consuming bay leaf may help combat diabetes 2 by restoring blood sugar and LDL-cholesterol to healthy and balanced levels.

Hibiscus Helping to rebalance digestion and liver function, the active acid in hibiscus (hydroxycitric acid) inhibits the production of amylase, an enzyme produced by the salivary glands and the pancreas to help the body digest carbohydrates. Hibiscus contains very high levels of vitamin C and is considered to restore digestive health with its gentle laxative properties.

Cocoa A decadent and frequently craved spice packed full of an abundance of phenolic antioxidants, cocoa also contains the feel-good amino-acid tryptophan, used by the brain to make the neurotransmitter serotonin, which helps restore a sense of life balance and give pause to the frenetic pace that occasionally overwhelms our lives with stress.

Basil Familiarly fragrant basil relieves stress, supports the adrenal glands, helps to restore and rebalance levels of cortisol and is being studied for its promising antiaging benefit. Basil's powerful antioxidant phytonutrients orientin and vicenin and the volatile oils eugenol and apigemen can aid in the rebalancing of stress hormones.

Saffron This beautiful bright-yellow stamen hides powerful properties in its most important phytochemical, crocetin. Studies have shown positive results that saffron in tea may help rebalance high-blood-pressure levels. This active phytonutrient compound in saffron may also help improve eye and vision health brought on by the onset of cataracts. Crocetin is also a strong anti-inflammatory that can help to restore lung function in those suffering from asthma by reducing inflammation in the lungs.

Garlic *The Russian Penicillin Spice*

'Garlic! Garlic! The secret of staying young!' So goes the opening line of a song dedicated entirely to garlic in the '90s Broadway musical *Dance of the Vampires*. The thousands of years of history, myths, beliefs and medical science surrounding garlic are mind-boggling. Chinese records dating from 2700BC indicate that garlic was used as a remedy for its heating and stimulating effects; Egyptian slaves building the great pyramids were fed garlic for strength; Ancient Greeks gave garlic to their soldiers and Olympic athletes were prescribed garlic tonics or simply chewed garlic as a remedy for any number of ills, from the common cold to deadly viruses and contagious diseases. Garlic was so revered that it was offered up at temples to the Greek gods. In the Middle Ages, Arabian physicians lauded garlic for its magical and astonishing curative power, while in Western Europe it was believed that the 'stink rose' smell of garlic would repel vampires! During World War II, it was called Russian penicillin because, after running out of penicillin, the Russian government issued its soldiers with cloves of garlic to keep them strong and healthy.

Garlic (*Allium sativum*) contains active organosulfur compounds, which are responsible for its health-giving properties (see below). Although the odour of fresh garlic causes some to avoid it, the overwhelming amount of positive health data should encourage you to include this superhero spice in your daily diet.

www.ncbi.nlm.nih.gov/pmc/articles/PMC3249897/

Garlic is used in kitchens all around the world: it is added to the classic dishes of Italy, France, Greece, Mexico, China and India, to name but a few. Choose garlic heads – they vary in size and can contain up to two dozen cloves – that are firm with no soft cloves, and store in an open container in a cool dry place rather than in the fridge, to prevent the garlic growing mould and passing its odour to the rest of the fridge contents! Properly stored, garlic will keep for up to three months. If it begins sprouting, simply cut away the green growth, which will be bitter. If you are using many cloves in a recipe, plunge whole cloves of unpeeled fresh garlic into boiling water for one minute, use a slotted spoon to scoop out, then immediately plunge into iced water until cool. The paper skin will then be soft enough to peel off easily. Garlic also comes in granulated or powdered form, which will keep for about a year.

Large mild-tasting cloves of elephant garlic are not in fact true garlic but a type of onion related to leeks. However, beautiful garlic scapes, sold in daffodil-like bunches, are the flowering stems of the garlic plant produced before the garlic bulbs mature. In season from early summer, scapes look like curling spring onions and are best eaten lightly sautéed and added to an omelette, or chopped and sprinkled over salads. You can also use them to make a scape and basil pesto.

---

6 Garlic owes its taste and odour to organosulfur compounds, which have been shown to have anticancer properties. When garlic is chopped or crushed, the enzyme allinase is released, which activates its anticancer, anti-inflammatory effect. It is therefore important to leave it for at least ten minutes after chopping before you cook it. Laboratory research and studies in humans have shown garlic's ability to reduce the formation of nitrosamines, which are chemical carcinogens. It is also possible that the reduction in nitrosamine formation is a result of garlic's antimicrobial properties. Research has shown that garlic modifies the metabolism of hormones, such as oestrogen and progesterone, through induction of cytochrome P450 enzymes. This could be extremely important in the regulation of hormone-dependent cancers such as prostate and breast cancer. Garlic and its various compounds seem to be able to block the carcinogenic action of various chemicals that target different tissues in the body. It is therefore logical to assume that it exerts its carcinogenic action through more than one mechanism. Allyl sulfur compounds present in garlic have anti-inflammatory effects and reduce the risk of cardiovascular and cerebrovascular diseases.

There is still much more to discover through research. 9

Eleni Tsiompanou, MD, PGDip, MSc Nutritional Medicine

Cardamom *The Spice Bomb*

The third most expensive spice in the world, cardamom, hailed the 'Queen of Spices', seduced emperors and adventurers for centuries with its sweet-tangy scent as a flavouring and as a medicine. A distant relative of the ginger family, it has been used as a traditional remedy for thousands of years for digestive problems from bad breath to stomach upsets. Its many volatile oils are also thought to help with lowering blood pressure, and its most active oil, cineole – impressively both antibacterial and antioxidant – has been recently trialled as an aid for asthma and other respiratory ailments.

This spice bomb is believed to have been discovered in the Cardamom Hills of Southern India. The tall cardamom bushes grow prolifically and are harvested commercially today primarily in India and Guatemala, the pods being picked from the base of each bush.

Cardamom's alluring aroma includes scents of citrus, evergreen, clove, camphor and black pepper. Hailed by many chefs as the most versatile spice in the cabinet, it is included – as whole pods, seeds or ground – in Indian and Chinese spice blends, slow-cooked stews, modern Asian fusion dishes and traditional Scandinavian breads and desserts, and it blends seamlessly with both sweet and savoury spices, including anise, cinnamon, clove, cumin, caraway, chili pepper, ginger, paprika, saffron and vanilla. Fifteenth-century writings tell of cardamom in rice dishes and 'sherbets' and it is still used today to give steamed rice a rich mysterious flavour. The majority of cardamom grown today is consumed in traditional coffee drinks in the Middle East and India, creating an unforgettable hot drink with a bright and lingering flavour. The wandering Bedouins of the Arabian Peninsula carry with them a special coffee pot with a tiny secret chamber to hold a cardamom pod. The white cardamom often favoured by British, European and Scandinavian countries is the green pod gently bleached to soften the camphor-like scent, which is thought to add additional sweetness.

Ideally, buy and use whole pods and choose smooth, smaller pods with an even greenish hue. They will last for years kept in an airtight container away from sunlight. Split open the pods to reveal the pungent seeds and grind a little at a time as the volatile oils quickly lose their punch and pungency. If you purchase ground cardamom, use it within six months.

Black cardamom, a closely related species, has a completely different flavour profile. When the pods are picked and dried, they exude a smoky flavour with peppery overtones that works well with slow-cooked meats, vegetables and stewed fruits.

'Cardamom offers much beyond its sweet aromatic allure. Its essential oils have been credited over the centuries for serving as an antiseptic (dental and oral health), antispasmodic (digestive, soothing and regularity), diuretic (urinary health), expectorant (pulmonary health) and stimulant (sense of wellbeing).

As a reservoir of antioxidants, cardamom promotes the body's protection against stress and common sicknesses. Animal studies have demonstrated its ability to increase glutathione, a key antioxidant enzyme native to our bodies. Above and beyond being a rich source of minerals (potassium, calcium, magnesium, manganese, copper and iron) and vitamins (riboflavin, niacin and vitamin C), it is now garnering interest to defend against cancers promoted by hormones. Cardamom contains key compounds indole-3-carbinol (I3C), which reduces oestrogen activity by disrupting activity at the oestrogen receptor, and di-indolyl-methane (DIM), which induces apoptosis, promoting an antiproliferative effect on cancer cells. These phytonutrients are commonly celebrated in the cruciferous vegetables such as broccoli, Brussels sprouts, cabbage, cauliflower and kale. I3C and DIM are being studied to reduce the risk of breast cancer, ovarian cancer and prostate cancer.

In the realm of cardiovascular health, cardamom showed efficacy in reducing blood pressure when studied in a small number of participants who consumed cardamom daily for three months. Research suggests that its action is similar to commonly prescribed antihypertensive medicines called calcium channel blockers.

(Safety note: cardamom pods should be used in small amounts since large quantities of this spice can irritate the gastrointestinal lining and promote stomach ulcers.)'

Param Dedhia, MD

Pomegranate *The Hippocratic Spice*

This jewelled 'fruit of paradise' originated in Persia and the Persian word is aptly translated. 'May food be your medicine and medicine be your food': so says the famous quotation attributed to Hippocrates, the father of modern medicine, who allegedly favoured this spice. He is said to have used pomegranate-seed extracts for numerous ailments, including skin and eye inflammation, as well as to aid digestion and cleanse the blood. In many ancient cultures, the pomegranate has been a symbol of health, luck, fertility and immortality.

The power of pomegranate comes from its active and extensive range of antioxidant polyphenols. Most parts of the pomegranate – including the flower, fruit rind, leaf, dried seed (anardana) and fresh seed, root and trunk bark, fresh fruit and juice – have been utilized medicinally worldwide in almost every traditional medicine discipline. Today, every bit of the pomegranate is under vigorous research and study to analyze the possible anticancer benefit of this remarkable fruit not only to help balance levels of the prostate-specific antigen marker (PSA) but also to enter non-toxic battle with, and possibly even reverse, prostate cancer (second only to lung cancer as the most deadly cancer for men). And pomegranate, deliciously packed with a medicine-cabinet's worth of natural remedies in its ruby-red sphere, has no side effects.

Pomegranate seeds have been used for medicinal purposes for thousands of years and today it is thought that the juice pressed and strained from the seeds may also be effective against heart disease, high blood pressure, inflammation as well as some cancers. The antioxidant oil shows promising high antiaging benefit when used on face and hands and is being studied for its preventative skin-cancer benefits. It also offers speedy recovery after a good run with thirst-quenching relief to rehydrate and refresh the body.

A single pomegranate contains about 500 seeds and yields one cup of seeds or half a cup of juice, with a sweet, tart, almost dry but refreshing taste from the nutrient-rich polyphenols.

Fresh whole pomegranate is available from autumn all through the winter and will keep for up to a month if refrigerated. Fresh seeds can be frozen for up to six months. Bottles of unopened juice, dried seeds, powder and molasses are all long-shelf-life staples, enabling you to enjoy and benefit from pomegranate every day. Try pomegranate molasses (made by reducing the juice to a thick molasses-like syrup) added to meat marinades, as a glaze for salmon, or simply drizzled over labneh with muesli and fresh berries. Or finish a healthy squash soup with a handful of fresh pomegranate and toasted pumpkin seeds and a squeeze of lime.

> Pomegranate is one of the most ancient fruits, considered sacred by many religions. It is symbolic of life, regeneration, birth, fertility, prosperity and a bright future. Pomegranate is rich in vitamin C, potassium and antioxidants as well as other chemicals. There is growing interest in its benefits in reducing the risk of prostate cancer, lymphoma, diabetes, high blood pressure and cardiovascular disease. Several laboratory and animal studies have shown that pomegranate has an effect on cell growth and tumour size. Human studies have also shown promising results on the reduction of PSA, the prostate cancer marker after surgery for prostate cancer, slowing tumour growth and therefore increasing survival and improving quality of life. It is also been shown to have antiviral and antibacterial properties against dental plaque. There are no side effects.

Eleni Tsiompanou, MD, PGDip, MSc Nutritional Medicine

Fenugreek *The Fascinating Spice*

What do New York nights and the spice fenugreek have in common? On humid nights when the wind was blowing moderately from West to East across the Hudson River that separates Manhattan from New Jersey, complaints would pour in to the 311 hotline about a mysterious odour. After many phone calls to and from the mayor and a bit of sleuthing, investigators discovered that the smell was coming from a factory in North Bergen, New Jersey, that processes fenugreek seeds! Even if you've never heard of fenugreek, it's likely you've tasted it in something: the fenugreek being processed by the New Jersey plant was probably destined as a flavouring ingredient in vanilla, maple syrup or butterscotch-flavoured syrups.

Like cinnamon, fenugreek exudes a sweet scent and is also being studied as a possible aid to reduce blood sugar, a vital concern for those with diabetes. Raw seeds soaked in water soften and expand and have been traditionally used to normalize digestion. Fenugreek is also considered in many cultures to increase libido in men, breast size in women and act as a powerful aphrodisiac. This makes complete sense as one of the active components in fenugreek has similar bio-identical properties to the hormone oestrogen. Sure beats rhino horn!

Fenugreek is one of the oldest cultivated medicinal plants: it is praised in Egyptian papyrus writings dating back to around 1500BC. Native to Southern Europe and Asia, it also grows in North and South America, North Africa and the Middle East.

A versatile annual plant that grows to about 60cm (2ft) tall, fenugreek produces light-green leaves similar to clover and small white flowers that can be used fresh as salad greens and, when dried, added to soups, stews and pastes. The long, slender, flat pods extending from the branches each contain 10–20 small, hard, golden-brown fenugreek seeds. The fresh seeds have a pungent aroma and a fairly bitter taste, which has been described as similar to burnt celery, but when lightly toasted, they smell of maple syrup. Toast the seeds carefully; if toasted too long, they'll become so intensely bitter they'll be inedible. Traditionally used in sauces, chutneys, pickles, long-cooking stews, naan bread and numerous grain recipes, fenugreek is also celebrated in this book with a sweet dish: Fenugreek Poached Pear with Dessert Dukkah (see page 206).

Look for fenugreek, which sometimes goes by the name 'menthi', at Middle Eastern grocers, specialty shops or online. Store whole seeds in an airtight glass container in a cool, dark place, where they should stay fresh for several months. Powdered or paste-form fenugreek should be kept in air-sealed packets in the fridge.

www.ncbi.nlm.nih.gov/pubmed/26098483

‘ Fenugreek shows itself to be a most interesting seed as it is bitter in taste in the raw form yet flavour-rich and aromatic if lightly roasted. This herb has honoured healthy living and wellness over the ages. Historically, it has been used to promote digestive wellness with its rich fibre content (non-starch polysaccharide) and to assist nursing mothers to release breast milk. It has been found to be a rich source of vitamins – A, C, K and B (the B vitamins include thiamine, riboflavin, niacin and pyridoxine) – and to supply key minerals – potassium, calcium, magnesium, manganese, copper, iron, zinc and selenium. Fenugreek has also been shown to reduce cholesterol and balance blood sugar.

The non-starch polysaccharides (NSPs) of fenugreek include saponins, pectin, tannins, hemicellulose and mucilage. In addition to aiding digestion, these NSPs, especially saponins, reduce the production of "bad" LDL-cholesterol by reducing the reabsorption of bile salts in the colon. Furthermore, they may reduce the risk of colonic cancers by binding toxins increasingly found in our food.

Fenugreek may help both type I and type II diabetes by two unique properties: its amino acid, 4-hydroxy isoleucine, which helps release insulin, and its natural fibre, galactomannan, which slows the rate at which sugar is absorbed into the bloodstream. Together these smooth the release and availability of sugar in our bloodstream.

As cardiovascular risk in men and women continues to increase, it is time to revisit traditional spices to balance cholesterol and sugar.

(Safety note: excess intake of fenugreek seeds by pregnant mothers can increase the risk of premature childbirth.) ’

Param Dedhia, MD

Thyme *The Breath of Life Spice*

Native to the Mediterranean and Southern Europe, common thyme (*Thymus vulgaris*) is part of the mint family and related to oregano. Hundreds of different species, cultivars and varieties of thyme are now grown, picked and savoured worldwide, including Variegated Lemon, Caraway, tangerine-scented Azores, Silver Queen, Goldstream and Bressingham Pink. Thyme prefers sunny, stony locations and its mid-summer flowers attract bees, which produce enchanting thyme-scented honey, and also help repel whiteflies.

Culinary thyme, hedge thyme, wild thyme and all the other thymes contain a great amount of the phytonutrient thymol, also found to a lesser degree in oregano and mint. Thymol is believed to help the lungs ward off a host of pulmonary symptoms and diseases. One sniff of fresh thyme makes you want to breathe in deeply and relax. The Greek word for thyme roughly translates as 'to fumigate' and the ancient Greeks and Romans burned branches of aromatic thyme as incense to purify their temples and homes while inhaling the smoke to invoke a sense of courage and strength.

From Hippocratic Greece until the 1930s, oil of thyme was used on surgical dressings and burned in hospital wards to fend off contagious diseases. The fresh and dried leaves, and the steam-extracted essential oil, are medicinally potent and thyme is one of the most versatile plants in traditional medicine. Thymol's commanding antibacterial talents are being analyzed in the search to discover new solutions in the war on MSRA (Methicillin-resistant *Staphylococcus aureus*) and other resistant bacterial strains. Thyme may also protect the body and brain from an alcohol-infused cocktail or pub-crawl-weekend hangover with its detoxifying properties, and its dominant active compound is added to mouthwashes and topical analgesic ointments. Ingesting large amounts of fresh or dried thyme has no adverse effect, but oil of thyme in extreme doses can be toxic. Consult with your doctor first.

Thyme leaves are a standard component of the classic bouquet-garni blend of thyme sprigs, bay leaf, parsley and rosemary that is used to infuse flavour into soups, stocks and many classic French dishes. Fresh and dried thyme are constant companions to recipes of many cuisines worldwide, but French, Greek and Italian dishes create a particular magic when thyme is added. One of the most used spices in your cupboard, thyme has a powerful scent with a gentle flavour and can be easily used in a cornucopia of ways. Try Lidia Bastianich's Pan-Roasted Monkfish with Thyme-Oil-roasted Tiny Tomatoes, Toasted Barley and Leeks (see page 196) or Courgette and Red Pepper Parcels (see page 24). Dark chocolate desserts or biscuits are scrumptious with a little thyme added and this herb also pairs well, in both savoury and sweet dishes, with citrus.

Fresh thyme stores best wrapped in damp paper and chilled. Six average sprigs will yield about a tablespoon of thyme leaves.

❛ Thyme, whose distinct fragrance is used widely in French cooking, is a spice whose flowers, leaves and oil are used as medicine.

Thyme leaves are administered orally to treat respiratory conditions, including bronchitis and coughs, and there is some evidence to support this use. It has also been used traditionally to treat gastrointestinal symptoms and as a diuretic. Thyme may have both anticoagulant and antiplatelet effects, so people taking "blood thinners" may want to avoid ingesting large quantities of thyme.

Thyme oil, rich in volatile compounds including thymol, is used as an antimicrobial in mouthwashes and liniments. Commercially, thymol has been combined with the antiseptic chlorhexidine as a dental varnish to prevent tooth decay. Thyme oil has also been used traditionally as a topical application: applied to the scalp to treat baldness and to the ears to fight bacterial and fungal infections. ❜

Linda Shiue, MD

SEEDED ANZAC THINS

Light and delicate, these crunchy, seeded, spice wafers are both surprisingly sweet and savoury. The maple-scented fenugreek works harmoniously with the other spices and, although you use only a small measure, it is one powerful spice! Traditionally added to curry, fenugreek is being studied as a therapeutic aid in weight loss and balancing cholesterol.

MAKES 24

125g (4½oz./1 cup) plain (all-purpose) flour

40g (1½oz./½ cup) desiccated unsweetened coconut

55g (2oz./⅔ cup) rolled oats, lightly toasted (don't use quick-cooking oats)

40g (1½oz./3½ tbsp) coconut or caster (superfine) sugar

1 tbsp sesame seeds

1 tbsp poppy seeds

1 tbsp fresh thyme leaves

1 tsp anise seeds

⅛ tsp ground fenugreek

1 tsp orange zest

1 tsp baking powder

¼ tsp salt

90–120ml (6–8 tbsp) extra virgin olive oil

1 egg white, for glazing

raw sugar and sea salt flakes, for glazing

Preheat the oven to 200°C (400°F/gas mark 6).

In the bowl of an electric mixer fitted with the paddle attachment, or in a large bowl using a spoon, mix the flour, coconut, rolled oats, sugar, sesame and poppy seeds, thyme leaves, anise seeds, fenugreek, zest, baking powder and salt until just combined.

In a small bowl, whisk the olive oil with 80ml (⅓ cup) of iced water. Add this to the dry mixture and mix until combined, scraping down the sides of the bowl as needed.

Shape a tablespoon of dough into a ball. Place four balls at a time on a piece of parchment paper, about 10cm (4in.) apart and cover with another piece of parchment or with cling film (plastic wrap). Roll out into very thin ovals, about 20cm (8in.) long. Transfer the dough and parchment to a baking tray. Lift off the top piece of parchment.

Whisk the egg white with 1 teaspoon of water, a pinch of salt and sugar until foamy. Brush the ovals with this glaze and sprinkle with a pinch of raw sugar and flake salt.

Bake, rotating the baking sheets halfway through, until the wafers are brown around the edges and in spots on top, about 8 minutes. (Check the wafers are cooking evenly and turn trays as needed; don't walk away and leave them as they can burn in moments!)

Transfer the wafers to a wire rack to cool, then store them stacked between layers of parchment paper in an airtight container.

THYME

SOUR CHERRY, THYME AND CHEDDAR SCONES

Originally created for Sausal El Segundo in Los Angeles, these scones are not too sweet and full of goodness, with grains, purported antiaging thyme leaves and high-anthocyanin brain-food cherries. The pepper is thought to increase the benefits of these active compounds as well as adding inviting toasty pepper aromas.

MAKES ABOUT 9 LARGE OR 15 SMALL SCONES

250g (9oz./2 cups) plain (all-purpose) flour

25g (1oz./3 tbsp) rolled oats (don't use quick-cooking oats)

2 packed tbsp soft brown sugar

1½ tsp chopped fresh thyme leaves, or ¾ tsp dried thyme

zest of ½ lemon

1 tbsp ground flax seeds

1½ tsp baking powder

½ tsp toasted ground black pepper, plus extra for sprinkling on top

¼ tsp kosher or sea salt

¼ tsp toasted ground star anise

55g (2oz./½ stick) butter, chilled, cut into 1cm (½in.) cubes

1 large egg, beaten

90ml (6 tbsp) sour cream, chilled

55g (2oz./½ cup) grated mature Cheddar, or Parmesan

1 egg beaten, for glazing

2 tbsp rolled oats, for sprinkling on top

185g (6½oz./⅔ cup) low-sugar cherry jam or compote

In a large bowl, whisk together the flour, rolled oats, brown sugar, thyme, lemon zest, flax seeds, baking powder, pepper, salt and star anise. Chop in the chilled butter with two forks or a pastry blender until the mixture resembles coarse cornmeal.

Add the beaten egg and cream and stir quickly and lightly with a fork until incorporated, being careful not to overwork the dough.

Turn the dough out onto a lightly floured surface and pat out or gently roll into a 1cm (½in.) deep rectangle, using additional flour sparingly. Sprinkle all but 3 tablespoons of the grated cheese on top.

Fold into thirds, seal sides gently and roll out again into a rectangle. Cut with a knife into 8cm (3in.) squares (or 15 smaller two-bite squares) and place on a parchment- or silicone-lined baking tray. Make a large thumbprint in the centre of each scone. Cover and chill for 30 minutes or until you are ready to bake, or wrap tightly and freeze for up to a month.

Just before baking, preheat the oven to 190°C fan (375°F/gas mark 5). Brush each scone with egg wash and sprinkle with the oats, remaining cheese and a few grinds of black pepper, then fill each thumbprint with about 2 teaspoons of cherry jam.

Bake for 15–17 minutes (12–14 minutes for smaller squares) until the tops are golden brown. Transfer to a wire rack to cool.

RESTORATIVE SPICE   187

GRILLED AUBERGINE PATE
(BAINGAN BHURTA)
Raghavan Iyer

'Traditionally in Northern Indian villages and in restaurants there, cooks drop aubergine (eggplant) directly onto hot coals in a bell-shaped, clay-lined oven (tandoor) that often generates intense heat (up to 370°C/700°F). It's easy to duplicate the same technique with a charcoal or gas grill. The smoky aubergine (eggplant) flavour offers an excellent backdrop to the subtle aromas of cloves and cinnamon in the garam masala. I often serve the pâté with naan, pita, or even slices of crusty crostini as a great starter to a meal.' RI

SERVES 6

2 small (about 450g/1lb. each) aubergine (eggplants)

2 tsp coriander seeds, ground

1 tsp cumin seeds, ground

1 tsp coarse sea or kosher salt

1 tsp garam masala

½ tsp ground cayenne pepper

¼ tsp ground turmeric

1 small red onion, finely chopped

115g (4oz./½ cup) passata (tomato sauce)

juice of ½ medium lime (1 tbsp)

1 tbsp freshly grated ginger

2 medium garlic cloves, finely chopped

25g (1oz./½ cup) finely chopped fresh coriander (cilantro) leaves and tender stems

2 tbsp ghee (clarified butter) or vegetable oil

1 tsp cumin seeds

1 large lime, cut into 8 wedges

Heat an oven grill (broiler) or heat coals or a gas grill for direct heat.

Pierce the aubergine (eggplants) with a fork in five or six places.

To grill (broil): grill (broil) the aubergine (eggplants) 5–8cm (2–3in.) away from the heat, turning them occasionally to ensure even cooking, until the skin is completely blackened and blistered, 20–25 minutes.

For cooking on the barbecue or grill: place the aubergine (eggplants) on the grill or directly onto hot coals, turning them occasionally to ensure even cooking, until the skin is completely blackened and blistered, 20–25 minutes. Transfer the aubergine (eggplants) to a large bowl, cover with cling film (plastic wrap) and set aside for about 30 minutes. The steam that rises from within will sweat the aubergine (eggplants) and help loosen the skin for easy peeling.

Peel and discard the skin and stem. Put the pulp in a bowl and mash using a potato masher, or with your hands, to a smooth consistency. Keep the juices and any liquid that pools at the bottom of the bowl.

Add the ground coriander and cumin, salt, garam masala, cayenne, turmeric, half the onion, the tomato sauce, lime juice, ginger, garlic and half the chopped coriander (cilantro); mix well.

Heat the ghee in a wok or deep 30cm (12in.) frying pan (skillet) over medium–high heat. Add the cumin seeds and allow them to sizzle and turn reddish brown, about 15 seconds. Immediately add the remaining onion and stir-fry until light brown around the edges, 2–3 minutes.

Add the aubergine (eggplant) mixture and stir-fry until almost all the liquid evaporates, 15–20 minutes.

Transfer to serving bowl and garnish with the remaining coriander (cilantro) and the lime wedges.

POMEGRANATE

POMEGRANATE SEED TABOULI

Nutty and nutritious, with those little bursts of the sweet–tart intoxicating flavour of healthy pomegranate, this is great as a side dish or packed into your lunchbox.

SERVES 4-6

200g (7oz./1 cup) kasha (toasted buckwheat) or farro

1–2 large shallots, chopped

120ml (½ cup) extra virgin olive oil

60ml (¼ cup) fresh lemon juice

1 tbsp pomegranate molasses

2 tsp cumin seeds, toasted and ground

3 bunches (175g/6oz.) finely chopped flat-leaf parsley

25g (1oz./1 cup) chopped fresh mint

zest of 1 lemon

4 tbsp pomegranate seeds

Put the kasha or farro in a small saucepan with 500ml (2 cups + 2 tablespoons) of water, cover and bring to the boil. Reduce the heat and simmer until tender, about 15–20 minutes. Cool.

Whisk together the shallots with the olive oil, lemon juice, pomegranate molasses and cumin. Season with salt and pepper.

In a large bowl, mix the cooled kasha or farro with the chopped parsley, mint and lemon zest, then fold in the whisked dressing and the pomegranate seeds. Serve cold.

GARLIC, CARDAMOM

RAW BEETROOT, FENNEL AND APPLE CRUNCH SALAD

This super nutrient-packed recipe makes an easy midday salad full of healthy spice heroes! Sprinkled with mint, pomegranate and toasted quinoa, this crunch salad will keep you going through the afternoon energy dips.

SERVES 4 AS A SIDE

115g (4oz.) fennel, thinly sliced, a few fronds reserved for garnish

½–1 small garlic clove, chopped

1 tbsp apple cider vinegar

1 tbsp grassy extra virgin olive oil

¼ tsp salt

115g (4oz./½ medium) red beetroot, finely grated

70g (2½oz./½ small) Granny Smith apple, cored and diced

20g (¾oz./3 tbsp) roughly chopped toasted walnuts, reserve a spoonful for garnish

10g (¼oz.) finely sliced spring onion (white part only)

15g (½oz./small handful) mint leaves, shredded thickly

1 tbsp chopped parsley

zest and juice of ½ lime

zest of ½ orange, juice of 1 small orange

2 tbsp grassy extra virgin olive oil

1 tsp ground cumin seeds, toasted and ground

½ tsp fennel seeds, toasted and ground

½ tsp cardamom seeds, toasted and ground

½ tsp smoked paprika

½ tsp pomegranate molasses

¼ tsp salt

10 grinds black pepper

1 tbsp toasted quinoa

Marinate the fennel and garlic in the vinegar, oil and salt and chill until softened, at least 30 minutes or overnight.

Mix together with all the remaining ingredients except the quinoa.

Garnish with the toasted quinoa and the reserved walnuts and fennel fronds.

GARLIC, SAFFRON, BAY LEAF

VEGETABLE PAELLA
(PAELLA DE VERDURAS)
José Andrés

'Paella is the quintessential rice dish of Spain. This recipe features saffron, which provides a distinctive flavour, as well as garlic – several special garlic varieties grow in Spain's countryside. The beauty of this recipe is its flexibility with the seasons. I love to shop at my local farmers' market with my daughters to select the vegetables for the weekend's paella. Ask about what's fresh at the markets near you.' JA

SERVES 4–6

60ml (¼ cup) Spanish extra virgin olive oil

1 bunch spring onions (scallions), thinly sliced

100g (3½oz./1 cup) button mushrooms, halved if larger

85g (3oz./½ cup) diced red (bell) pepper

70g (2½oz./½ cup) diced courgette (zucchini)

70g (2½oz./½ cup) diced carrots

1 tsp minced garlic

55g (2oz./¼ cup) sofrito (see below)

240ml (1 cup) dry white wine

pinch saffron

1.2 litres (5 cups) mushroom or vegetable stock

200g (7oz./1 cup) Spanish Bomba rice (if using Valencia rice, use only 1 litre/4¼ cups stock)

40g (1½oz./¼ cup) fresh green peas

alioli, for serving (see below)

For the sofrito (makes about 3 cups):

10 ripe plum tomatoes, sliced in half

350ml (1½ cups) Spanish extra virgin olive oil

4 small Spanish onions, finely chopped

1 tsp sugar

1 tsp salt

1 tsp pimentón, or Spanish smoked paprika

3 bay leaves

For the alioli (makes 1 cup):

1 small egg

240ml (1 cup) Spanish extra virgin olive oil

1 garlic clove

1 tsp sherry vinegar or fresh lemon juice

sea salt, to taste

First make the sofrito. Place a grater over a mixing bowl and grate the open side of the tomatoes down to their skins. Discard the skins. Heat the oil in a pan over medium–low heat. Add the onions, sugar and salt. Cook, stirring occasionally, until soft and caramelized, about 45 minutes. Stir in the grated tomatoes, pimentón and bay leaves and cook over medium heat until the tomatoes have broken down and the oil has separated from the sauce, about 20 minutes. Discard the bay leaves and store the sauce in the refrigerator, covered, until ready to use.

To make the alioli, put the egg, 2 tablespoons of the olive oil, the garlic and the vinegar or lemon juice into the bowl of a food processor fitted with a steel blade. Process the ingredients at high speed until the garlic is fully puréed and the mixture becomes a loose paste. While processing, slowly begin to add the remaining olive oil drop by drop. If the mixture appears too thick, add a teaspoon of water to loosen the sauce. Continue adding the oil until the sauce becomes rich and creamy and light yellow in colour. Season with sea salt to taste.

To make the paella, heat the olive oil in a 33cm (13in.) paella pan over medium–high heat. Add the onions and sauté until soft and lightly browned, about 3 minutes. Add the mushrooms, red (bell) pepper, courgettes (zucchini), carrots and garlic and cook for 2 minutes more. Stir in the sofrito and cook for 1 minute. Pour in the white wine and let it reduce by half, about 2 minutes.

Crumble the saffron into the pan and pour in the stock. Increase the heat to high and bring to the boil. Let boil for 2–3 minutes, then add the rice and peas and stir until well combined. Reduce the heat to medium–high, season with sea salt to taste and cook for 4 minutes. Do not stir the rice again as this can cause it to cook unevenly.

Reduce the heat to low and cook for another 7 minutes. Remove the paella from the heat, cover with a clean cloth and let rest for 5 minutes. Serve with the alioli.

'SPAGHETTI AND MEATBALLS'
WITH THYME OIL AND GARLIC

A healthier take on the classic comfort food, the 'pasta' here is made from spaghetti squash. If unavailable, use courgettes, peeled into ribbons and steamed or pan-simmered. The 'meatballs' are vegan but the texture and taste are so much like beef you may consider surprising friends and family with this super-healthy vegan variation!

SERVES 4

For the 'meatballs':

150g (5½oz./¾ cup) dried brown lentils, rinsed and picked over

3 garlic cloves, sliced

10 thyme sprigs, plus extra to garnish

3 tbsp Thyme Oil (see below)

100g (3½oz./1 small) onion, roughly chopped

350g (12oz./3½ cups) white mushrooms, roughly chopped

3 tbsp low-salt tomato purée (paste)

1½ tbsp Dijon mustard, or to taste

85g (3oz./1 cup) rolled oats, toasted and roughly ground

1½ tsp dried thyme

240ml (1 cup) vegetable stock

additional oil or oil spray for baking

For the 'spaghetti':

1kg (2lb. 4oz.) spaghetti squash (yields about 750g/1lb. 10oz./4 cups)

2 tbsp thyme oil (see below)

a few saffron strands (optional)

Preheat the oven to 180°C (350°F/gas mark 4). Put the lentils, garlic and thyme sprigs in a small saucepan with 350ml (1½ cups) water. Bring to a boil, then simmer over low heat for 10 minutes – the lentils will be crunchy. Remove from heat, drain and cool slightly, discarding the thyme sprigs. Set aside.

Add the thyme oil to a sauté pan and cook the onions over medium heat until translucent, about 4 minutes. Add the mushrooms and cook for an additional 4–5 minutes, until the mushrooms release their liquid.

Transfer to a food processor, add the lentil mixture and pulse until puréed but with a few chunky bits.

Put the tomato purée (paste) into the pan and cook for 2 minutes to caramelize, then add the lentil mixture, mustard, oats, dried thyme and vegetable stock. Stir and cook until the liquid is absorbed and the mixture is fragrant. Season with salt and pepper and set aside to cool.

When cool to touch, shape into about 20 balls (each about 25g/1oz.) and place on a lined, oiled baking tray.

To make the 'spaghetti', split the spaghetti squash in half and scrape out the seeds for another use or discard. Add the thyme oil, a few saffron strands (if using) and 60ml (¼ cup) of water. Place the squash cut side down on an oiled baking tray and bake for 30–40 minutes, or until fork tender. Ten minutes through baking the squash, add the 'meatballs' to the oven to bake until browned, about 20–25 minutes.

Remove the squash from the oven and turn cut side up to cool for about 10 minutes. Using a fork, scrape the squash with a fork to make the 'spaghetti'. Drizzle with thyme oil, a few thyme sprigs and season to taste.

Arrange the 'spaghetti' on four plates and add five 'meatballs' to each. Serve with your favourite pasta sauce or a tin of warmed chopped tomatoes.

THYME OIL

MAKES 350ml (1½ CUPS)

350ml (1½ cups) extra virgin olive oil   about 15 fresh thyme sprigs

Insert the thyme sprigs in a bottle that will hold them upright. Using a funnel, slowly pour the oil into the bottle until it is completely covering the thyme. Press the sprigs deeper into the bottle so they remain submerged.

Seal the bottle and store in a dark cool pantry. The oil will be ready to use in a week and will keep, tightly sealed, for a month in a cool pantry or for 2 months in the fridge.

PAN-ROASTED MONKFISH
WITH THYME-OIL-ROASTED TINY TOMATOES, TOASTED BARLEY AND LEEKS
Lidia Bastianich

I worked with Lidia several years ago at a beachfront resort that hosted the then top food and wine event in the world, 'Cuisines Of the Sun', on Big Island, Hawaii. Lidia inspired me with her passionate discipline of Italian classic cooking techniques, her endless spirit and her infectious joy of food and life. She created simply flavourful fish-centric tastes seasoned with the plentiful produce available. This dish, adapted from a recipe in her cookbook Lidia's Italian Table *(William and Morrow, 1998) captures her simple, unfussy and mouth-watering cuisine.*

SERVES 6

300g (10½oz.) baby cherry tomatoes on the vine (or regular-sized cherry tomatoes, halved)

4 garlic cloves, unpeeled

9 long thyme sprigs

5 tbsp Thyme Oil (see page 194)

200g (7oz./1 cup) barley or fregola

450g (1lb./about 3 medium) leeks, cut into small rounds

1kg (2lbs. 4oz.) monkfish fillets

175ml (¾ cup) extra virgin olive oil

50g (1¾oz./generous ⅓ cup) plain (all-purpose) flour

3 garlic cloves, sliced finely

240ml (1 cup) dry white wine

120ml (½ cup) fish or vegetable stock

45g (1½oz./3 tbsp) unsalted butter

2 tbsp chopped fresh Italian parsley

¼ preserved lemon, thinly shredded

a few thyme leaves, to garnish

Preheat the oven to 120°C (250°F/gas mark ½). Spread the tomatoes and garlic cloves on a lined baking tray scattered with five thyme sprigs. Drizzle with 3 tablespoons of the Thyme Oil and season with salt and pepper. Bake for 35 minutes or until roasted and lightly caramelized. Set aside until ready to plate the fish.

Put the barley into a large pan and pour over 600ml (2½ cups) of water. Cover with a lid and bring to a rolling boil then lower the temperature to a simmer. Gently simmer, covered, for about 45–55 minutes until just tender and the water has been absorbed. Transfer to a baking tray, spread out and leave to cool.

Blanch the leeks in a medium pan of boiling salted water for 3 minutes. Drain thoroughly then leave to cool.

Using a paring knife, remove the outer mottled grey membranes and any dark-red portions from the fish fillets. Slice the fish on a slight angle into 1cm (½in.) thick medallions. Place the medallions a few at a time between two sheets of cling film (plastic wrap) and pound them lightly with the flat side of a meat mallet or the bottom of a small heavy saucepan to flatten them slightly.

In a large frying pan (skillet), heat 3 tablespoons of olive oil over medium–high heat. Add the blanched leeks and barley. Season with salt and pepper and cook, turning often, until nicely golden brown, about 12 minutes. Remove the pan from the heat and cover to keep warm.

Meanwhile, sprinkle the monkfish with salt and lightly dust with flour, tapping off any excess. In a large pan, heat the remaining olive oil and the sliced garlic over medium heat. Add as many of the monkfish slices as will fit in a single layer and cook turning once, until golden brown on both sides, about 5–7 minutes. Remove the monkfish to a plate and keep warm; repeat with the remaining monkfish.

Drain the remaining oil from the pan. Add the wine and bring to a boil, scraping the sides and bottom of the pan. Add the fish stock, butter and remaining four thyme sprigs and season lightly with salt and pepper to taste. Simmer until the sauce is reduced by about half and lightly thickened, about 7 minutes. Strain the sauce through a sieve and check the final seasoning.

To serve, stir the parsley into the barley and leek mixture, then spread over the base of a warmed serving dish. Drizzle with the remaining Thyme Oil. Top with the monkfish slices, spoon the sauce over the fish, then sprinkle with thyme leaves and preserved lemon and scatter the roasted tomatoes and garlic around the plate.

★

SPICY SPAZCHOOK
WITH BAHARAT HASSELBACK PARSNIPS

Created for a long summer's day barbecue in New Zealand with a fresh organic chicken from the local butcher, then raiding my spice shelves and garden pots full of herbs, I came up with what is now fondly referred to as Spicy Spazchook. Splitting the backbone open so the bird lays flat as it cooks is called spatchcocked. Chickens being called chooks in the southern hemisphere had a ten-year-old guest shouting 'good spazchook'! Try your own herb and spice blends in either hemisphere: it will be a hit whether oven-grilled (broiled) or cooked on the barbecue. The parsnip side dish is a riff on the classic hasselback 'slinky' potato dish; here parsnips are roasted with a baharat spice oil.

SERVES 4

1 whole large chicken, cleaned and split at backbone

2 large onions

For the marinade:

2 tbsp dry mustard powder

2 tbsp sweet pimentón, powder

½ tsp cracked cardamom pods

3 or 4 garlic cloves, minced (1 tbsp minced)

2 tbsp lemon juice

1 large handful fresh mixed herbs (parsley, basil, thyme, oregano, rosemary, sage)

20 grinds black pepper

1 tsp sea salt

2 tbsp brown sugar

240ml (1 cup) grapeseed or vegetable oil

For the fenugreek baharat spice oil:

120ml (½ cup) olive oil

2 tsp maple syrup or honey

1 tbsp toasted ground black peppercorns

1 tbsp paprika

2½ tsp ground cinnamon

2½ tsp coriander seeds, toasted and ground

2½ tsp ground cloves

2 tsp fennel seeds, toasted and ground

1 tsp ground nutmeg

¾ tsp cumin seeds, toasted and ground

½ tsp ground fenugreek

¼ tsp cardamom seeds, toasted and ground

For the baharat hasselback parsnips:

8 x 2.5–4cm (1–1½in.) thick parsnips, scrubbed then trimmed so each parsnip is the same length for even cooking

fenugreek baharat spice oil (see above)

120ml (½ cup) hot vegetable stock or water

12 fenugreek leaves, fresh or dried

knob (small piece) butter

Mix all the marinade ingredients in a small bowl and smear on the chicken. Place the 'spazchook' in a sealable plastic bag and marinate for 3 hours or overnight.

Mix all the ingredients for the fenugreek baharat spice oil together in a bowl.

Preheat the oven to 200°C (400°F/gas mark 6). Remove the chicken from the fridge.

Peel the parsnips on one side to make a flat surface to prevent rolling. Tuck a chopstick either side of the parsnip and gently 'saw' the vegetable in 3mm (¹/₈in.) slices. (The chopsticks will prevent the knife from cutting all the way through.) Use the tip of the knife to wiggle open the cuts. Drizzle the spice oil into the openings and lay the parsnips in a casserole dish. Pour in hot stock or water to a depth of 5mm (¼in.), add the fenugreek leaves and drizzle additional spice oil on top. Season with salt. Cover with foil and cook for 30–40 minutes until tender.

If oven grilling (broiling) the chicken, preheat the grill (broiler) to 180°C (350°F/gas mark 4). Slice unpeeled onions into five or six thick disks and arrange in an oiled roasting tin. Place the chicken breast-side down on top. Grill (broil) for 20 minutes, turn over and cook a further 20–25 minutes until juices run clear. Remove from oven, cover and let rest for 15–20 minutes. While the chicken rests, return the parsnips to the oven, uncovered, and cook for an additional 15 minutes to brown. To barbecue the chicken, grill off direct heat. Allow about the same cooking and resting times as above. Carefully remove the parsnips from the casserole dish and serve with the Spazchook Chicken. If there is any liquid left in the pan, whisk in a knob (small piece) of butter to thicken and spoon over the parsnips.

KIMCHI

Judy Joo

'Korean food is known for its gutsy and vibrant flavours and much of that comes from punchy ingredients such as ginger, garlic and chilies. Kimchi is a classic dish that showcases Koreans' love for spice. It is Korea's national dish and is eaten every day with every meal. My mum used to make huge quantities of this fermented cabbage dish once a year and store it in clay pots underneath our porch outside. It definitely smells a bit funky, so do wrap it well. You can eat it freshly made, put it in stews, stir-fries and use the 'juice' to kick up any recipe nicely. After one taste, you'll see why kimchi is popping up on menus around the world.' JJ

MAKES 1 LARGE JAR

2.5kg (5½lb./about 1½ –2) heads Korean cabbage (napa or Chinese cabbage)

325g (11½oz.) Korean coarse salt

150g (5½oz.) spring onions (scallions), cut into 5cm (2in.) pieces

200g (7oz.) carrots, cut into matchsticks using a julienne peeler

200g (7oz.) daikon (or Korean radish), cut into matchsticks using a julienne peeler

For the dashima stock:

7 medium dried anchovies, guts and heads removed

6 dried shitake mushrooms

5cm (2in) square of seaweed/kelp dashima

3 spring onions (scallions) (55g/2oz.), roughly chopped

1 small onion (115g/4oz.), roughly chopped

3 large garlic cloves (13g/½oz.), crushed

For the spice paste:

80g (3oz.) garlic (about 18 cloves)

40g (1½oz.) fresh ginger, grated

100g (3½oz.) seojutt (Korean salted shrimp)

20g (¾oz./5 tsp) granulated sugar

130g (4½oz.) gochugaru (Korean chili flakes)

100g (3½oz./scant ½ cup) Korean anchovy sauce

First brine the cabbage. Wash the cabbage well and split into quarters by cutting the bottom roots and pulling the tops apart. Dissolve half of the salt in 60ml (¼ cup) of water. Spread the remaining salt over and in between the leaves of the cabbage. Immerse the cabbage, cut side up, in the salted water (add more water if necessary) and weigh down with a plate so it is completely immersed. Leave overnight in the fridge.

The next day, rinse the cabbage well under running cold water two or three times and drain very well. Gently squeeze out any excess water and leave in a colander to drain further.

Make the dashima stock. Soak the anchovies, mushrooms and kelp for 20 minutes in 500 ml (2 cups plus 2 tablespoons) of cold water, then place in a pot over high heat. Add the spring onion (scallion), onion and garlic and bring to the boil, then lower to a simmer and cook for 20 minutes. Remove and strain. Allow to cool completely.

Make the spice paste. Combine the garlic, ginger, seojutt, sugar, gochugaru and anchovy sauce in a food processor and blend until smooth. Add just enough of the cooled dashima stock to make a smooth paste, about 200–250ml (about 1 cup) should be adequate. Stir in the spring onions, carrots and daikon.

Rub the spice paste all over the cabbage and in between each leaf. Place in a large container with a tight-fitting lid and store in a cool place (at around 2°C/35°F) to ferment for 2–3 weeks, then store in the fridge, where it will keep for at least a year – if it lasts that long!

POMEGRANATE PISTACHIO PARFAIT

With chia seeds full of protein and seductive ruby-red pomegranate juice packed with anthocyanins and prostate-healthy antioxidants, this light and easy-to-make pudding sweetened with honey is a dairy-free delight – refreshing, romantic and healthy!

SERVES 4

For the chia cream:

3 tbsp chia seeds

240ml (1 cup) almond milk

⅛ tsp almond extract

pinch salt flakes

2 tbsp honey

¼ tsp ground cardamom

For the pomegranate gelatin:

475ml (2 cups) pure pomegranate juice

1 tbsp honey

4 gold gelatin leaves (see page 46, or 3¼ tsp powdered gelatin)

For the vanilla labneh:

¼ tsp vanilla extract

¼ tsp granulated sugar, or to taste

pinch ground cardamom

85g (3oz./⅓ cup) labneh

To serve:

25g (1oz./3 tbsp) pistachios, chopped

2 fresh figs, quartered or torn, or dried figs, roughly chopped

a few drops rose water

To make the chia cream, mix together all the ingredients in a bowl, cover and chill for 3 hours or overnight.

Cover the gelatin leaves in ice-cold water and leave until soft. In a small saucepan, warm the pomegranate juice with the honey to dissolve. Drain and squeeze excess water from the gelatin then stir it into the juice. Divide the liquid among four dessert glasses. Chill until firm.

Whisk the vanilla, sugar and ground cardamom into the labneh.

Spoon the chia cream layer on top of the pomegranate gelatin layer then top with vanilla labneh. Sprinkle over some chopped pistachios and garnish with figs. Sprinkle over a few drops of rose water.

CARDAMOM CARAMEL ORANGE ICE CREAM

A bit of spiced decadence, this recipe is nevertheless a leaner style of ice cream containing no egg yolks and only half the amount of double (heavy)/whipping cream.

MAKES 1 LITRE (1 QUART)

For the caramel:	For the ice cream:
5 black cardamom pods, cracked	240ml (1 cup) coconut cream
1 tsp (about 8–10) green cardamom pods, cracked	240ml (1 cup) whipping cream
120ml (½ cup) fresh orange juice, strained	100g (3½oz./½ cup) granulated sugar
1 tbsp lemon juice	large pinch salt
zest of ½ orange	1 tbsp white rum (optional)
300g (10½oz./1½ cups) granulated sugar	2 egg whites, at room temperature
1 vanilla pod (bean), split and cut into 8 pieces	
120ml (½ cup) double (heavy) cream	
1 tbsp coconut oil	

Dry-toast the cardamom in a small pan then roughly grind the pods and seeds in a mortar and pestle.

For the caramel, in a small pan, heat the orange and lemon juice, orange zest, sugar, cardamom, half the vanilla pod (bean) pieces (reserve the remainder for the ice cream) and a pinch of salt to a simmer, taking care it doesn't bubble over. Stir occasionally and cook until the sauce is as thick as honey. Whisk in the cream and coconut oil until well blended. Let it stand for 10 minutes off the heat, then strain out the larger pieces of cardamom and cool completely. Cover and chill until needed.

To make the ice cream, in a medium pan, heat the coconut cream and whipping cream with three quarters of the sugar, the reserved half vanilla pod (bean) pieces and a large pinch of salt until steamy and the sugar has dissolved. Turn off the heat, whisk to help cool and add the rum if using. Cover and chill until cold.

Beat the egg whites in a bowl with a whisk or electric mixer until frothy. Stream in the remaining sugar and continue to whip until the whites form shiny stiff peaks.

Fold the cream into the meringue in stages until incorporated.

Freeze in an ice-cream maker according to manufacturer's instructions. Scoop one third of the ice cream into a container then spoon the caramel on top. Repeat the layers. Cover with cling film (plastic wrap) and freeze until firm.

FENUGREEK-POACHED PEAR
WITH DESSERT DUKKAH

As a 14-year-old budding dancer, I was obsessed with making steamed pears with Cool Whip topping sprinkled with cinnamon sugar. A tad more sophisticated in flavour, texture and colour, these Fenugreek-poached Pears are sublime sitting on a bed of Dessert Dukkah. The toasty maple characteristics of the fenugreek swirl on the tongue, but be mindful not to overtoast or you may have to start again.

SERVES 4

350g (12oz./1¾ cups) granulated sugar

2 tbsp lemon juice

½ cinnamon stick, toasted

2 allspice berries, toasted

½ tsp fenugreek seeds, toasted

3 fenugreek leaves

4 pears such as Bosc or Concorde, with stems

60ml (¼ cup) dessert wine, e.g. Sauternes, Botrytis Semillon or Riesling

2 strips lemon peel

Dessert Dukkah (see below), to serve

labneh or softly whipped cream, to serve (optional)

Put the sugar, lemon juice, cinnamon, allspice berries and fenugreek seeds into a 2-litre (2-quart) heavy metal pan and add 120ml (½ cup) of water. Bring to a simmer on medium–high heat, gently swirling the liquid occasionally, and reduce until syrupy and amber in colour. Carefully add a further 350ml (1½ cups) of water (be careful as it will bubble up). Stir to dissolve the caramel, then add the fenugreek leaves, pears, wine and lemon peel. Place a piece of damp muslin (cheesecloth) or a circle of parchment paper with a small cut in the middle over the pears inside the pan to keep them gently submerged. Poach until tender but still firm, about 18 minutes.

Remove the pears from the liquid, then chill the poaching caramel in an ice bath. Return the pears to the liquid caramel and cover and chill until needed. Make the Dessert Dukkah (see below).

To serve, arrange 1 heaped tablespoon of dukkah on each of four plates. Using a sharp knife, level the bottom of the pears so they stand flat. Arrange each pear in the middle of the dukkah and serve with the pear-poaching caramel sauce and labneh or softly whipped cream if wished.

DESSERT DUKKAH

MAKES 140g (5oz./1 CUP)

⅛ tsp fenugreek seeds

½ cinnamon stick, broken into chips

1 tbsp flax seeds

2 tsp coriander seeds

1 tsp cumin seeds

½ tsp caraway seeds

25g (1oz./¼ cup) pecans, toasted and cooled

25g (1oz.¼ cup) sliced almonds, toasted and cooled

40g (1½oz./⅓ cup) pumpkin seeds, toasted and cooled

2 tsp date or raw sugar

1 tsp salt flakes

¾ tsp vanilla powder (optional)

In a small pan over low heat toast the fenugreek seeds very lightly for just a few minutes and remove to the spice grinder to cool. Turn the temperature to medium then toast the cinnamon chips. Cool and finely grind together and transfer to a small bowl. Toast the flax, coriander, cumin and caraway seeds together over medium heat until you can smell the spices. Cool then grind finely.

Using a mortar and pestle, pound the pecans, almonds and pumpkin seeds together until roughly ground. Add to the small bowl with the spices, sugar, salt and vanilla powder (if using) and mix well.

Stored tightly covered in a cool place, the dukkah will keep for up to 3 weeks, or freeze it for up to 2 months.

CARDAMOM

CARDAMOM CHAI TISANE

This warming drink is spicy, aromatic and does not contain any caffeine or dairy. The spices are simmered slowly to allow them to infuse all of their delicate, health-boosting flavour into the drink. Perfect for the colder months, this will help to fend off sniffles and is also a good appetite suppressant to fend off late-afternoon growling tummies. The addition of warm and frothy coconut or almond milk makes this the perfect caffeine-free alternative to your usual afternoon latte.

SERVES 2

1 star anise

6 green cardamom pods, lightly crushed

2 cloves

2 black peppercorns, cracked

1 tbsp chopped fresh ginger

5cm (2in) piece of vanilla pod (bean), split, or ½ tsp vanilla paste

160ml (⅔ cup) coconut or almond milk (optional)

½ tsp honey or agave nectar

Pour 450ml (2 cups) of filtered water into a pan and bring to a gentle simmer over a low heat. Add the star anise, cardamom pods, cloves, peppercorns, ginger and vanilla pod or paste, cover the pan and leave to simmer for 30 minutes, stirring occasionally.

Meanwhile, warm the coconut or almond milk in a small pan until small bubbles start to appear on the surface. Remove from the heat and stir in the honey. Keep warm.

Pour the tisane through a colander and into a jug to strain out the spices. Divide the strained liquid between two cups.

Transfer the warm milk to a screw-top jam jar and seal the lid. Shake the milk until frothy and then pour over the tisane. Serve immediately.

Calming spice

In the chaos and busyness of today's world, which so often switches on our reactive fight-or-flight hormone cortisol, we need a pocket of peace to reorganize our thoughts and rebalance our life. These spices contain an abundance of phytonutrients that may help to soothe the body and calm the mind.

Calming Spice Health Heroes
Sage ★ Basil ★ Saffron ★ Mint ★ Lemongrass

Like sipping a comforting cuppa in your Nana's favourite teacup, these calming spices provide a soothing support with their inherent active phytonutritive natural soothing compounds. Many of these spices are rich in natural calming antidepressants while others help to relax and relieve body systems. Take five minutes of meditative peace and serenity then rejoin the day with clearer vision, purpose and focus. Not long ago people used to alleviate stress by taking a break to have a cigarette, but now you can nurture yourself by replacing unhealthy stress-reducing habits with a calming spice infusion, or make a recipe from the calming recipes in this book.

Basil, the eugenol-scented plant, supports the heart and adrenal-gland health with its multi-antioxidant phytophenols that may calm and reverse the levels of reactive, corrosive fight-or-flight cortisol hormones that are released when you're in stressful situations. The subtle yet powerful crocetin – the natural drug carotenoid chemical compound found in saffron flowers – has been used for centuries as a natural antidepressant. Lovely lemongrass can calm the nerves and refocus scattered thoughts and worries. The smoke of burning sage is revered for its negative-energy-clearing talents amongst Native American tribes, and sage is being studied for its mind-calming, meditative and thought-focussing properties. Mint is not only a frequently recommended carminative (relieving gas) for digestion but can also offer relief for nerve pain, quiet the mind and calm anxiety, and studies show positive results for on-going stress management.

Other calming spice heroes

Nutmeg This precious spice offers relief and support for a large number of complaints, including anxiety and depression as well as memory loss and low libido. The active compound found in nutmeg, myristicin, is a powerful natural narcotic, however, so care should be taken not to over-use it medicinally.

Oregano The classic Italian spice balances the acid–alkali scales in the digestive system, fending off free radicals that can wreak havoc with their corrosive effect, speeding up body-system aging. It offers a calming effect to the stomach and intestines, relieving pain and discomfort in the digestive system with its active compounds carovol and thymol.

Rosemary Studies have shown that rosemary can help relieve depression-like symptoms in animals as effectively as fluoxetine, a prescription antidepressant of the selective serotonin reuptake inhibitor (SSRI) class, with its concentrated and multiple antioxidant essential oils rosmarinic acid, carnosic acid and carnosol. According to the *International Journal of Medical Science*, human studies indicate that rosemary can improve memory, while in traditional medicine, it is used as a calming nerve tonic.

Ginger The calming gingerol compounds in ginger soothe and calm the symptoms of nausea brought on by migraines, seasickness, morning sickness and the after-effects of necessary prescription medications, such as chemotherapy. Ginger also acts as a carminative, soothing the digestive system and relieving it of gas.

Citrus Zest More effective than the scent of lavender, the smell and taste of citrus peel has a calming and lifting effect and may also reduce stress and anxiety. Lemon, orange and especially grapefruit peel can aid in refocusing the mind to help you work better on challenging analytical tasks.

Turmeric Among its plethora of talents, turmeric is lauded not only for its potential pain relief from joint inflammation, but also for being naturally soothing. Turmeric's active compound, curcumin, is a natural sedative: it calms and quiets nerves, settles those pre-performance jitters and, in a cup of turmeric milk tea, can help you sleep. A recent test study showed that taking 1000mg a day of curcumin may have the same results as taking an antidepressant and can also offer relief to those suffering from insomnia.

Sage *The Meditation Spice*

Sage has been culturally and religiously significant to many cultures for millennia: the ancient Greeks and the druids of Ireland used it to invoke clear, calm and meditative serenity while Native American tribes burnt it as incense to ward off negative or evil energy, increase clarity and purify the home.

Of nearly a thousand types of sage, a plant native to the Mediterranean and naturalized throughout Europe and North America, only a handful are edible. These include garden sage, true sage, sweet clary, purple sage and the fruity pineapple sage from Mexico. Hardy and drought tolerant, this sacred spice of Native Americans is often made into a tea to clear and calm the mind and to relieve sore throats and colds. Clary sage, a mild and sweet variety, has long been used as an eye treatment in many traditions. In Chinese traditional medicine, the root rather than the leaves of Chinese sage, also called red sage, is infused into a tonic called danshen that is prescribed primarily for its soothing and healing qualities and is also used to treat cardiovascular disease. Food production and processing use the volatile oil in sage to improve the stability and shelf life of cooking oils.

The familiar evergreen perennial shrub thrives in full sun and well-drained lean soil and has long, light-green leaf stalks that grow tender but strong oval-shaped leaves. The veined leaves have a velvet texture with soft tiny-toothed edges and some types can grow the size of salad leaves (up to 5cm/2in. in length). Generally green-grey on the top, sometimes bearing purple-tinged edges with a lighter shade of grey on the underside, the sage plant exudes a strong pungent, piney and aromatic scent. Sage blossoms, attractive to honey bees, bloom in mid-summer with small white, blue or purple flowers.

Sage is popularly used in rich, hearty Italian, German and Greek main courses, including the classic Roman dish Saltimbocca alla Romana, a sage-infused veal and prosciutto dish. Fresh sage also figures prominently in British cheeses and is an integral ingredient in the classic Sunday roast side dish hastily assembled from sage and onion stuffing mix.

The bitter-tasting fresh leaves are best used in cooked dishes or quickly blanched to soften the bitterness. A fun way to enjoy freshly picked sage, and a great topping for soups, salads and main courses, is to flash-fry sage leaves until crispy (see page 230). Sage is sold fresh and dried. Rubbed sage is the finest type of dried sage and I recommend it, as it is minimally ground and delivers a full flavour and aroma, but remember to use dried sage sparingly as it is far stronger than fresh: 1 teaspoon of dried rubbed sage is the equivalent to about 1 tablespoon of fresh sage.

> This herb has been used in the Mediterranean for literally thousands of years: it's often found carved into the beautiful statues of Roman figures, who treated it as a sacred, ceremonial plant. From a medicinal standpoint, sage has one of the longest histories of use of any medicinal herb.
>
> The many terpene [strong-smelling organic compound] antioxidants found in sage are why it was so often used as a preservative for meat before the days of refrigeration.
>
> Interestingly, it also has some significant potential to help with memory and prevent Alzheimer's disease. A placebo-controlled, double-blind, crossover trial on sage involving 44 participants showed significantly improved, immediate and several-hours-later measures of word and cognitive recall. The results represented evidence that sage is capable of acutely modifying cognition in healthy young adults.
>
> The polyphenolic constituents, which are the antioxidant powerhouses, can provide substantial neuroprotection, which might decrease the likelihood of developing the amyloid plaques found in Alzheimer's disease.

Geeta Maker-Clark, MD

http://www.ncbi.nlm.nih.gov/pubmed/12895685; Adv Exp Med Biol. 2015;863:95-116. doi: 10.1007/978-3-319-18365-7_5.

Basil *The Reverence Spice*

The name basil is derived from Medieval Latin and early French languages from the Greek word 'basilikos', meaning royal. Another relative of the mint family, basil relieves stress, supports the adrenal glands, normalizes levels of cortisol and is being studied for its promising antiaging benefit. Basil is full of free-radical activity in its antioxidant phytonutrients orientin and vicenin and the volatile oils eugenol and apigemen, which can aid the rebalancing of stress hormones. Currently under study, basil shows promise in reducing levels of the flight-or-flight hormone cortisol and the overwhelmed stress-out enzyme creatine (both of which are corrosive when called upon in excess).

The numerous varieties of basil include Thai, lemon, sweet, purple (or opal) and holy basil (tulsi). All can be grown from seed and thrive in warm conditions with full sun, well-watered roots and protected from strong breezes until established. Pick leaves frequently to encourage growth.

Basil is best used fresh or preserved in oil: when dried, it loses the aroma of fresh leaf although it still contains all the active health benefits in a concentrated form and is the best choice to season long-cooked dishes. When purchasing fresh basil, buy only what you will need for a few days as the leaves will blacken and bruise easily once picked and refrigerated.

All types of basil work readily in numerous cuisines and recipes. Nothing could be simpler than the three-ingredient Italian salad of buffalo mozzarella, tomato and basil drizzled with olive oil and balsamic vinegar; or handfuls of basil, garlic, pine nuts and olive oil whizzed together to make a heavenly pesto ready to fold into cooked fresh pasta. Thai basil is a perfect finish to stir-fries, seafood dishes and salads. The agrodolce on page 228 celebrates sweet basil folded into red onion and sour-cherry-glazed sweet potatoes to serve as a side or main, while Mindy Segal's addictive Cinnamon Basil Ice Cream (see page 248) is a perfectly decadent spice pairing.

Holy (or tulsi) basil has smaller leaves but is heartier so stands up to curries, poultry and meat dishes and is used primarily to season Malaysian, Indian and Indonesian cuisine. Native to, primarily grown in and revered in India, holy basil, or tulsi, is a popular tea blend worldwide and often includes fragrant and soothing rose petals. Holy basil got its name from its use in Indian ceremonial religious gatherings. Its clove-like aroma is due to its higher content of eugenol oil, the active phytonutrient compound found in clove and allspice (see page 18). It is also available in dried form and as a nutritional supplement.

❛Basil, a very fragrant herb whose many varieties are used widely in Mediterranean and Asian cuisine, has volatile chemicals similar to those in thyme. These volatile chemicals possess antimicrobial and antioxidant properties. Basil is also rich in nutrients and contains many vitamins and minerals that are cardio-protective, including vitamin A, magnesium, beta-carotene, vitamin C and vitamin K, as well as calcium, iron, folate and omega-3 fatty acids.

Holy Basil is a different species from sweet or Thai basil, which are more commonly used in cooking Italian and Thai foods, respectively. Holy basil is native to India, where it is known as tulsi, and has been used for thousands of years in Ayurvedic medicine. Medicine is made from the leaves, stems and seeds. In Ayurvedic medicine, holy basil is considered an "adaptogen" – a substance that helps people manage life stress and anxiety. In addition to these uses, holy basil has been used for treating the common cold, influenza, asthma, bronchitis, diabetes, heart disease, malaria and tuberculosis. It has also been used as a mosquito repellent and to counteract snake and scorpion bites. Topically, holy basil is applied to the skin for ringworm. There has been recent interest in using holy basil seed oil for cancer, though there are only preliminary animal studies.

Note: holy basil may interact with blood-thinning medications.❜

Linda Shiue, MD

Saffron *The Seductive Spice*

The most expensive spice in the world is the dried bright-yellow stigma from a small purple crocus. Each flower creates only three long, delicate stigmas and it takes about 250,000 of these threads to make 1kg (2lb. 4oz.) of pure saffron – that's over 4,000m² (about an acre) of flowers! This seductive, costly spice is intensely aromatic when released into food or drink, so thankfully a little goes a long way.

Saffron has been used since ancient times to treat a variety of ills, including depression, anxiety and hormonal imbalances and disorders in both men and women. Saffron's most important active phytochemical is crocin, a carotenoid phytonutrient that possesses free-radical-fighting activity and antitumor qualities. Saffron protects the body from the ravages of oxidant-induced stress and bacterial infection. Saffron has been vigorously tested and there is evidence that it exerts a significant chemopreventive effect against liver cancer. Bountiful in minerals and vitamins, especially potassium and vitamin C, saffron is also considered helpful in lowering blood pressure, calming the heartbeat and easing digestion.

Some of the first mentions of saffron in Ancient Greek times date back to the eighth century. During the Middle Ages, despite its high cost, people were crazy about saffron and it was added for flavour, colour and health to a range of dishes like 'pottage' a thin, porridge-like meat and grain stew, and the popular blancmange, often sweetened with honey and with or without meat.

Saffron's golden allure crosses cultures and cuisines – it truly is an international spice and can be found growing from Spain, Greece, Italy, Turkey and Iran to India and even Tasmania and New Zealand. Saffron is used to flavour dishes from most cultures: think of Mexican arroz con pollo, Italian risotto milanese, Spanish paella, the French peasant fish stew bouillabaisse with rouille, Indian biryranis, Scandinavia's traditional lussekatter and England's Cornish saffron bread (see the Cornish Saffron Popovers on page 222 for an inspired take on this).

Buy whole saffron threads in their purest form: the darker the yellow-orange colour the more active crocin and fragrance it contains. To make sure your saffron is authentic, drop a few stigmas in a small bowl of warm water. True saffron will dissolve, turning the water a yellow-orange colour, ready to add to your recipe; turmeric and other imposters won't. Saffron will keep up to three years tightly packaged away from air, light and moisture, so foil-wrap the clear glass vial or plastic box it often comes in. The finest way I've found to prepare saffron for a dish is described by Chef Todiwala on page 36.

> Saffron is one of the most ancient spices and certainly the most expensive. Aiani in Northern Greece, Iran and Spain are major exporters of this precious spice, which takes its name from the Arab word 'asfar' or 'za'faran', meaning yellow, due to the golden-yellow colour it gives to foods. One shouldn't confuse saffron with turmeric, the golden and much less expensive spice from India. Saffron has been found to have numerous effects, including antitumour, antidepressive, anti-inflammatory and antioxidant activity, which are currently being researched. Used in conjunction with modern medicine, it can assist in health preservation and recovery from many diseases. But remember, as with any substance that has pharmacological effects in the body, if you take too much, it can be toxic. The quantities that are used in food will not harm anyone. You can find high-quality saffron in Persian or Middle Eastern shops, where it is often cheaper than in high-street supermarkets.

Eleni Tsiompanou, MD, PGDip, MSc Nutritional Medicine

Mint *The Chill-out Spice*

A versatile multi-climate plant that thrives easily in fields, marshes, mountains and your windowbox, mint grows year round. True mint is of the genus *Mentha*, of which there are estimated to be between 12 and 25 species, but there are also many hundreds of hybrids, cultivars and varieties of mint, and their names are a delight: there's lemon and orange, bergamot, apple and pineapple, plus slender, wrinkled-leaf and even chocolate mint. Commercially, the two most commonly grown, known and used are spearmint (*M. spicata*), and peppermint (*M. piperita* – a true mint pairing of *M. spicata* and water mint, *M. aquatica*).

Spearmint is differentiated by its lack of leaf stock and by its toothy-edged leaves with mosaic-textured tops. In plant mythology, it is considered to convey wisdom. This white-blossomed creeper prefers semi-shade and moist conditions and should be ringed or potted if you don't want mint wandering all through your garden. Spearmint's distinctive flavour is milder than that of peppermint as its aromatic primary compound is the volatile oil carvone. Spearmint also contains the flavonoid thymonin, caffeic acid derivatives, rosmarinic acid and limonene.

Spearmint is a safe remedy for children with its milder minty flavour and gentler active compounds. For childhood fevers, make a tea of spearmint and white horehound (related to mint), which will help relieve minor aches, pains and chills. In Japan in 2001, a group of medical researchers reported that essential oil of spearmint showed significant bactericidal activity against such disease agents as *Staphylococcus aureus*, *E. coli* and *Helicobacter pylori*.

Menthol, the main active ingredient of peppermint (*M. piperita*), is found in the leaves and flowering tops of the plant. It provides the cool sensation of the herb and these are often dried and used as a culinary spice or for beneficial heath use. Peppermint is primarily cultivated for its oil, which is extracted from the leaves of the flowering plant by steam distillation. The content of menthol determines the quality of its essential oil, which is used as a carminative (relieving gas) and stimulant, for its derivative menthol and for flavouring, especially chewing gum, breath mints and to mask the taste of what would be an unpalatable pill to swallow.

The medicinal parts of peppermint are derived from the whole plant and include a volatile oil, flavonoids, phenolic acids and triterpenes (precursors to steroids). The essential volatile oils, in addition to menthol, are arementhone and menthyl acetate. Menthyl acetate is what gives peppermint its 'minty' flavour.

Peppermint tea can stimulate the immune system and ease congestion of colds, fevery flus and upper respiratory infections. The German Commission E (see page 94) has officially recognized peppermint's ability to reduce inflammation of nasal passages. When menthol vapours are inhaled, nasal passageways are opened to provide temporary relief of nasal and sinus congestion. A plant with potent antiviral properties, peppermint can also help fight viruses that cause ailments such as the flu, herpes, yeast infections and mumps. Peppermint has also been used traditionally as an earache remedy, to dissolve gallstones, ease muscle tightness, relieve stress and anxiety and ease menstrual cramps.

Mint is also used in a myriad of ways in food and drink, from mint sauce, minted pea soup and salads to chocolate bonbons, ice cream and cocktails.

‘ The mint family includes many different plants, including the well-known spearmint and peppermint. Mint oil has a lovely refreshing taste that has been used to flavour everything from mouthwash to candy, and is used as a mouth refresher for the very reason that it is an antibacterial.

I use peppermint oil often in my practice for people with digestive issues, particularly irritable bowel syndrome. Some excellent studies have shown that peppermint can reduce the symptoms of abdominal pain and gastrointestinal upset that accompany such a diagnosis. These need to be taken in enteric-coated capsules, however, as the pure oil is far too strong to be taken internally.

A simple peppermint tea can achieve some digestive relief, though it can worsen heartburn!

As an antibacterial, antifungal, digestive and analgesic, the entire mint family is an easy-to-grow and well-regarded medicinal plant. ’

Geeta Maker-Clark, MD

http://www.ncbi.nlm.nih.gov/pubmed/16121521

Lemongrass *The Soothing Spice*

Softly scented graceful lemongrass (*Cymbopogon citratus*) is native to Sri Lanka and South India and is now widely cultivated in the tropical areas of the Americas and Asia. In many countries, such as Brazil, a centuries-old traditional medicinal drink called *abafado* is a popular remedy for anxiety that is enjoyed several times a day. Fold and bruise some fresh lemongrass leaves then plunge them into boiling water, steep for 10–15 minutes and pour into a cup. I like to add a little freshly grated ginger and coconut sugar, too. The delicately scented lemongrass steam gives you pause to stop and enjoy, and this soothing tea calms jangled nerves and will help you focus your scattered thoughts – a bit like reorganizing your brain's to-do list.

A tufted grassy perennial with a tangle of fresh pale yellow-green leaves and rhizome-type bulbs, the hardy lemongrass grows easily in tropical to sub-tropical climes throughout the world, from Australia to the Americas, the Pacific Isles to the Caribbean and even in garden pots in Cornwall.

Traditional lemongrass health benefits are numerous and promising. Ancient Thai remedies use lemongrass to treat gastrointestinal disorders and fevers and it is also believed to increase circulation.

In other cultures, it is used as an analgesic pain reliever, an antifungal and antiseptic and as a remedy to treat nervousness. A cup of lemongrass tea every four hours is recommended to reduce fevers. Many studies show the plant sterols in lemongrass can be effective to block the absorption of dietary cholesterol.

The light playful scent of this spice pairs perfectly with broths (see the Waygu Beef Carpaccio with Green Tea Noodles, Lemongrass and Ginger on page 246) and it is commonly used in teas and curries, too. It is also suitable for poultry, fish and seafood and is an important ingredient in Thai and Vietnamese cuisine.

Lemongrass is available dried and preserved but I recommend you buy and use fresh lemongrass if possible. (Or buy a whole lemongrass plant: it will happily grow in a plant pot and will add a little bit of the tropics to your garden or balcony.) It is usually sold in bunches – look for firm stalks – and, if you buy more than you need, you can freeze it, tightly wrapped in a zipped plastic freezer bag. When adding it to liquid, either mince the bulb into little wheels or bruise and bash the entire bulb to release the oils and then add to your recipe. As with bay leaf, unless you chop it into tiny bits, it is best to remove the stalks before serving.

> Lemongrass has been traditionally used as a tea and in aromatherapy. As a rich source of volatile oils, it contains citral, which serves as an antioxidant by turning on the body's key detoxifying enzyme, glutathione S-transferase, which can defend cells from damage by free radicals. Free radicals are a factor in most chronic diseases such as atherosclerosis.
>
> In addition to containing B vitamins (folate, thiamin, pyridoxine and pathothenic acid) and minerals (zinc, calcium, iron, copper, magnesium and manganese), lemongrass is noted beyond its citrus scent as a multifaceted folk therapy as well as a modern science opportunity in both animal and human studies. Historically, it has sought to reduce gastrointestinal symptoms, depress the central nervous system and to promote sedation. Whereas animal studies have suggested beneficial activity as anti-inflammatory, anticancer, antiallergic and antianxiety nutrient, small human studies have shown assistance with other modalities to address chronic periodontitis and oral thrush (fungal infection) in HIV-positive patients. Although it was not as strong as antifungal pharmaceuticals, it showed antifungal properties against pityriasis versicolour—a common fungal skin infection of the upper and lower torso. Early studies demonstrate that the brief inhalation of the essential oil may accelerate the recovery of anxiety as compared to controls.
>
> (*Safety note*: as a topical oil, lemongrass can cause skin irritation in some individuals when used in cosmetics, perfumes and as a massage oil.)

Param Dedhia, MD

CORNISH SAFFRON POPOVERS
WITH SWEET SAFFRON BUTTER

Inspired by the classic British Yorkshire pudding, 'popovers' are baked in a similar fashion and are often made with cheese. Using traditional Cornish saffron bread ingredients, here is a recipe for quick-as-you-can popovers that are great for afternoon tea or an after-dinner bit of something sweet and surprising using this most alluring and expensive spice.

MAKES 24 MINI OR 10–12 STANDARD-SIZED POPOVERS

⅛ tsp saffron strands, lightly toasted

2 tbsp orange juice

zest of ½ orange

125g (4½oz./1 cup) plain (all-purpose) flour

1 tsp sea salt

240ml (1 cup) full-fat (whole), milk warmed to 38°C (100°F)

4 large whole eggs, beaten

1 tbsp grapeseed oil

For the sweet saffron butter:

⅛ tsp saffron threads, lightly toasted

3 tbsp granulated sugar

100g (3½oz./scant ½ cup) softened butter

½ tsp lime zest

½ tsp ground cardamom seeds

large pinch salt

2 tbsp currants plumped with 1 tbsp water or brandy

To make the sweet saffron butter, rub the toasted saffron threads into the sugar until combined. Put into a small bowl with all the remaining ingredients and whisk by hand or with a mixer until smooth and creamy. Cover and chill until needed.

To make the popovers, crumble the toasted saffron and dissolve in the orange juice. Set aside.

Mix the flour and salt together in a bowl. Add the warm milk a little at a time. Whisk until smooth, then add 80ml (⅓ cup) of cold water and the saffron orange juice, whisking until bubbly. Incorporate the beaten eggs, transfer to a jug, cover and chill for 30 minutes or up to a day.

When ready to bake, preheat the oven to 240°C (475°F/gas mark 9). Brush mini- or standard-sized muffin cups with oil and put them on a baking tray. Place in the oven on the lower shelf until smoking hot.

Rewhisk the chilled batter, then carefully remove the trays from the oven, pour the batter into the hot tins to about three quarters full and return them to the oven. Do not the oven door while they are cooking or they will not rise.

Bake mini popovers for 8–10 minutes, standard-sized ones for about 20 miniutes, then reduce the temperature to 200°C (400°F/gas mark 6) and bake for a further 8–10 minutes until brown, crisp and risen.

Serve the popovers warm with the sweet saffron butter.

CHICKPEA SALAD
WITH MINT VINAIGRETTE
Francesco Carli

'Delightful, simple, cooling and packed with easily digestible legume protein from the chickpeas, this salad is easily doubled and a cinch to prepare for picnics, parties and lunchboxes. Peppermint, which is higher in cooling menthol flavour than spearmint, releases an intense freshness to the senses when consumed and has excellent properties to assist digestion and fight infection. The last-minute addition of sweet, soothing, softly textured mango to the dish adds a sublime richness to this simple Brazilian-style salad.' FC

SERVES 4

2 tbsp olive oil	125g (4½oz.) cherry tomatoes, halved
2 tbsp lemon juice	½ cucumber, seeded and chopped
1 tsp lemon zest, or to taste	½ red (bell) pepper, seeded and chopped
1 tbsp apple cider vinegar	60g (2¼oz./½ medium) onion, chopped
3 garlic cloves, minced	30 peppermint leaves, chopped
400g (14oz.) can chickpeas, drained	100g (3½oz.) mango flesh, diced

In a medium bowl, mix together the olive oil, lemon juice and zest, vinegar, garlic and salt and pepper to taste.

Toss together the chickpeas, tomatoes, cucumber, (bell) pepper, onion and peppermint leaves. Check the seasoning and correct if necessary. Finally stir in the diced mango.

Serve immediately or cover and refrigerate for a while before serving.

SAGE, BASIL, GINGER, TURMERIC

BRIDGE STREET ROASTED PUMPKIN RAVIOLI
WITH PIÑON SAGE PESTO

These ravioli filling ingredients not only taste delicious but the acid–alkali balancing maple syrup, restorative garlic, spicy warming ginger and the prairie-pine, mind-clearing flavour of sage have added health benefits.

SERVES 6

For the filling:

120ml (½ cup) double (heavy) cream

350g (12oz.) roasted pumpkin or butternut squash flesh

175g (6oz/1½ cups) Turmeric Melted Onions (see page 146)

40g (1½oz./3 tbsp) butter

2 tbsp maple syrup or brown sugar

1 tbsp roasted garlic purée (2 cloves)

1½ tsp freshly grated ginger

1 tsp ground turmeric

large pinch each ground cinnamon, allspice and fenugreek

½ tsp kosher salt, or to taste

¼ tsp fresh cracked pepper, or to taste

1–2 tsp fresh lemon juice, or to taste

225g (8oz./1 cup) ricotta

For the ravioli dough:

2 whole eggs plus 1 yolk

2 tsp extra virgin olive oil

175g (6oz./1⅓ cups) bread flour

85g (3oz./⅓ cup) semolina

1½ tsp salt

To finish:

3 tbsp toasted pepitas (pumpkin seeds)

To make the filling, simmer the cream in a saucepan over medium heat, then add the squash, onions, butter, sugar, garlic purée and spices. Season to taste with salt, pepper and lemon juice. Purée with a stick blender until smooth. Fold in the ricotta by hand until well combined. Cover and chill until just ready to make the ravioli.

To make the ravioli dough, whisk the eggs and oil in a small bowl. In a medium bowl, stir together the bread flour, semolina and salt. Make a well in the centre, add the egg and oil mixture and stir to combine. Add 1 tablespoon of water, knead and shape into a pad. Cover with cling film (plastic wrap) and chill for 30 minutes.

On a lightly floured surface roll out the dough, then roll through a pasta machine to #5 thickness or roll out using a rolling pin to 5mm (¼in.) thick. Cut into two equal-sized sheets. Dot spoonfuls of the filling 3cm (1¼in.) apart on one pasta sheet. Run a wet finger around each spoonful of filling, then lay the second sheet on top. Seal each ravioli from the centre outwards to push out any air, then, using the dull edge of cutter, press around the filling to seal. Using a cutter one size larger, cut through the ravioli, transfer to a lightly floured tray and chill.

Gently drop the ravioli into a pan of simmering salted water a few at a time and cook to al dente. Drain well, arrange on a serving plate and spoon the pesto over. Garnish with a few toasted pepitas (pumpkin seeds) and serve.

PIÑON SAGE PESTO

MAKES ABOUT 480ml (2 CUPS)

50g (1¾oz.) cashew nuts

50g (1¾oz.) piñon (pine nuts)

20g (¾oz./⅔ cup) sage leaves, roughly chopped

15g (½oz./½ cup) basil leaves

2 tbsp parsley leaves

4 garlic cloves, peeled and chopped

squeeze of lemon juice

240ml (1 cup) extra virgin olive oil or pumpkin seed oil

55g (2oz./⅓ cup) grated Parmesan

salt, pepper and ground chipotle chilli or smoked pepper, to taste

Put the nuts, sage, basil, parsley, garlic and lemon juice in the bowl of a food processor with an S blade and pulse to chop. Scrape down the sides of the bowl, then, with the motor running, drizzle in the oil in a steady trickle until combined to form a green paste. Spoon the pesto into a medium-sized bowl and gently stir in the grated Parmesan. Season with salt, pepper and ground chipotle chili or smoked pepper to taste.

BASIL, ROSEMARY, TURMERIC

SWEET POTATO AGRODOLCE

Agrodolce is a traditional Italian sweet-and-sour sauce. This version, served with sweet potatoes, is packed with brain-food-anthocyanin-loaded cherries and spices and finished with a generous handful of the familiar, fragrant, antioxidant-rich basil leaf.

SERVES 4-6

3 tbsp dried cherries, roughly chopped

350g (12oz.) red sweet potatoes, kumara or yams, peeled and cut into 1cm (½in.) pieces

3 tbsp pumpkin seed, extra virgin olive or grapeseed oil

2 tsp cumin seeds, toasted and ground

60ml (¼ cup) balsamic or orange vincotto vinegar

2 jalapeño chilies, seeded and thinly sliced in rings

½ tsp ground turmeric

2 tbsp honey

2 medium-sized red onions (about 450g/1lb.), thinly sliced

2 rosemary sprigs

2 thyme sprigs

1 garlic clove, thinly sliced

20g (¾oz./¾ cup tightly packed) fresh basil leaves, plus extra for garnishing, torn

Preheat the oven to 200°C (400°F/gas mark 6).

Put the dried cherries into a small bowl, cover with hot water and leave to soften for 10 minutes. Drain and set aside.

Put the sweet potatoes in a bowl and toss with 2 tablespoons of the oil, the cumin and some salt, then spread out evenly on a baking tray. Roast, tossing occasionally, until golden brown and fork tender, 17–20 minutes. Remove from the oven, leave on the tray and set aside to cool.

In a small saucepan, mix the drained cherries with the vinegar, jalapeños, turmeric and honey and season with salt. Cook, stirring, until the sauce reduces to a thin syrup, about 5 minutes.

Heat the remaining 1 tablespoon of oil in a large pan over medium–high heat. Add the onions, rosemary and thyme and sauté until golden brown. Add the garlic, cook for about 3 minutes more, then add the cherry mix and reduce.

Gently fold in the sweet potatoes. Add the basil then gently toss again. Spoon onto a platter or individual serving plates. Garnish with extra torn basil leaves and serve immediately.

SAGE, BASIL

VEGETARIAN 'BURNING LOVE'
WITH BROWN BUTTER AND SAGE
Mette Helbak

'"Burning love" is a Danish classic comfort food dish of mashed potatoes with fried bacon and onions on top. This is a vegetarian version with lots of different vegetables, where the umami comes from sage brown butter and mushrooms.' MH

SERVES 4 AS A MAIN COURSE

For the mash:

500g (1lb. 2oz.) celeriac, peeled and coarsely chopped

500g (1lb. 2oz.) potatoes, peeled and coarsely chopped

50g (1¾oz./½ stick) butter, cut into cubes

2 tbsp coarsely chopped sage

2 tbsp coarsely chopped basil

a little bit of the water used for boiling celery and potatoes

For the brown butter:

85g (3oz.) butter

leaves of 5 sage sprigs

For the 'love':

150g (5½oz.) mushrooms

4 onions, diced

200g (7oz.) carrots, cut into cubes

200g (7oz.) parsley root, cut into cubes

200g (7oz.) Brussels sprouts, cut into quarters or halves

1 tsp salt

To make the mash, put the celeriac and potato into a pan, cover with water and boil for 20 minutes or until tender. Drain, reserving about 240ml (1 cup) of the liquid. Add the butter, sage and basil and mash with a whisk. Season with salt and add the reserved liquid a little at a time until the mash is soft and creamy.

To make the brown butter, melt the butter in a small saucepan and let it slowly turn brown over medium heat for 10–15 minutes. When it smells of roasted hazelnuts, it is done. Remove from the heat and add the sage.

To make the 'love', cut or tear the mushrooms apart into smaller pieces and fry them in a dry, hot frying pan for 3–4 minutes. Turn down the heat to medium and add the rest of the vegetables and a couple of tablespoons of the brown butter. Cook until the vegetables are turning brown and a little soft, about 4–5 minutes.

Serve the fried vegetables and brown butter on top of the mash.

WAIMATE CORN FRITTERS AND MUSSELS
WITH SAGE-RUBBED BACON AND SMOKED-TOMATO AIOLI

One of the oldest farming communities in New Zealand, Waimate North grows luscious sweetcorn and hosts the country's oldest agricultural show, the Bay of Islands Pastoral and Industrial Show. Pungent and aromatic sage often appears dusty, fuzzy and grey, but don't be fooled: it is packed with mind-clearing compounds and can help relieve sore throats, too!

SERVES 4

4–6 rashers streaky or back bacon

1 tsp rubbed sage

¾ tsp sage honey

½ tsp chipotle powder

4–8 green-lip mussels, steamed in shells

baby greens, to serve

For the smoked-tomato aioli:

1 large egg yolk

1 garlic clove, minced

pinch sea salt

zest and juice of 1 lemon

2 tsp honey

20g (¾oz./¼ cup) semi-dried smoked tomatoes, finely chopped

120ml (½ cup) grapeseed oil

For the fritters:

500g (1lb 2oz./3 cups) fresh, raw or defrosted corn kernels

3 large eggs

1 tbsp finely chopped chives

¼ tsp hot chili sauce

1 tsp dried, rubbed sage

½ tsp baking soda

70g (2½oz./scant ½ cup) rice flour

85g (3oz./½ cup) chopped courgette (zucchini)

a little vegetable oil, to fry

Preheat the oven to 160°C (325°F/gas mark 3).

To make the aioli, in a small bowl or using a stick blender, whisk the egg yolk with the garlic, salt, lemon zest and juice, honey and tomatoes until well blended. Continue to whisk while drizzling in the oil in a slow, steady stream until the sauce begins to come together and thicken. If too thick, whisk in an additional teaspoon of water until well combined. Cover and chill for up to 2 days until ready to use.

Lay the bacon rashers on a parchment-lined baking tray. In a small bowl, mix the sage, honey and chipotle powder to a paste with a pinch of salt. Brush onto the bacon, then cover with another piece of parchment and top with another tray to keep the bacon flat. Bake for about 12 minutes until browned and crispy. Set aside.

To make the batter for the gluten-free fritters, cover the corn with boiling water, let it stand for 3 minutes then drain well. Put half the corn in a food processor with the eggs and chives and blend to a chunky purée. Add the hot chili sauce, sage, baking soda, rice flour, a pinch of salt and a few grinds of pepper, then pulse to form a thick batter. Stir in the reserved corn and the courgette (zucchini).

Heat a little oil in a heavy pan and cook in batches over medium heat, pouring about 3 tablespoons of batter for each fritter. Cook until golden brown and cooked through, about 3–4 minutes each side. Add oil to pan between batches if needed.

Place a fritter in the centre of each plate, top with a little aioli then repeat twice more. Arrange two mussels, sage, a piece of bacon broken in two and a little more sauce on the fritters. Scatter with baby greens and serve immediately.

DOVES BAY BOUILLABAISSE
WITH SPICY RED PEPPER ROUILLE

This classic French dish is transported to the southern hemisphere with the freshest of New Zealand's fish and shellfish. In the far north, where snapper is plentiful, the fishermen will often smoke their catch, infusing it with an intoxicating smoky sweetness that adds an amazing depth of flavour to this dish. The addition of kawakawa pepper to the stock creates a gentle spicy undertone to the soup that is heightened by the subtle, smoky heat of the paprika-scented red pepper rouille that is served alongside.

SERVES 8

For the smoked snapper stock:
bones of 2 smoked snapper or other smoked fish
2 onions, unpeeled, cut in quarters
3 carrots, cut in large chunks
1 celery stalk
small handful parsley
1 bay leaf
4 kawakawa or 6 wild pepper leaves, torn in pieces
8 peppercorns
½ lemon, cut in half

For the rouille:
1 red (bell) pepper, roasted (see page 24), peeled, seeded and roughly chopped
2 garlic cloves, roughly chopped
1 slice white bread, torn into pieces
1 egg yolk
1 tbsp Dijon mustard
juice of 1 lemon

¼ tsp smoked paprika or chipotle powder
120ml (½ cup) extra virgin olive oil
16 slices baguette, to serve

For the bouillabaisse:
4 medium new potatoes, cubed
2 large onions, cut into large dice
1 litre (4¼ cups) smoked snapper stock (see above)
240ml (1 cup) dry white wine
8 Roma (plum) tomatoes, peeled, seeded and cut into large dice
12 saffron threads
2 kawakawa pepper leaves or 4 wild pepper leaves, torn
350g (12oz.) scallops
350g (12oz.) whole king prawns (jumbo shrimp), peeled
225g (8oz.) smoked snapper, flaked (2 cups flaked)
1 large lobster tail, shelled and sliced
16 mussels, washed and beards removed
20g (¾oz./⅓ cup) chopped parsley, to garnish
8 thyme sprigs, leaves picked, to garnish

First make the stock. Put all the ingredients in a stock pot, add water to cover and bring to a very low simmer. Simmer for 2 hours, then cool and strain.

To make the rouille, put the red (bell) pepper, garlic, bread, egg yolk, mustard, lemon juice and paprika or chipotle powder in a food processor with an S blade and purée until smooth. With the machine running, slowly drizzle in the oil until the mixture becomes thick and smooth. Season to taste and set aside.

For the bouillabaisse, pour 700ml (3 cups) of salted water into a 1-litre (1-quart) pan and bring to the boil. Reduce to a simmer and add the potatoes and half the onion. Cook for 10 minutes, or until fork tender, then drain. Transfer the potatoes and onions to a large chopping board and spread out to cool.

Heat the grill (broiler) to high and arrange the baguette slices on a grill (broiler) pan. Grill (broil) until lightly golden, turning the slices halfway through. Set aside.

Put the stock, wine, saffron, pepper leaves, tomatoes, potatoes and all the onions into a large stock pot over medium heat. Bring to a gentle simmer, then add the fish and shellfish and cook gently for 2–3 minutes until the mussels have opened. Discard any that remain closed. Season to taste.

Preheat the grill (broiler) to high. Spread the toasted baguette slices with the rouille and place under the grill (broiler) until golden and bubbling. Ladle the bouillabaisse into individual serving bowls and garnish with parsley and thyme. Serve each bowl with two slices of the spicy rouille-topped bread.

RED MULLET POACHED IN SAFFRON BROTH
WITH KABOSU LEMON AND AMARETTO
Anne-Sophie Pic

*Colourful, healthful and fragrant, with steaming Kabousu lemon-and-saffron-butter sauce,
this fish 'portrait' is a stunning work of art and flavour.*

SERVES 10

10 x 150–200g (5½–7oz.) red mullet, or pink snapper
or sea bass

olive oil, for searing fish and brushing

Maldon salt, to finish

For the Kabosu lemon butter:

55g (1¾oz./½ stick) salted butter, at room temperature

55g (1¾oz./½ stick) unsalted butter, at room temperature

zest of 2 Kabosu lemons

For the pickles:

300g (10½oz.) baby red beetroot

90ml (6 tbsp) white balsamic vinegar

85g (3oz./scant ½ cup) sugar

For the garnish:

2 small parsnips (or 5 mini celeriac)

30g (1oz./2 tbsp) salted butter

100g (3½oz.) daikon (or Korean radish or celeriac) shavings

3 pieces of mini (or 'Golden Ball') turnip

100g (3½oz.) celeriac, peeled and chopped

100ml (scant ½ cup) milk

For the sauce:

5 saffron threads

½ tsp dried lemongrass

zest of ½ lemon

Kabosu lemon butter (see above)

30ml (2 tbsp) amaretto

To make the Kabosu butter, mix the butters together with the Kabosu lemon zest.

For the beetroot pickles, cut the beetroot into 50 wedges, reserving a tiny slice of red beetroot to cut into matchsticks, as pictured, for finishing. Arrange the wedges, separating the colours into sous-vide bags. Bring the balsamic vinegar and sugar to the boil then pour an equal amount over the wedges in bags and cool completely. Vacuum-seal the bags and set the sous-vide cooker at position 3. Leave to steam for 1½ hours. Alternatively, put the wedges in separate pans, pour over the boiling marinade and simmer gently until fork tender.

For the garnish, peel the parsnips and blanch them in salted water, then roast them in a beurre noisette (brown butter) until lightly and evenly coloured. Chill, then cut them into 1 x 4cm (½ x 1½in.) matchsticks.

Using a mandoline, cut the daikon 1mm thick then trim using a 4.5cm (1¾in.) diameter pastry (cookie) cutter. Peel and turn the mini turnips to give them a rounded shape. Cook them in butter then cut them in quarters.

Cook the celeriac in the seasoned milk, drain and purée, then immediately whisk in the Kabosu lemon butter, adjusting the seasoning with Kabosu lemon zest and salt if necessary.

For the sauce, heat 100ml (scant ½ cup) of water to 75°C (165°F), infuse the saffron, lemongrass and lemon zest for 15 minutes, then taste and infuse for a further 5 minutes if necessary. Strain through a muslin (cheesecloth) strainer then whisk in the Kabosu butter. Add the amaretto and adjust the seasoning as necessary.

Descale and clean the red mullet then lift and debone the fillets. Sear the fillets, skin-side down, on a griddle in a little olive oil. Cook the fillets evenly, remove them from the griddle, turn them over, check they are cooked, then brush a little olive oil on the skin side.

To serve, butter the daikon, parsnips and turnip. Arrange parsnip sticks next to each other and lay two daikon petals and a quarter of mini turnip on top. Add two dots of celeriac purée on either side. Add two red mullet fillets with a little Maldon salt on the skin side then place five alternating coloured wedges of beetroot in between the fish fillets. Carefully pour the sauce around the sides of each bowl to just cover the bottom. Serve immediately.

ROASTED FREE-RANGE QUAIL
WITH SAFFRON RISOTTO
Simone Cerea

'One of the most well-known dishes in Italy is the Risotto alla Milanese, It is also one of my favourites, originating in Milan, an area close to where I come from. The aroma and colour of the saffron is distinctive and enhances the simplicity of the dish. More complexity is delivered through the complementary flavours of the quail and the saltiness of the pancetta, which reminds me of family Sunday lunches. Dolcetto is a variety of black Italian wine grape, like Nebiolo from the Piedmont region. "Lardo di Colonnata" is the smooth, pure back fat of pigs aged in marble troughs with herbs and spices. These pigs are raised on a diet of chestnuts and acorns, near the town of Colonnata in northwestern Italy.' SC

SERVES 4

For the saffron risotto:

2 tbsp olive oil

5g (⅛oz.) finely chopped white onion

140g (5oz./⅔ cup) carnaroli rice

1 tbsp dry white wine

350ml (1½ cups) boiling chicken stock

pinch saffron powder

20g (¾oz./4 tsp) unsalted butter

20g (¾oz./1¾ tbsp) grated Parmesan

For the chicken mousse:

100g (3½oz.) chicken breast

10g (¼oz.) Lardo di Colonnata

2 tsp double (heavy) cream

2 tsp milk

5 pistachios, skin removed, lightly toasted and chopped

½ date, skin and seeds removed, finely chopped

2 amaretti biscuits, crumbled

1 sage leaf, finely chopped

For the bacon-wrapped quail:

4 whole free-range quail (semi-boned) (about 85g/3oz. each)

chicken mousse (see above)

20g (¾oz./4 tsp) butter

4 sage leaves

8 thin slices Pancetta Steccata

For the butternut squash:

200g (7oz.) butternut squash, peeled and cut into rings 2cm (¾in.) thick

1 garlic clove, chopped

1 fresh thyme sprig

20g (¾oz./4 tsp) butter

1 tbsp olive oil

For the mulled-wine reduction:

475ml (2 cups) Dolcetto d'Alba

1½ cinnamon sticks

4 cloves

1 star anise

3 juniper berries, cracked

⅓ orange, sliced

2 tbsp brown sugar

15g (½oz./1 tbsp) butter

To garnish:

2 tsp olive oil

16–20 individual Brussels sprout leaves

pinch saffron flowers (optional)

To make the saffron risotto, heat up a pan, add the olive oil and fry the onions until lightly golden. Add the rice and let the rice toast for 3 minutes.

Add the white wine and reduce completely before gradually pouring in the boiling chicken stock. Keep boiling until the grains are al dente, about 18 minutes. Add the saffron powder about 15 minutes into the cooking. Just before the rice is ready, remove the pan from the heat and add the butter and Parmesan. (Removing from heat will prevent the cheese from splitting.) Season with salt and pepper to taste.

Meanwhile, prepare the bacon-wrapped quail. Start by making the chicken mousse. Remove the skin from chicken breast and blend it in a food processor with the Lardo di Colonnata, adding cream and milk at the last minute to get a soft mixture. Stir in the remaining ingredients using a spatula and season with salt and pepper to taste.

Preheat the oven to 190°C (375°F/gas mark 5).

Turn the whole quail with thighs facing up and cut along the backbone. Remove the carcass by cutting around the bone, but preserve the legs and wings. Season with salt and pepper and place the mousse in the middle, keeping the skin on the outside. Recompose the quail as a whole and secure using a toothpick. Brush butter on the skin and hold the quail in place by wrapping it in foil. Bake in the oven for approximately 8 minutes, or until the skin turns golden brown.

Remove the quail from the oven, place a sage leaf on top of each one and wrap with two slices of pancetta steccata. Return the quail to the oven and cook for a further 4 minutes.

Remove and leave to rest for 5 minutes before serving. Reduce the oven temperature to 180°C (350°F/ gas mark 4).

Put the butternut squash rings in a baking tray, scatter over the garlic and thyme, dot with butter and drizzle over the olive oil. Bake in the oven for 10 minutes until the squash rings have turned golden brown.

To make the mulled-wine reduction, mix all the ingredients except the butter together in a saucepan and let it simmer until the wine is reduced by a fifth of the total volume. Whisk in the butter before serving to achieve the right consistency.

Meanwhile, add 2 teaspoons of oil to a hot sauté pan and quickly flash-fry the Brussels sprout leaves for about 10 seconds – they should retain their crunchiness. Drain on kitchen paper and set aside for serving.

To serve, arrange a large serving spoonful of warm risotto on each of four plates, then top with the quail. Arrange the butternut squash to the side, scatter with the Brussels sprouts leaves and the saffron flowers (if using), then drizzle the mulled-wine sauce over all. Serve immediately.

Illustrated on pages 238–9

MINT

TURKISH LAMB STEW
John Gregory-Smith

'This humble stew is packed full of smoky flavours from the pepper paste and Turkish pepper flakes. Dry mint adds another dimension that mellows into the rich sauce as it cooks slowly. Marinating the lamb overnight in yogurt, pepper paste and spices tenderizes the meat, ensuring that it is beautifully soft, and gives it an extra depth of flavour. This is a simple trick that I use for any similar stew or casserole.' JGS

SERVES 4

600g (1lb. 5oz.) lamb leg, cut into 2.5cm (1in.) cubes

4 tbsp olive oil

2 onions, thinly sliced

3 Turkish green (bell) peppers, seeded and thinly sliced

400g (14oz.) can chopped tomatoes

2 tbsp Turkish red pepper paste

2 tbsp tomato purée

1 tsp Turkish (Aleppo) pepper flakes

1 tsp dried mint

cousous and a green salad, to serve (optional)

For the marinade:

4 tbsp Greek-style yogurt

3 garlic cloves, crushed

2 tbsp mild Turkish red pepper paste

2 tbsp tomato purée

2 tsp Turkish (Aleppo) pepper flakes

1 tsp dried mint

½ tsp ground cinnamon

Put all the ingredients for the marinade into a mixing bowl. Add a good pinch of salt and mix together. Add the lamb and mix well so it all gets completely coated. Cover and marinate overnight in the fridge.

Remove the lamb from the fridge to come to room temperature.

Meanwhile, heat the oil in a casserole over a medium heat and add the onions and (bell) peppers. Cook, stirring occasionally, for 6–8 minutes or until lovely and golden.

Add the tomatoes, red pepper paste, tomato purée, Turkish pepper flakes, dried mint and a good pinch of salt and pepper. Pour in 100ml (scant ½ cup) of boiling water and mix together. Add the lamb and mix well. Cover, reduce the heat to low and cook, stirring occasionally, for 1½–2 hours or until the lamb is beautifully tender, removing the lid for the last 30 minutes of cooking so that the sauce can reduce.

Serve immediately with couscous and a green salad.

LEMONGRASS PORK PEARLS
WITH MANGO RELISH

Graceful lemongrass soothes the body and mind with its plant-sterol-rich oil, citral. It adds a luscious fragrance and flavour to this light, fresh, spicy dish, which is a go-to for cocktail parties – it's fun to make your own 'foldovers' – as well as making a delicious main course. If you like, you could serve it with little bowls of toasted chopped peanuts or almonds and additional mint to sprinkle on top.

SERVES 2 AS A MAIN OR UP TO 6 AS A SHARING PLATTER

For the pork pearls:

450g (1lb.) minced (ground) pork

3 large garlic cloves, minced (about 2 tbsp)

1 bunch (10g/¼oz./¼ cup) thinly sliced chives

1 stalk (10g/¼oz.) lemongrass, tough outer layers removed, lower 15cm (6in.) of tender bulb finely chopped

1 tbsp freshly grated ginger

1 tsp fish sauce (e.g. *nuoc mam* or *nam pla*)

1 tsp Sriracha sauce (hot Thai chilli sauce)

½ tsp sesame oil

1½ tsp palm or brown sugar

¾ tsp salt

½ tsp pepper

For the relish:

1 medium avocado, peeled, pitted and diced

½ small mango, peeled, pitted and diced

¼ small jicama or Asian pear, peeled, cored and diced

1 or 2 jalapeños, sliced in rings

juice and zest of 1 lime

juice of 1 passion fruit (strain seeds optional)

1 tbsp chopped coriander (cilantro) leaves

1 tbsp chopped Thai basil leaves

½ tsp Sriracha sauce (hot Thai chilli sauce)

For the sauce:

2 tbsp passion fruit juice and 2 tbsp water

2 lemongrass stalks

2 tsp fish sauce

1 tbsp toasted sesame seeds

1 tbsp sugar

½ tsp salt

To serve:

90g (3¼oz.) buckwheat soba noodles, cooked and tossed with 2 tsp oil

55g (2oz.) carrot, grated (about 1 cup grated)

12–16 lettuce leaves, e.g. butter or Little Gem lettuce

15g (½oz./½ cup) coriander (cilantro) leaves

To make the pork pearls, put all the ingredients into a large bowl and, using your hands, mix together, then form the mixture into 5g (⅛oz.) balls. Arrange the 'pearls' on a plate, cover and refrigerate for at least 30 minutes, until firm.

Preheat a pan to medium–high and add a little oil. Cook the pork pearls, swirling the pan until browned all over, about 3–4 minutes.

To make the relish, gently combine the avocado, mango, jicama, jalapeño, lime juice, passion fruit juice, coriander (cilantro), basil and Sriracha in a bowl. Cover and refrigerate until ready to serve.

To make the sauce, whisk all the ingredients together in a small mixing bowl. Season with more vinegar or sugar, depending on your preference.

To serve, arrange the noodles, carrot, lettuce leaves and coriander (cilantro) leaves on a serving platter. To eat, spoon some noodles into a leaf, top with the pork pearls, relish, coriander (cilantro) leaves and sauce. Fold over the lettuce leaf to enclose and have a bite!

WAGYU BEEF CARPACCIO
WITH GREEN TEA NOODLES, LEMONGRASS AND GINGER

A simple, quick, light dish – from fridge to bowl in 15 minutes. The scent of lemongrass as the broth is poured over the beef, noodles and vegetables soothes and calms the mind and soul and may even help to lower 'bad' cholesterol.

SERVES 4

200g (7oz.) Wagyu sirloin or other sirloin beef

1–2 tsp white miso paste

200g (7oz.) green tea or buckwheat soba noodles

½ tsp fresh wasabi or 1 tsp wasabi paste, or to taste

350ml (1½ cup) vegetable stock

2 or 3 lemongrass stalks, thinly sliced

1 x 30g (1oz.) piece ginger, peeled and sliced into matchsticks

200g (7oz.) choy sum ('Chinese flowering cabbage') or bok choy

150g (5½oz.) firm tofu, cut into cubes

10–12 chives cut in matchsticks, for garnish

In advance, freeze the beef, tightly wrapped in plastic.

Take the beef out of the freezer and slice, while still firm, into 8–12 thin strips. Using the back of a spoon or your thumb, spread the beef strips with miso paste on one side, then set aside on a small plate.

Boil 1 litre (4¼ cups) of water in a saucepan, then add the noodles and simmer for 4–5 minutes. Drain the noodles into a colander under running cold water, drain, then tip into a small mixing bowl and stir in the wasabi to combine. Set aside.

Warm the vegetable stock in the same pan with the lemongrass and ginger. Add the choy sum and simmer for 2 minutes.

Divide and mound the noodles into four bowls. Using a slotted spoon, remove the choy sum and ginger from the broth and arrange on top of the noodles. Pour the broth into individual pitchers or teapots. Arrange the beef on top of the noodles, miso side-up, scatter with tofu and chives. Pour hot broth over all, inhale the lemongrass-ginger-miso steam to savour, and enjoy it slowly.

CINNAMON BASIL ICE CREAM
Mindy Segal

'This ice cream was inspired by some beautifully roasted peaches that I bought one year at the farmers' market for a special dessert. I decided that it needed a little of the garden in the ice cream I served them with so I steeped fresh basil in my cinnamon ice cream. Eureka – delicious! It's also good served with poached berries. Indonesian (Ceylon) cinnamon is a milder, softer flavoured cinnamon also known as true cinnamon. Cassia cinnamon is also fine to use but as the flavour is stronger, the basil-cinnamon balance will have a stronger cinnamon taste when using the cassia variety.' MS

MAKES 1 LITRE (1 QUART)

4–6 fresh Indonesian cinnamon sticks

475ml (2 cups) double (heavy) cream

475ml (2 cups) full-fat (whole) milk

13 large egg yolks

225g (8oz./1 cup) cane sugar

leaves from 1 bunch (70g/2½oz.) cinnamon basil, regular basil or Thai basil, finely chopped

½ tsp fresh ground cinnamon

pinch sea salt

¼ tsp pure vanilla extract

Put the cinnamon sticks on a baking tray and toast in the oven until hot to touch.

Meanwhile, in a heavy-bottomed pan, heat the cream and milk to a simmer.

Remove the cinnamon sticks from the oven and crush into pieces. Put the pieces into the warm milk and cream mixture and leave to steep for 1 hour.

Combine the egg yolks and sugar in a 2-litre (2-quart) bowl, whisk thoroughly and set aside.

Strain the cinnamon sticks from the milk and cream mixture and discard them. Return the liquid to the pan and bring to the boil, then pour the liquid over the eggs and sugar, mixing thoroughly.

Pour back into the pan and cook over medium–low heat, stirring constantly until the custard coats the back of a spoon (nappe). Pour the hot custard into a bowl and set over an ice bath.

Steep the chopped basil in the hot custard until cool. Add the ground cinnamon and salt and mix thoroughly.

When cool, strain the custard through a fine mesh strainer then whisk in the vanilla extract.

Freeze the custard in an ice-cream maker, following the manufacturer's instructions.

The Contributing Chefs

José Andrés, who has been named one of *Time* magazine's '100 Most Influential People' and awarded 'Outstanding Chef' by the James Beard Foundation, is an internationally recognized culinary innovator, author, educator, television personality, humanitarian and chef/owner of ThinkFoodGroup. A pioneer of Spanish tapas in the US, he is also known for his avant-garde cuisine. Andrés' award-winning group of restaurants includes locations in Washington D.C., Miami, Puerto Rico, Las Vegas, Los Angeles and Mexico City. In 2012, Andrés formed World Central Kitchen, an NPO that uses the power of food to empower communities and strengthen economies. *thinkfoodgroup.com*
Recipe on page 193.

Lidia Bastianich is an Emmy Award-winning public television host, best-selling cookbook author, restaurateur and owner of a flourishing food and entertainment business. She is the chef/owner of four acclaimed New York City restaurants (Felidia, Becco, Esca and Del Posto) as well as Lidia's Pittsburgh and Lidia's Kansas City, with her daughter Tanya. She is also founder and president of entertainment company Tavola Productions, has a line of pastas and all-natural sauces called LIDIA'S and is co-owner of Eataly, the largest artisanal Italian food-and-wine marketplace in New York City, Chicago and São Paolo, Brazil. *lidiasitaly.com*
Recipe on page 196.

April Bloomfield is the executive chef and co-owner with Ken Friedman of the Michelin-starred restaurants The Spotted Pig and The Breslin Bar & Dining Room in addition to The John Dory Oyster Bar, Salvation Taco, Tosca Café and Salvation Burger. She is also the author of two cookbooks, *A Girl and Her Pig* and *A Girl and Her Greens*. A native of Birmingham, England, April began her culinary studies at Birmingham College and went on to hone her craft through cook positions in various kitchens throughout London and Northern Ireland, including Kensington Place, Bibendum and The River Café. *Instagram & Twitter: @AprilBloomfield*
Photo credit: Melanie Dunea
Recipe on page 78.

Neil Brazier's quirky outlook is reflected in a very inventive but approachable menu. Neil travelled extensively throughout the UK, America and Asia, working in various Michelin-star-rated restaurants and elite country house hotels, before returning to New Zealand as an executive chef for some of New Zealand's finest eateries and lodges, including the award-winning Kauri Cliffs in the Bay of Islands. Currently Peter Gordon's Executive Chef at The Sugar Club and Belotta, Neil draws inspiration from the various cultures he has experienced and combines them to create food that is as unique as it is elegant. *facebook.com/neil.brazier1*
Recipe on page 83.

Francesco Carli arrived in Rio de Janeiro from his native Italy more than 20 years ago and has since remained in Brazil, where he has become renowned for quality Italian cuisine. He has written several books and won many awards. During his tenure as Executive Chef responsible for all the restaurants within the Belmond Copacabana Palace in Rio de Janeiro, its Hotel Cipriani Restaurant was elected by the American magazine *Hotel* as one of the top ten hotel restaurants in the world. Francesco is currently Head Chef at the Country Club of Ipanema in Rio de Janeiro. *linkedin.com/in/francesco-carli-59b09480*
Recipe on page 224.

Simone Cerea's culinary journey began with a chance meeting with a cruise-ship chef who sparked a passion for cooking in him. Born and raised in Bergamo, Italy, he was mentored by the esteemed Italian chef and restaurateur Angelo Paracucchi. His culinary approach is as simple and straightforward as his love for quality ingredients, allowing the natural flavours to flourish in the dish. With more than three decades of experience and a 15-year tenure with Four Seasons Hotels and Resorts – he is currently Executive Chef at Regent Singapore – Simone's greatest satisfaction still comes from an empty plate and a satisfied smile from a diner. *regenthotels.com/EN/Singapore*
Recipe on pages 240–1.

Anne Conness' unique blend of creativity and drive have forged a career path that has taken her from painting to television production to cooking, and now, as co-owner and chef of Sausal, to creating a soul-satisfying Nuevo Rancho Cuisine. Sausal opened in September 2015 in El Segundo, California, to much critical acclaim. With a Mexican-inspired menu that pays homage to the history of Alta California cooking, Conness, along with Pastry Chef Natasha MacAller, brings that rich history forward with a new type of modern-rustic cooking they refer to as Nuevo Rancho Cuisine.
Instagram: @sausalelsegundo
Recipe on page 40.

Suzanne Goin''s six LA restaurants (Lucques, a.o.c., Tavern, The Larder at Maple Drive, The Larder at Burton Way and the new Larder at Tavern at the Tom Bradley International Terminal at LAX) reflect her passion for seasonal cooking. Her artistry has earned her numerous accolades, including the coveted 'Outstanding Chef of the Year' in 2016. In December 2013, Suzanne and her business partner Caroline Styne launched The Larder Baking Company, a wholesale operation for breads and bakery goods developed with master baker Nathan Dakdouk. Goin is the author of two award-winning cookbooks, *Sunday Suppers at Lucques* and *The a.o.c. cookbook*.
Instagram: @suzannegoin
Recipe on page 30.

Peter Gordon was born in Whanganui, New Zealand, and collated his first cookbook aged just four. At 18 he moved to Melbourne where he lived for five years, training and working as a chef in various restaurants. Eventually his spirit of adventure and culinary curiosity led him to travel through Asia for a year, from Indonesia to India. This life-changing experience was to become a major influence on his culinary style, and he went on to earn an international reputation as the 'godfather' of fusion cuisine. Peter lives in Hackney, London, and has restaurants in both Auckland and London.
Instagram: @chefpetergordon
Recipe on page 150.

John Gregory-Smith is a chef and food writer who specializes in Turkish cuisine. He is passionate about Turkey, having explored the country extensively over the last ten years, and regularly hosts Turkish pop-ups and secret supper clubs in London. *Turkish Delights*, John's third book, follows the success of *Mighty Spice Cookbook* and *Mighty Spice Express*. John is also a presenter, who has appeared in the UK and US and who hosted *The Telegraph*'s Fabulous Foodies 2015. He has written for, and his recipes have been widely featured in, numerous UK publications, including *GQ*, *Sainsbury's Magazine*, *The Times* and the *Daily Mail*.
Instagram: @johngs
Recipe on page 242.

Mette Helbak is a Danish chef, food stylist and food writer with a love for creating beauty and great taste with vegetables, and she focuses on them both at her restaurants in Copenhagen and in her cookbooks. She began her career in food writing about other chefs' kitchen skills as a food critic and restaurant-guide editor, but wanted to create a restaurant where super-simple food cooked using the best seasonal ingredients fresh from local farmers would be presented at its best. Her restaurant, Stedsans, located inside the greenhouse of Scandinavia's first rooftop farm, ØsterGRO, is that dream come true.
Instagram & Twitter: @mettehelbak
Recipe on page 230.

Raghavan Iyer is a cookbook author, culinary educator, spokesperson, consultant to numerous national and international clients and host of Emmy Award-winning documentary *Asian Flavors*. From 2014 to 2015, he was President of The International Association of Culinary Professionals. He is the author of several cookbooks, including *660 Curries*, a companion video series of which won him the James Beard Award of Excellence in 2016, and has gained several other awards, notably the International Association of Culinary Professional's Award of Excellence for Cooking Teacher of the Year (2004).
raghavaniyer.com
Recipe on page 188.

Sarah Johnson was born and raised in California. Upon graduating from university, she moved to Berkeley to work at Alice Water's acclaimed Chez Panisse Restaurant. It was during that time that Sarah found her life's passion for cooking. This led her to travel through Europe, visiting kitchens in Ireland then Italy. Upon returning to California, Sarah continued her training in pastry at Chez Panisse and in 2014 she accepted the position of Senior Pastry Chef at Skye Gyngell's Spring Restaurant. Today Sarah collaborates with Skye and the biodynamic farm Fern Verrow to create dishes that are fresh, innovative and celebrate the fruits of the season.
Instagram: @johnson_sarita
Recipe on pages 168–9.

Judy Joo is a chef and host of the new and hugely successful cooking and travel show, *Korean Food Made Simple* (Food Network, worldwide). Her book of the same title was published in May 2016. After studying at the French Culinary Institute and working as a recipe developer for, and contributor to, *Saveur* magazine, American-born Judy moved to London to work at renowned restaurant Gordon Ramsay. A regular face on the Food Network/Cooking Channel, Judy made a name for herself as the only female Iron Chef UK. She has written for and been featured in numerous publications worldwide. Judy looks to her Korean heritage to add Eastern flavours and spices to her dishes.
judyjoo.com
Recipe on page 200.

Michael Kempf has been Head Chef at Facil in Berlin, Germany, since 2003. That year, he received his first Michelin star, at the age of only 26. More awards followed, including Up-and-Coming Chef of the Year from Gault Millau in 2010, and in 2013, he was honoured with his second Michelin star. Chef Kempf's cuisine is an exercise in elegant simplicity, combining exquisitely prepared main ingredients with fresh, unexpected accompaniments and focusing on light, modern preparations of vegetables and aromatic sauces. His love of fresh, healthy cuisine is more than just professional interest: in his free time, he is a long-distance runner.
facil.de
Recipe on page 75.

François Kwaku-Dongo was raised on the Ivory Coast but moved to New York in 1981 to study Literature. He worked in NYC restaurants while attending school, was bitten by the gourmet-cuisine bug and within a few years became sous chef at Remi in NYC, where he met Wolfgang Puck. He moved to LA and within 10 years was voted one of the best upcoming young chefs and became executive chef of Wolfgang's flagship restaurant Spago Hollywood. In addition to frequent TV and radio appearances, he has featured in various print media. François is currently Executive Chef at David's Soundview Catering in Stamford, Connecticut.
Instagram: @fkdongo
Recipe on page 116.

Christine Manfield is one of Australia's most celebrated chefs and a writer of several successful books, including *Dessert Divas, Tasting India, Fire, Spice, Stir, Paramount Cooking* and *Paramount Desserts*. One of Australia's leading culinary ambassadors, her professional life as restaurateur has included three groundbreaking, award-winning restaurants: Paramount (Sydney, 1993–2000), East@West (London, 2003–5) and Universal (Sydney, 2007–13). Her range of spice pastes and condiments, the Christine Manfield Spice Collection, is widely available at retail stores throughout Australia.
Instagram: @christinemanfieldchef
Recipe on page 114.

Anne-Sophie Pic is the only French woman to have been awarded three Michelin stars. She has also received numerous other awards and distinctions, including being named by Veuve Clicquot as 'World's Best Female Chef' in 2011. Her story is that both of an illustrious lineage of chefs and of a self-taught young woman who graduated from business school. This career path has enabled her to create an intuitive and exciting cuisine that is characterized by its innovative mixing of flavours and the constant search for complexity and aromatic intensity, which is revealed with finesse in her dishes.
Instagram & Twitter: @annesophiepic
Recipe on page 236.

Rachel Pol is a pastry chef, chef-owner of Tomato restaurant in Panama and hosts the Panama cooking TV show *Soy Rachel, Soy Foodie*. She also caters for the city's most exclusive events and is a consultant to hotels and restaurants and a regular guest chef and speaker at culinary events and conferences. Rachel is currently making and branding her own chocolate from bean to bar, using Panamanian organic cacao beans, promoting fair trade for local growers. Her project will educate about the sustainable use of the land and create educational centres for children in these communities.
Instagram & Twitter: @rachelfoodie
Recipe on page 110.

Mindy Segal specializes in contemporary American cuisine, placing a modern twist on traditional classics. Segal was awarded the prestigious James Beard Foundation award for Outstanding Pastry Chef in the Country in 2012. Her Chicago restaurant, Hot Chocolate, is the culmination of 25+ years of dedication to her craft. Her bestselling cookbook *Cookie Love* was released in 2015. Mindy has appeared on *The Today Show, The Martha Stewart Show, The Food Network* and in *Food & Wine, Bon Appétit* and *The New York Times*.
Instagram & Twitter: @mindysegal
Recipe on page 248.

Cyrus Todiwala, OBE, 2014 'BBC Food Personality of the Year', cooks, teaches and runs three successful restaurants: Mr Todiwala's Kitchen, Café Spice Namaste and Assado. He has also teamed up with Scottish Chef Tony Singh in the hit BBC2 series *The Incredible Spice Men*, is a regular on *Saturday Kitchen*, has authored six cookbooks and appears regularly at top food festivals around the world. He is Fellow of the Royal Academy of Culinary Arts and the Master Chefs of Great Britain and one of only a handful of British Asian chefs with an entry in *Who's Who*.
Twitter: @ctodiwala
Recipe on pages 36–7.

The Contributing Medical Doctors

Param Dedhia, MD, serves as a passionate internal medicine, integrative medicine and sleep medicine physician at Canyon Ranch in Tucson, Arizona. From lectures to one-on-one consultations, Param brings the science of medicine to the experience of individuals, helping them to live more healthily. His medical practice and lecturing explores the connections between nutrition, exercise, stress and sleep to attain optimal health.
Linkedin.com/in/param-dedhia-0066235

John La Puma, MD, is a board-certified internist, professionally trained chef and author of *ChefMD's Big Book of Culinary Medicine* and *The Realage Diet*. His current research focuses on improving the symptoms of aging and optimizing personal medical health with culinary and nature prescriptions. He is based in Santa Barbara, CA.
Linkedin & Twitter: @johnlapuma

Geeta Maker-Clark, MD, is a Clinical Assistant Professor, Coordinator of Integrative Medical Education and Director of the Culinary Medicine curriculum at the Pritzker School of Medicine, University of Chicago. She relies heavily on the use of food as medicine in her approach to healing, as well as herbs, botanicals, breathwork, conventional medicines and healing practitioners in the community.
drgeetamakerclark.com

Linda Shiue, MD, is a board-certified internal medicine physician and chef who believes that the best medicine is prevention, based on healthy food and a healthy lifestyle. She is the Director of Culinary Medicine at The Permanente Medical Group in San Francisco, CA, where, in addition to treating patients in the clinic, she also teaches healthy cooking as a building block of health. Her recipes and writing have appeared in numerous publications, including several cookbooks.
facebook.com/thedoctorsspicebox

Eleni Tsiompanou, MD, PGDip, MSc Nutritional Medicine, is an Integrative Physician trained in modern Nutritional Medicine and Ayurvedic Nutrition. She is also a practising Consultant Physician in Palliative Medicine. She is the founder of the Health Being Institute, where nutrition, physical activity, psychological and spiritual interventions as well as modern medical approaches are used to prevent and treat disease and improve health and wellbeing. Dr Eleni provides regular evidence-based training on diet and nutrition to doctors, nurses and other healthcare professionals.
healthbeing.co.uk / Twitter: @DrEleni

Luigi Fontana, MD, PhD, is Professor of Medicine at Washington University, where he is co-director of the Longevity Research Program, and at the University of Brescia, Italy.

Richard Lee, MD, is Medical Director of the Integrative and Supportive Oncology Program at the UH Seidman Cancer Center and Visiting Associate Professor at CWRU School of Medicine in Cleveland, OH.

Margaret Papoutsis, DO, Raw Dips (SN) (NT), MBANT, CNHC, is a registered osteopath and nutritional therapist. At her London practice, she successfully integrates nutrition, exercise and other complementary therapies within her osteopathic treatment recommendations.
margaretpapoutsis.co.uk

INDEX

THE AUTHOR

NATASHA MACALLER spent 30 years as a professional ballerina performing with New York's prestigious Joffrey Ballet and Boston Ballet, finishing her exhilarating career in the Broadway and Los Angeles productions of *The Phantom of The Opera*. Turning her artistic spirit to the kitchen, she now channels the same passion, diligence and precision that made her a successful dancer into her love of creative cooking. She divides her time between Los Angeles, London and New Zealand, where she teaches cookery courses and writes. She's also a highly sought-after restaurant consultant.

Spice Health Heroes, her second cookbook, blossomed from her passion for the distinctive, varied spices she cooks with while travelling and consulting. Her first book, *Vanilla Table* (Jacqui Small, UK), was published in 2015. Some 33 widely applauded international chefs contributed recipes. The book attracted great acclaim, resulting in television appearances and dazzling reviews in blogs, newspapers and magazines. *dancingchef.net / Instagram: @dancingchefnatasha*

ACKNOWLEDGEMENTS

Thank you for your generous contributions:

Spice Health Heroes was photographed in New Zealand and ingredients donated by: Wayne Fraser, owner thespicetrader.co.nz; Fenton Wood of Coppers folly purewasabi.co.nz; meats by Greylynnbutchers.co.nz; Cate Bacon, owner, theflipside.co.nz, organic saffron; Alexa Bell and Sandra Goodwin, owners flourflower.co; The Old Packhouse Market, theoldpackhousemarket.co.nz. Props supplied by: Collis Studio collis.co.nz; Republic Home www.republichome.com; Father Rabbit fatherrabbit.com; The Props Department thepropsdepartment.co.nz.

To you all with huge thanks for your support, help and humour:

Wendy & Dr. Graham Dobson, Sherry Yard, Rochelle Huppin, Jim Dodge, Elaine Skeete, Anna Seechran, Penny Subbotin, and Krystal Burtrum for your talented translations from German to English!
Testers and tasters: Tami MacAller, Sally MacAller, Matilda Lee, Ben Chevre, Neil Brazier, Alexa Bell, Roy Goodwin, Sue Lyon, Marita Hewitt, bread-pudding queen Merran Kenworthy and Kathy Kordalis.
Special thanks for your advice and assistance: John La Puma MD, Seth Crosby MD, Tim S. Harlan MD, Elmo Agatep MD, Rachelle Bross PhD, Lucy Dahill, Becky Cortese, Peter Gordon, Rosalinda Monroy, Sue Knight and Janice Wald Henderson.

Many thanks to my very patient, tireless editors, Anne McDowall and Fritha Saunders, Maggie Town for the beautiful design and Manja for the stunning-as-ever photographs.
Jacqui, thank you for the spark – and I'm still hoping to taste your world-famous curry!
And finally, thank you to each and every one of my inspiring contributing chefs and doctors; thank you for helping *Spice Health Heroes* come to life!

SUPPLIERS

UK
thespiceworks.co.uk
tfcsupermarkets.com
spicemountain.co.uk
boroughmarket.org.uk
thespiceshop.co.uk
thespicery.com

USA
thespicehouse.com
rareteacellar.com
spicestationsilverlake.com
worldspice.com
savoryspiceshop.com
laboiteny.com

CANADA
silkroadspices.ca/about-silk-road

FRANCE
anne-sophie-pic.com/boutique/epicerie
epices-roellinger.com

AUSTRALIA
herbies.com.au
harrisfarm.com.au
thespicelibrary.com.au

SPICE BOOKS AND WEBSITES

Cumin, Camels, and Caravans Gary Paul Nabhan
Culinary Herbs & Spices of the World Ben-Erik Van Wyk
The Flavour Thesaurus Niki Segnit
Healing Spices Bharat B. Aggarwal, PhD
Pepper Marjorie Shaffer
Food In History Reay Tannahill
World Spice At Home Amanda Bevill and Julie Kramis Hearne
The Spice Routes Chris and Carolyn Caldicott
The Oxford Companion to Food Alan Davidson and Tom Jaine
On Food and Cooking Harold McGee
The Modern Preserver Kylee Newton

drweil.com Dr. Andrew Weil, MD, FACP
drlowdog.com Dr. Tieraona LowDog MD
drlibby.com Auz/NZ Dr. Libby Weaver, nutritional biochemist
ncbi.nlm.nih.gov/books/NBK92774/Herbs and Spices in Cancer Prevention and Treatment